CRIME AND PUNISHMENT IN SOVIET OFFICIALDOM

Contemporary Soviet/Post-Soviet Politics

CRIME AND PUNISHMENT IN SOVIET OFFICIALDOM

Combating Corruption in the Political Elite, 1965-1990

 **William A. Clark**

Routledge
Taylor & Francis Group

LONDON AND NEW YORK

First published 1993 by M.E. Sharpe

Published 2015 by Routledge
2 Park Square, Milton Park, Abingdon, Oxon OX14 4RN
711 Third Avenue, New York, NY 10017, USA

Routledge is an imprint of the Taylor & Francis Group, an informa business

Library of Congress Cataloging-in-Publication Data

Clark, William A., 1958–
Crime and punishment in Soviet officialdom: combating corruption in the political elite, 1965–1990/William A. Clark
p. cm.
Includes bibliographical references and index.
ISBN 1-56324-055-6 (cloth)
ISBN 1-56324-056-4 (pbk.)
1. Political corruption—Soviet Union—History.
2. Bureaucracy—Soviet Union—History.
3. Misconduct in office—Soviet Union—History.
I. Title.
JN6529.C6C58 1993
354.47009′94—dc20
92-45245
CIP

ISBN 13: 9781563240560 (pbk)
ISBN 13: 9781563240553 (hbk)

To my sister, Joan Gregory,
and her sons, Sean and Daniel

CONTENTS

PREFACE

The demise of the Union of Soviet Socialist Republics on the final day of 1991 did not erase the multitude of social, economic, and political problems that had developed over the course of the previous seventy-five years. Just as the Bolsheviks were forced to address a number of pressing concerns that they inherited from both the tsarist and provisional governments, so too the individuals who make up the post-Soviet leadership in the former territories of the USSR have been saddled with the legacies of communist rule. The possible solutions to these already well-chronicled problems are as numerous as the different languages and cultures of the resultant independent states of the region. While their specific responses will in all likelihood be quite different, conditioned as they are by a great number of different historical and cultural forces, many of the most pressing problems in the post-Soviet states may be quite similar in their origins.

In this book, I seek to shed some analytical light on one rather pervasive social and political problem that was seemingly unsolvable by Soviet authorities: official corruption. The pages that follow contain an honest attempt to present the nature of the problem in its most objective form. Unlike a number of works appearing over the years on the topic of Soviet political corruption or elite privilege that have sought primarily to affix moral blame to this or that individual or to this or that mode of social organization, I have sought to relegate any such ethical calculation to the realm of the reader's own judgment. That is to say, despite the fact that there is no doubt quite an abundance of blame to be distributed on this score, such an exercise is not the goal of this book. The achievement of such a goal at this time would add very little to that which is already understood, for previous works have in all probability succeeded in evaluating ethically the phenomenon of political corruption in Soviet Russia and have raised the appropriate measure of penance for all offenders.

Rather, my hope is that the present treatment of political corruption raises more provocative questions. I have adopted a theoretical and comparative perspective on the social phenomenon of corruption in the Soviet Union during that state's last quarter-century of existence, with the explicit assumption that the study of the Soviet Union and its resultant independent states can be furthered by discounting the once predominant notion that the USSR and its politics are *sui generis,* and hence uncomparable. Substantively and methodologically, it is arguable that such a predisposition did as much damage as it did good in analysis of the post-Stalin period.

To approach the "fulfillment of this plan," as it were, attention has been paid to the theoretical academic literature in organizational behavior, economics, administrative ethics, and political development, as well as to the more traditional areas involving Russian and Soviet history, culture, and politics. As a scholarly exercise, the conscious attempt to view developments in the Soviet Union from a more broad-based and comparative perspective, informed as such by an array of diverse forces, risks challenging one's comfortable assumptions about both the generic theoretical literature and the specific realities of Soviet politics. I hope that such a juxtaposition facilitates some refinement of each body of literature.

A number of individuals have contributed in various ways to the successful completion of this manuscript. My administrative superiors, both at the University of South Carolina and, subsequently, at the Louisiana State University, have made the research and writing of the book much easier. In this respect, Michael Welsh, director of the James F. Byrnes International Center at the University of South Carolina, and Cecil L. Eubanks, chairman of the Department of Political Science at Louisiana State University, each provided the needed organizational support to allow the project to progress apace. Similarly, Michael Weber, executive editor for the social sciences at M.E. Sharpe, Inc., displayed from the start a great deal of faith in the project and provided continued encouragement and patience when the tumultuous political events in the Soviet Union necessarily caused delays and changes in the writing of the manuscript. Special thanks should also be extended to Peter Reddaway, who read the entire manuscript in draft form and offered both bibliographic direction and substantive guidance, both of which effected improvement in the final product. Finally, a debt is owed to Gordon B. Smith, who some years ago sensitized me to the importance of law and issues of legality in Soviet politics. While it is clear that each of these individuals improved the content of the manuscript in his own particular way, all are of course free of responsibility for any errors of fact or interpretation, which remain the sole possession of the author.

CRIME AND PUNISHMENT IN SOVIET OFFICIALDOM

1

INTRODUCTION
Corruption, Politics, and Soviet Society

If the study of corruption teaches us anything at all, it teaches us not to take a political system or a particular regime at face value. Corruption, after all, may be seen as an informal political system.

—James C. Scott[1]

Conceptualizing Corruption

Despite the popular perception of an accepted universal understanding of "corruption," different conceptualizations of the term exist. What is more, many of these conceptualizations contradict other notions of the term, or emphasize quite different aspects of the phenomenon. Such being the case, it is important at the outset to explore these varying and competing notions of corruption, to evaluate their claims, and to settle in on a useful usage of the term for the present purposes of examining official corruption in the Soviet setting.

Most standard accepted definitions of corruption fall into one of three basic categories, or, rather, highlight three distinct metaphors. First, corruption frequently is conceived of in terms that bring to mind physical decay, decomposition, and disintegration. Here, corruption is seen as unwholesome or putrid. Second, corruption is used to describe a decline in morality, a fall from grace, a loss of innocence, or a deterioration from a state of purity. Finally, and more relevant to our concern for the corruption of public officials, corruption has been defined as involving the perversion of an official's public duties, usually for personal gain. In this sphere of official corruption, the trust society places in public officials is betrayed, the office itself is corrupted, and a general decline in the legitimacy of the public authorities obtains if such practices come to be perceived as symptomatic of public officials as a whole. This conceptualization highlights the fact that "corruption" shares the same root as "rupture"; both words originate from the Latin *rumpere* or *ruptus:* to break/broken. What follows is a list of definitions that accentuate this third conceptualization of corruption.

1. "Corruption is behavior of public officials which deviates from accepted norms in order to serve private ends."[2]
2. "Corruption is behavior which deviates from the formal duties of a public role because of private-regarding . . . pecuniary or status gains; or violates rules against the exercise of certain types of private-regarding influence."[3]
3. "The cry 'You are corrupt!' is moral and political more than a legal accusation, and the connotations of decay, depravity, secretiveness and self-interest are well understood as being incompatible with official position in public office: public trust is betrayed."[4]
4. "There is fairly general agreement in the literature on what corruption means: namely, the use of public office for private advantage."[5]
5. "Corruption can be said to exist whenever a power-holder who is charged with doing certain things . . . is by monetary or other rewards not legally provided for, induced to take actions which favor whoever provides the award and thereby does damage to the public and its interests."[6]
6. "Corruption is an extra-legal institution used by individuals or groups to gain influence over the actions of the bureaucracy."[7]
7. "Corruption, like the concept of power, is a *relational* term . . . that implies a serious violation of standards or expectations associated with a broader set of public relationships and processes."[8]
8. "Corruption [is defined] as the behavior of public officials which diverges from the formal duties of a public role to serve private ends."[9]
9. "At its most basic level, corruption is the abuse of public roles and resources for private benefit."[10]

10. "An agent is *personally corrupt* if he knowingly sacrifices his principal's interest to his own, that is, if he betrays his trust. He is *officially corrupt* if, in serving his principal's interest, he knowingly violates a rule, that is, acts illegally or unethically albeit in his principal's interest."[11]

Each of these ten definitions of corruption, however, opens up several thorny issues regarding just what constitutes the "public interest," or the expectations of those who hold public office. The public interest changes over time and place, and is defined at any given time in different ways by different societal groups. Moreover, the behavior of public officials is also subject to different ethical criteria; in a word, different people at different times expect different types of behavior from those who hold the public "trust."

Meier and Holbrook have recently made the useful distinction between corruption and ethics, and such a distinction is apposite for any attempt to conceptualize corruption in a comparative setting. As they put it, corruption "is probably only a small subset of the behaviors that might be considered unethical."[12] The authors point to Paul Appleby's work on morality and administrative ethics, in which the latter argues that unethical behavior is generally considered substantially more than just illegal activity (the operational definition of corruption defended below). For example, Appleby includes as unethical official behavior such "legal" behavior as the unwillingness to assume the responsibilities associated with a public office, the inability to deal with constituents of that office, the failure to use institutional resources efficiently, and the failure to anticipate bureaucratic problems. None of these activities violates the law, yet they may in varying degrees violate the public "trust" or the public "interest." This concern is perhaps best summarized by John Waterbury: "A legally corrupt person may arouse no normative reprobation; [and] a person judged corrupt by normative standards may be legally clean."[13]

Comparative research into corruption, then, with the differing cultural forces, varying sets of expectations on official behavior, to say nothing of the lack of consistency in these factors over time, magnifies these problems of the ethics–corruption connection. Ethics cannot be usefully defined as merely the compliance with formal regulations; nor can such compliance be a guarantee of ethical behavior. As one student of corruption puts it, "corrupt behavior is condemned and censured.

'Corruption' is a pejorative term. However, applying the label to behavior on the part of public officials in many non-Western countries immediately poses a dilemma of intriguing dimensions."[14] In sum, one must conclude that to study corruption is not to study ethics, per se. Attempts to equate the two render comparative research into the phenomenon of corruption especially problematic.

Conceptualizing Corruption in Comparative Perspective

Despite the existence of a sizable body of literature that deals with the phenomenon of official corruption on moral or ethical grounds, the concept of corruption is most appropriately seen as a *legal* construct. This is not to say, of course, that moral and ethical considerations are inappropriate to any discussion of corruption; on the contrary, the persistence in every society of corrupt practices, as well as the particular motivations of individuals who engage in "corrupt" behaviors, often raise normative concerns. Indeed, as stated above, in normal parlance the word "corruption" implies moral decay, disintegration, degradation, and deterioration—all of which carry an obvious pejorative flavor. This fact notwithstanding, however, scholars interested in examining the phenomenon of "corruption" in a comparative perspective must approach their subject matter legalistically, not normatively, if meaningful and valid generalizations are to be attained.

Traditionally, comparative research has been subject to charges of "bias," "cultural imperialism," "ethnocentrism," and the like. This is no less true for research into governmental, or official, corruption. Much of the cross-national research into this social phenomenon has entailed the implicit, and often explicit, application of Western standards of official conduct and societal mores to non-Western settings, resulting many times in the condemnation of the latter based on a set of ethical "rules of the game" that do not even exist within that society. What is considered "corrupt" behavior in the United States, for instance, may be considered acceptable and legitimate in another society within which different sets of social mores obtain. For example, the bestowal of gifts by private individuals upon public officials may raise eyebrows (and legal charges) in Washington, but may be seen as part of traditional custom in a regional capital of an African state. In like fashion, the concept of corruption varies temporally as well as spatially. For example, what is presently considered electoral "fraud" and "corruption" in the United States might not have merited comment during the period of the so-called "Spoils System." That is, what was ethically acceptable in the early 1800s might be considered morally wrong today.

What the above details, then, is the fact that the utilization of "corruption" strictly as a universal moral or ethical construct is fraught with a variety of threats to valid inference. There is nothing inherent in a behavior that makes it "corrupt." Whether an action is corrupt depends on the social context within which it occurs. As one set of researchers put it:

> Actions are "situated" within socio-cultural contexts. . . . Corruption [can] be regarded as a negotiated classification of behavior rather than as an inherent quality of behavior. Such a classification is accomplished by the application of certain tacit, common sense interpretative criteria, dependent on specific social contexts and embedded in stocks of knowledge.[15]

To argue otherwise leads the researcher to impute or superimpose the label of "corruption" onto a set of behaviors that may not be so considered by the society within which those behaviors took place. It would lead, likewise, to the application of such pejorative labels on past behaviors that were considered absolutely acceptable and appropriate by the society at the time the acts were performed. To do so would, again, allow other cultures to determine the morality of our own, other eras to apply their morality to ours. In the interest of objective social scientific analysis, this state of affairs is unacceptable. Because of this non-universality of societal norms over time and place, scholars must rely on the specific set of *institutionalized* values that obtain or obtained in the society under study. The quotation cited above referred to "corruption" as a "negotiated classification." In each society, the politics of the day go a long way in determining the outcome of these "negotiations." The politics of meaning is, like other political games, determined in large part by the distribution of power within the system. As Berger and Luckmann aptly put it, "He who has the biggest stick has the better chance of imposing his definitions of reality."[16] Whatever the outcome of the political "negotiations" over meanings, the laws of the system that prevail at any given point in time codify these classifications and, as "proxies" for the public interest, are the most appropriate guides to follow. It is in this sense that concepts like "corruption" are *legal* constructs. Inasmuch as they function as the institutionalized representation of the "public interest," it is the prevailing legal codes that determine if an act is "corrupt" or not.

The understanding of "corruption" as essentially a legal concept points to a number of other characteristics of the phenomenon that merit elaboration here. The concept of governmental, or "official," corruption, the focus of this work, presupposes the existence of a significant level of public institutionalization. The law-based notion of official corruption, which may be defined as behavior of public officials aimed at the acquisition of forbidden or circumscribed benefits and made possible as a result of their official duties or position, can exist only in those societies that have a relatively well-developed notion of public office. That is, those traditional or "patrimonial" societies that support no real distinction between "private" and "public," no notion of "public" office separate from the pursuit of private ends, no institutionalized set of structures by and through which "public" ends are pursued, and no set of codes that describe and place limits on the range of socially approved behavior, have no real conception of corruption, per se; there may be disloyalty, there may be betrayal, there may be broken or disrupted relationships, but not "corruption." Such systems do not possess a formal "legal" system and thereby do not exhibit official corruption. In the sense, then, that corruption is a legal construct, it exists only in those societies throughout history that have experienced some level of institutionalization or, as some have put it, "modernization."

Indeed, a large number of scholars believe it is exactly this period of modernization that gives rise to a sort of cultural schizophrenia that is defined, on the one hand, by the persistence of traditional patrimonial customs and, on the other hand, by the development of rational-legal approaches to governance. The process of institution building, considered by many the hallmark of modernization, creates a formal system of governing that must, if it is to gain legitimacy, overcome a legacy of informal, localized patrimonial rule. As Joseph S. Nye has argued,

> [B]ehavior that will be considered corrupt is likely to be more prominent in less developed countries because of a variety of conditions involved in their underdevelopment—great inequality in distribution of wealth; political office as the primary means of gaining access to

wealth; conflict between changing moral codes; the weakness of societal and governmental enforcement mechanisms; and the absence of a strong sense of national community.[17]

Such transitional societies are unstable, by and large, precisely due to the low level of legitimacy enjoyed by these newly emerging structures and the values they entail. This period of instability, according to Joseph Nye, Samuel Huntington, and others, is marked by the conflict between old customs and new legal standards. Not surprisingly, it is during this period that certain types of behavior deemed inappropriate by the new institutions are labeled "corrupt" and are dealt with as such. It is only with the development of modern rational-legal structures, then, that the concept of official corruption emerges. It is for these reasons that in changing societies, where traditional practices tend to lag behind institutionalization norms, corruption as a social phenomenon is so marked. As Huntington puts it,

> Corruption in a modernizing society is thus in part not so much the result of the deviance of behavior from accepted norms as it is the deviance of norms from the established pattern of behavior.[18]

Because those behaviors that are proscribed by the respective legal systems of different societies vary widely, identical actions in two different societies may be totally acceptable in one, yet considered "corruption" in another. For example, the vast majority of economic crimes that existed under Soviet law were legitimate practices in American society. The Soviet crime of "speculation," a serious transgression punishable in extreme cases by death, involved in many cases little more than the everyday activity of retailers in the United States: the procurement and re-selling of goods and/or services with a view toward the acquisition of profit. What is "corrupt" behavior in one setting may be a highly valued practice in another. This example points to the difficulty of constructing any notion of "corruption" based on non-legal principles.

It may be useful to consider corruption as an extra-legal system for the production and distribution of services. Considered in this sense, corruption entails an alternative to the formal system whereby goods and services are provided. The formal system, supported by governmental institutions, the legal codes (and the agencies that enforce them), and in most instances the approbation of the populace, may or may not be a more efficient or more equitable system of producing and distributing services. In fact, in some situations the development of "corrupt" practices on a wide scale becomes necessary and possible because the formal system is seen by a significant number of people as being less efficient and/or less "fair" than should be the case. The political "machines" of American urban settings may, viewed from this perspective, share much in common with the "black market" that thrived in the Soviet Union. Each in its own way seeks to provide an alternative to the formal system that was perceived to disenfranchise and discriminate against identifiable groups within society.

The above comparison between machine politics in the United States and the black market in the USSR highlights the degree to which the above-mentioned characteristics of corruption overlap. It is interesting to note that it is precisely those groups in each setting that felt isolated and betrayed by the "alien" norms that supported the emerging formal power structure (European immigrants in the United States, ethnic minorities in the Soviet Union) that were disproportionately active in the "corrupt" practices. Both the machine politics of urban America and the Soviet black market system represent less formal, more patrimonial, and more traditional ways of allocating goods and services in a society for precisely those individuals and groups whose traditional values were most threatened by the rational-legal institutions with which they were required, formally, to interact. Political machines withered away in the United States largely as a result of the perceived increases in the efficiency and fairness (and resultant legitimacy) of the formal system; the black market flourished in the Soviet Union for precisely the opposite reasons.

Corruption and Soviet Society

Corruption has been an issue of concern in Soviet society since the first months of the regime's life, and institutional efforts to combat it over the years have taken a variety of forms. The problem of the black market in the Soviet Union presented itself almost immediately to Lenin and his Bolshevik administrators upon their seizure of power. The severe dislocations of World War I and the subsequent Russian civil war between the Bolsheviks and the so-called "White" movement of various and sundry alternatives to the newly established government in Petrograd produced a thriving black market trade. While Lenin created the infamous All-Russian Extraordinary Commission for Combating Counter-Revolution and Sabotage (it came to be known as simply the "Extraordinary Commission"—*Chrezvychainaia Komissiia*—or Cheka) on December 7, 1917, primarily for the purpose of dealing with the political enemies of the Bolsheviks, a significant amount of the Cheka's original work dealt with countering the rampant speculation (i.e., private trading) associated with the burgeoning black market. Reflecting this concern, within a week of its creation, the phrase "and the combating of speculation" was appended to the Cheka's official title.

Despite a shocking lack of administrative control or regularized "due process" associated with Cheka activities during its December 1917–February 1992 life span (Cheka head Felix Dzerzhinsky once remarked: "We stand for organized terror"), the Cheka was unable to uproot the illegal private trade that developed as a result of the inability of the formal institutions of the state to supply the population with the needed economic goods. As a leading scholar on the activities of the Cheka remarked, "The prevalence of profiteering was such as to defeat the combined efforts of the courts and the Chekas; it was not until the New Economic Policy (NEP) of 1921 removed its causes that the phenomenon of speculation virtually vanished, or rather was legalised."[19]

The Cheka's failure to deal with the black market was certainly not the result of a lack of attention to the problem. A variety of methods were employed to shut down the illegal trade, and large numbers of people were arrested under the new Bolshevik legal prohibitions against such activity. Citing the evidence from Moscow, for example, it seems as though the Cheka between December 1918 and November 1920 arrested 26,692 individuals for speculation.[20] In terms of the actual anti–black market legislation of Lenin's regime, on July 22, 1918, Lenin signed a decree on combating speculation; this decree prescribed rather severe legal penalties (including up to ten years of hard labor and the confiscation of personal property) for those convicted of such activity. In addition, the Cheka was busy dispensing its own set of penalties for speculation and profiteering. During the first two years of its existence, the Extraordinary Commission executed over 900 individuals for speculation and the misappropriation of goods.[21] Social conditions under War Communism were such, however, that official efforts to crush private trading were destined to fail.

In such an environment, moreover, official corruption too became a point of concern for the new Bolshevik government. Officials connected to Soviet food and economic supply organizations were especially vulnerable to black market approaches. Many were unable to resist the temptation to exploit their official positions for personal gain. Here again the Cheka attempted to discourage these illegal activities by executing those found to be the most corrupt. Some have argued that over 600 state officials were shot for economic crimes during 1918 and 1919.[22] The failure of the regime to control the behavior of its officials prompted Lenin in late 1919 to sign a *Sovnarkom* (the acronym for the *Sovet Narodnikh Komissarov,* or Council of People's Commissars) decree aimed at raising further the stakes in the anti-corruption campaign. The decree established a Special Revolutionary Tribunal, attached to the Cheka, the purpose of which was to deal with the wide array of offenses associated with illegal trading: speculation, profiteering, bribery, theft, and so on. In terms of its mission, the Tribunal was less a judicial body and more a punitive organ of the Cheka. According to the wording of the decree, " The Special Revolutionary Tribunal is guided in its judgments solely by the interests of the Revolution, without being bound by any forms of legal procedure. . . . Its sentences are final and not subject to appeal."[23] As was the case with many early Bolshevik institutions, the Special Revolutionary Tribunal was short-lived, being abolished and replaced in the spring of 1920 by the Supreme Revolutionary Tribunal.

The same 1919 *Sovnarkom* decree that established the Special Revolutionary Tribunal also created a Special Inter-Departmental Commission, composed of prominent Chekists and jurists. The function of this commission was to provide oversight and coordination to the anti-corruption efforts, with special attention being paid to studying the causes of the problem (bureaucratic red tape, lack of inventory controls, sloppy record keeping, and the like). With this in mind, a Special Section was organized within the Cheka in January 1920 to deal specifically with official misconduct. Here, these activities of the Cheka clearly overlapped with non-police functions having to do with addressing the production and distribution problems of the Soviet economy. In the Bolshevik drive to bring greater and greater proportions of the economy under centralized state control, the precedent of employing the coercive organs of the state for non-traditional police work was established.

This precedent was, as has been well chronicled, extended to almost unbelievable lengths under Lenin's successor. Stalin's revolution from above after 1928 entailed extreme levels of social mobilization, which in other societies has tended to exacerbate crime. Stalin's formula for exacting control over society during this upheaval involved a tremendous increase in the coercive power of the state. In 1930, Stalin called for "the highest development of state power so that the state would become the mightiest and strongest" ever.[24] The "withering away of the state" would have to wait.

Throughout the late 1920s and early 1930s the legal penalties for varying categories of crime were raised from the "lax" levels of the NEP period. Capital punishment was restored in many areas of the legal code. In 1933, the OGPU (Stalin's secret police, the Unified State Political Administration) was given the power to execute those convicted of misdeeds. What is more, Soviet officials suddenly found their performance subject to criminal evaluation. In the politicized environment of the 1930s, managerial inefficiency was translated into sabotage, with obviously high costs. According to Peter Juviler,

> To stop what seemed rightly a disruptive menace, the indiscipline, absenteeism, corruption, and negligence, Stalin introduced a whole new list of crimes. Capital offenses multiplied. The death penalty came to threaten many economic criminals, from hoarders of silver coins to railroad workers unintentionally causing wrecks through negligence. Stalin's theory of intensification of the class struggle lent support to a criminal policy marked by an "unjustified increase in punishment for certain crimes and in court practice an unfounded trend toward general increase of repression" to the point that maximum sentences specified for offenses became minimum sentences in practice, and even uncommon crimes of everyday life were regarded and treated as "counterrevolutionary."[25]

Armed with such a legal disposition, the coercive organs of the state were flooded with cases; it is estimated officially that convictions in the Russian Republic rose 44 percent between 1928 and 1933.[26] This increase would have been much higher had the jurisdiction for lower-level crimes not been transferred out of courts and into the non-professional comrades' courts.

The general intensification of legal penalties in Soviet society under Stalin did not ignore Soviet officials. The category of crime labeled "misconduct in office" covered many white-collar crimes and, again according to Juviler, "became an even wider means of repression" than the new laws dealing with theft of public property.[27] Convictions for official misconduct in the Russian Republic alone rose from roughly

86,000 (or 7–8 percent of all convictions) during the last year of the NEP to 398,000 (or approximately 25 percent of convictions) in 1933. Especially vulnerable to charges of official misconduct were Soviet officials directly administering production-oriented organizations; many *kolkhoz* chairmen and enterprise managers had very short tenures on the job. Stalin's need for internal scapegoats to explain away the economic dislocations brought about by his policies of crash industrialization supported by forced collectivization logically made those responsible for running Soviet industry the most likely "suspects" if production faltered.

It should be noted that despite the high political (and physical) stakes of official misconduct, whether real or imagined, during Stalin's time in power, corruption, both within Soviet officialdom and in the greater society, still existed at some level. Unfortunately for those implicated in such matters, ordinary crimes such as hooliganism, theft, and murder instantly became politicized into the "wrecking" activities of "enemies of the people," or individual "lapses" of socialist construction. The penalties exacted for such political crimes were much more severe than "everyday" crimes. In such an environment, and given both the level of terror that existed and the almost total lack of judicial integrity in the meting out of social control, neither societal nor official "corruption" in the normal sense of the word reached high levels during the final quarter-century of Stalin's reign.

From the perspective of law and jurisprudence, one of the paradoxes of the Stalin period after the initial assault on Soviet society was the reversal of the revolutionary ethos of Soviet law. This concept of law as an active arm in furthering the revolution, pushed by such "legal nihilists" as E.B. Pashukanis, N.V. Krylenko, and P.I. Stuchka, embraced a very elastic notion of crime and punishment. It was eventually abolished in favor of what Robert Sharlet has called a "romanist" ethos.[28] While the former elevated a "jurisprudence of terror" to the center of revolutionary justice and was critical in Stalin's desire to destroy the NEP and to collectivize the peasantry, once Stalin had succeeded in the early stages of this revolution from above, the adoption of an integrated system of stability, formality, and professionalism allowed the general secretary to institutionalize these social changes in the law. Thus, from the perspective of the law, the Stalin period is somewhat paradoxical in that his rule is associated with both a "jurisprudence of terror" and legal elasticity, and the development of the stable, integrated legal system that serves as the basis of the Western bourgeois conception of law. This is not to say that terror as a political instrument was abandoned during the final years of Stalin's rule (or subsequently for that matter); nonetheless, and perhaps inevitably, Soviet legal affairs during this time period did indeed come to be patterned less on revolutionary justice and more on institutionalized, regularized, and professional criteria.

The problems of official and societal corruption had again begun to assume especially disturbing levels as early as the beginning of the 1960s. In spite of Prosecutor General Rudenko's accompanying claim that in the Soviet state "coercion has never been a major weapon in the fight for socialist justice,"[29] Khrushchev in 1961 publicly raised the stakes in the struggle against corruption. First, on May 5, 1961, the Presidium of the USSR Supreme Soviet passed the resolution "On Intensifying the Struggle against Especially Dangerous Crimes." Article 22 of the Principles of Criminal Legislation of the USSR and the Union Republics was to be altered. Newly listed in this article among this category of "especially dangerous" crimes, joining such likely offenses as high treason, espionage, sabotage, terrorism, banditry, and premeditated murder, was the economic crime of "the pilfering of state or public property in especially large amounts."[30] Like the other crimes in this "especially dangerous" grouping, the theft of state property was again punishable by "the application of the death penalty by shooting." Not since May 26, 1947, the day Josef Stalin abolished the death penalty for such a crime, could the theft of socialist property result in execution by firing squad.[31]

The level of Khrushchev's seriousness with respect to the issue of corruption was demonstrated later in the year. State and party officials must have become agitated when Khrushchev ordered that the traditional distinction under Soviet law between "indirect theft," such as that which occurred in report padding and general abuse of authority, and "direct theft," as in cases of outright embezzlement, be erased. Suddenly, Soviet officials found guilty of report padding (a very common sin of Soviet bureaucratic officials, as shall be seen in later chapters) could, under certain circumstances, find themselves charged with a capital offense. It is interesting that the decree was signed by the man who would later, after Khrushchev was overthrown in a palace coup, reverse this implied threat of Soviet officialdom: the then-chairman of the Presidium of the USSR Supreme Soviet, Leonid Brezhnev.

Khrushchev's war on corruption continued in the summer of 1961 with a further expansion of the list of crimes punishable by the death penalty. *Izvestiia* reported in its July 2, 1961, edition a second decree of the USSR Supreme Soviet Presidium: "On Increasing Criminal Responsibility for Violating Currency Regulations." In it, the Presidium resolved to permit the application of capital punishment by shooting "for speculation in *valuta* [foreign currency] valuables or banknotes" if such speculation took the form of a continuous business or if such speculation entailed especially large amounts. In addition, lesser criteria applied to persons convicted of *valuta* violations a second time.

The tacit threat to Soviet officials engaging in corrupt behavior was emphasized a third time by Khrushchev early in the following year. In yet another decree from the USSR Supreme Soviet Presidium, Khrushchev made another common practice of Soviet officials punishable by death; here the focus was bribery. The decree stated, somewhat incorrectly as it turns out, that bribery was one of the "shameful and odious survivals of the past bequeathed to our society by capitalism," one that was "alien and completely intolerable to the Soviet state."[32] While the Bolsheviks did indeed inherit a tradition of Russian bribery that was certainly well developed (as shall be discussed at length in the next chapter), future history would certainly show that bribery was not at all alien to Soviet administrative behavior. The fact that in 1961, after almost half a century of Bolshevik rule, the regime felt compelled to raise the penalties for bribery certainly demonstrates that the problem did not disappear with the full-scale building of communism.

The decree, like the two others cited above, made the taking of bribes "in the presence of especially aggravating circumstances" punishable by the firing squad. An interesting twist to the decree, and one that must have introduced an additional element of concern for Soviet officials not unaccustomed to bribery, was its stipulation that a person who had given a bribe (extorted or given willfully) would be relieved of any criminal liability if he voluntarily reported his actions to the authorities.

Conclusion

The message of this initial discussion is quite clear and presents the challenge of the following pages. Conceptually, corruption is a difficult phenomenon to handle. While the ethical components of the term are self-evident, attempts to address this component directly present serious obstacles to objective analysis. Here, a law-based, or legalistic, understanding of corruption has been advanced over those based in ethics or morality. Such a compromise seems to be necessary if the chapters that follow are to avoid assuming the form of biased *ad hominem* attacks on the behavior of morally suspect public officials. As will be shown, corruption in the Soviet setting (and during the transition away from communist rule) reflected quite a diverse range of causes and consequences, both of a functional and dysfunctional nature. Thus, any ethical evaluation of official corruption in Soviet officialdom is much more difficult than it may seem at first glance; such evaluations will be left to the discretion of the reader.

To these concerns one must add the fact that by its very nature corruption, whether conceived of in ethical or legal terms, is hidden behavior. Unlike the usual social phenomena studied by political scientists, whether they be elections, parliamentary behavior, constitutions, political parties, interest groups, or governmental institutions, the topic of corruption raises some obvious threats with regard to the soundness of the data. The fact that the social force under consideration is illicit makes efforts to determine its scope and impact on society somewhat problematic.

Students of Soviet politics have long ago grown accustomed to the so-called "data problem" that inheres in their subject matter. Like so much else of importance to understanding the political system associated with the seventy-five-year history of Soviet power, the study of political corruption within the Soviet scheme of things must be undertaken in full awareness of the limitations posed by the subject matter. In the present case, the burden facing the investigator is that the subject matter under study is itself inherently illusive; the burden is doubled by the fact that this illusive social characteristic manifested itself in what was essentially a closed society.

Finally, it is important to make explicit the conviction that is especially axiomatic among students of the Soviet Union: the imprecision of our concepts and the weakness of our data in no way render the phenomenon under study any less important to understanding social and political life in the USSR. The fact of the matter is that societal corruption, both private and public, reached rather shocking levels in the Soviet Union for rather specific reasons having to do with the strengths and, more to the point, the weaknesses of the system. It is in this sense that the effort to study the symptoms as best we can helps in the diagnosis of the more general disease.

Notes

1. James C. Scott (1972), *Comparative Political Corruption* (Englewood Cliffs, NJ: Prentice Hall): 2.

2. Samuel P. Huntington (1968), *Political Order in Changing Societies* (New Haven, CT: Yale University Press): 59.

3. Joseph S. Nye (1967), "Corruption and Political Development: A Cost–Benefit Analysis," *American Political Science Review*, Vol. 51 (No. 2): 419.

4. Michael Clarke, ed. (1983), *Corruption: Causes, Consequences and Control* (New York: St. Martin's Press): xiv.

5. Leslie Palmier (1983), "Bureaucratic Corruption and Its Remedies," in Michael Clarke, ed., *Corruption: Causes, Consequences and Control* (New York: St. Martin's Press): 207.

6. Carl J. Friedrich (1966), "Political Pathology," *Political Quarterly*, Vol. 37 (No. 1): 74.

7. Nathaniel H. Leff (1964), "Economic Development through Bureaucratic Corruption," *The American Behavioral Scientist*, Vol. 8 (No. 3): 8.

8. Philip H. Jos (1992), "Empirical Corruption Research: Beside the (Moral) Point," unpublished paper presented to the Annual Meeting of the South Carolina Political Science Association, p. 2.

9. John Kramer (1977), "Political Corruption in the USSR," *Western Political Quarterly*, Vol. 30 (No. 2): 213.

10. Michael Johnston (1986), "The Political Consequences of Corruption: A Reassessment," *Comparative Politics*, Vol. 18 (No. 2): 459.

11. Edward C. Banfield (1975), "Corruption as a Feature of Governmental Organization," *Journal of Law and Economics*, Vol. 18 (No. 4): 587–588.

12. Kenneth J. Meier and Thomas Holbrook (1992), " 'I Seen My Opportunities and I Took 'Em': Political Corruption in the American States," *Journal of Politics*, Vol. 54 (No. 1): 135–155.

13. John Waterbury (1973), "Endemic and Planned Corruption in a Monarchical Regime," *World Politics*, Vol. 25 (No. 4): 533.

14. David H. Bayley (1966), "The Effects of Corruption in a Developing Nation," *Western Political Quarterly*, Vol. 19 (No. 4): 721.

15. Steven Chibnall and Peter Saunders (1977), "Worlds Apart: Notes on the Social Reality of Corruption," *British Journal of Sociology*, Vol. 28 (No. 2): 145.

16. Peter L. Berger and Thomas Luckmann (1967), *The Social Construction of Reality* (New York: Penguin): 127.

17. Joseph S. Nye (1967), "Corruption and Political Development," p. 418.

18. Samuel P. Huntington (1968), *Political Order in Changing Societies*, p. 60. See also Steven J. Staats (1972), "Corruption in the Soviet System," p. 44.

19. George Leggett (1981), *The Cheka: Lenin's Political Police* (Oxford: Clarendon Press): 214–215.

20. Ibid., p. 215

21. Ibid.

22. Ibid., p. 216.

23. Cited in Leggett (1981), *The Cheka*, p. 216.

24. Cited in Peter H. Juviler (1976), *Revolutionary Law and Order: Politics and Social Change in the USSR* (New York: The Free Press): 43.

25. Ibid., p. 49.

26. Ibid., p. 50.

27. Ibid., p. 51.

28. Robert Sharlet (1977), "Stalinism and Soviet Legal Culture," pp. 155–179 in Robert C. Tucker, ed., *Stalinism: Essays in Historical Interpretation* (New York: W.W. Norton).

29. *Izvestiia*, May 7, 1961, p. 5.

30. Ibid.

31. Stalin abolished capital punishment on this date, but reinstated it on January 12, 1950, for the crimes of treason, espionage, and sabotage.

32. *Vedmosti Verkhovnogo Soveta SSSR*, No. 8, February 2, 1962, Article 85, pp. 221–222.

2

PUBLIC ADMINISTRATION AND THE STRUCTURE OF CORRUPTION IN SOVIET OFFICIALDOM

It seems a fair generalization that
all Soviet managers are, ipso facto,
criminals according to Soviet law."

—David Granick[1]

Russia, whether in tsarist or soviet form, has traditionally been primarily a bureaucratic entity. Political power in Russia and the Soviet Union alike never rested with elective posts, but fundamentally with appointive offices, arranged hierarchically. For precisely this reason, the role of the official has been historically much more salient as a telling characteristic of Russian and Soviet society than has been the case in the western world. Dating back prior to the 1722 introduction of the Petrine Table of Ranks, which established a strict hierarchy of administrative ranks and the possibility of attaining noble status through state service, the Russian and Soviet empires were marked by the predominance of officialdom. The bureaucratization of public life in Russia was well established long before Bolshevik reformers embarked on their first of several "scientific" attempts at restructuring the machinery of state politics. In this sense, then, the existence of structured bureaucratic government in Russia is not a Bolshevik creation.

Given the influence of such a tradition, it is advisable in studying the characteristics of Soviet officialdom—whether focusing on the recruitment of officials, their backgrounds, or their behavior—to resist the temptation, frequently succumbed to by students of the Soviet period, to treat post-1917 Soviet Russia as *sui generis*. A variety of forces beyond the particular motivations of Soviet planners molded the specific nature of Soviet officialdom, both in its structure and function, and therefore merit attention herein. In addition to the historical legacies that influenced the development of Soviet officialdom, phenomena of a more generic nature are at work as well. Much of the theoretical literature on organizational behavior and bureaucratic tendencies is certainly applicable to a society that has been referred to as a "bureaucracy, *writ* large." To the degree that such appellations are valid, any attempt to describe and analyze the structure of official corruption in the Soviet Union requires a more comprehensive approach than has traditionally been adopted.

This chapter seeks to explicate structural forces that have had an impact on the specific manifestations of official corruption in the Soviet system. The utility of such an approach is based on the assertion that the social behaviors of *apparatchiki* can be explained in good part by examining the organizational structure within which they operate. This is not to say that Soviet officialdom was comprised of blind automatons whose actions were determined inexorably by organizational forces beyond their ability to control or manipulate. Rather, what follows seeks to shed light on the logic of the bureaucratic system that governed the Soviet Union and the manner in which this bureaucratic logic has conditioned the specific set of behaviors exhibited by individuals associated with the operation of the Soviet administrative organs. That such an approach seems worthwhile in deciphering official behavior at both a micro and macro level of analysis seems to be justified by a corpus of scholarship that has focused on the impact of organizational structures on social behavior, both directed at the principles of organization, per se, as well as those of Russia and the Soviet Union particularly.

To this end, the treatment of the subject that follows is divided into three parts. The first provides a brief, but focused, overview of the social characteristics associated with various forms of public organization. Here, a more generic and theoretical approach will be adopted to describe the conclusions of scholars who have investigated the nature of bureaucracy, its impact on individual and collective behavior, and the "symptoms" that seem to inhere in specific types of organizational schemes. Second, the chapter will examine the nature of pre-Soviet forms of governmental bureaucracy in Russia to establish the historical record of official behavior prior to the development of Bolshevik forms of public administration. Finally, aspects of the Soviet organization of political power will be explored with a view toward discerning those characteristics specific to the exercise of power by Soviet authorities.

Of course, the organizing principle of the chapter revolves around the search for structural factors that may account for the pervasive official corruption that obtained in the USSR. In this way, one of the goals of what follows is to isolate the specifically Soviet contribution to the legacy of official corruption that continues to manifest itself in Russia. This goal is by no means easily attained. As Paul Gregory has argued, "one of the most difficult problems of studying Soviet bureaucracy is to distinguish particularly 'Soviet' features from those that are common to any large bureaucratic organization."[2] This chapter, nonetheless, seeks to untangle the various major influences that combined to determine the behavior of Soviet officialdom.

Bureaucratic Organization and Bureaucratic Behavior

Much has been written about the behavior of large complex organizations that have adopted bureaucratic structures. It is worth noting at the outset that a bureaucratic structure is but one of a variety of organizational structures that may be adopted or developed over time. The process of bureaucratization involves the development of specific characteristics that mark the operation of organizational activity. According to Rowney and Pintner,

> Bureaucratization is the formation of activities in an organization into compartments of activity that are separated from one another according to perceived differences in the formal objectives of participants in the activity, differences in the training or preparation of the participants, and differences in the career experiences of participants.[3]

In this sense, bureaucratization is not synonymous with organization or with a body of officials, per se, but can be said to develop within an already existing organization that may have been originally organized along different lines. Organizations, societies, and aspects of economic endeavor such as farming and manufacturing can be said to be "bureaucratized" as the manner by which tasks are confronted assumes in greater degree this organizational flavor.

Other characteristics that have been cited as requisite to the concept of bureaucracy are the following: (1) a hierarchical command structure, (2) a specialization of functions, and (3) a rational arrangement of official positions according to the performance of necessary tasks. Such ideal characteristics, as cited by Max Weber and other students of public administration, are present in bureaucracies at varying levels and at various times. However, to the degree that a specific organization becomes bureaucratized, it will exhibit these operational tendencies. It is worth noting that Weber and others saw the bureaucratization of modern affairs as an improvement over preexisting modes of organization in that bureaucracy, by its very nature, is technically superior to these other forms by virtue of its greater efficiency. The specialization, rationality, efficiency, and impersonality of bureaucratic modes of operation are considered superior to prebureaucratic forms in much the same way that a machine is considered superior to non-mechanical modes of production and transportation.

At the micro level, Anthony Downs, in his influential analysis of bureaucracy, puts forth and defends three central hypotheses that seek to explain how bureaucracies and their staff operate.[4] First, he postulates that bureaucratic officials seek to attain their goals in a rational manner. As "utility maximizers," officials over time act efficiently, given the set of constraints imposed upon their behavior. These constraints may entail the limited capabilities of the actors themselves, the lack of complete information in decision making, the standard operating procedures of the bureaus themselves, and the like. Second, according to Downs, despite a relatively wide array of individual goals that motivate the behavior of bureaucratic officials, such as power, wealth, loyalty, and pride, every official is significantly and primarily motivated, even in his or her official capacity, by self-interest. Finally, and for present purposes most importantly, Downs posits that every organization's social functions are conditioned by, and help to influence, its internal structure and behavior. That is, for Downs there exists an inexorable link between the fashion in which an organization is structured and the way its officials behave in its social *milieu*.

This alleged superiority of the bureaucratic organization, though, is not without its own particular set of problems. Indeed, a dominant theme in the analysis of bureaucracies has been the explication of those specific dysfunctional characteristics that almost inexorably develop as side effects of the adoption of bureaucratic modes of organization. For present purposes, these operational characteristics can be divided into categories with particular reference to problems associated with organization size, organization age, and organization control. Without doubt, this tripartite separation is artificial and is justifiable only on the grounds of emphasizing these salient characteristics. As shall be shown, organizational size and the behavioral consequences of size cannot be separated out from those consequences associated with the age of an organization (e.g., bureaucracies tend to grow larger over time), or the problems of internal control (e.g., larger bureaucracies are more difficult to control than are smaller ones). However, it is useful for strictly analytical reasons to treat them separately.

Factors Related to the Size of Bureaus

According to Downs, all organizations have inherent tendencies to expand. Because bureaucrats are keen on maximizing their own individual power, or at least maximizing their self-interest, bureaucratic organizations tend to grow in size as these individuals widen the areas of responsibility over which they exercise some degree of leverage. As the resultant collective drive of the organization—the embodiment of these aggregate desires—is concomitantly to grow larger, additional responsibilities are adopted, and staff size grows. Internal functions are forced, then, to become more specialized and routinized if the organization is to succeed in its attempt to digest these additional responsibilities and staff.

One ramification of this tendency of bureaus to grow entails the continual efforts on the part of individual officials, on the one hand, and the entire organization, on the other, to justify and expand on their original *raison d'être*. That is to say, in the course of efforts to expand both individual and organization prerogatives, organizations very often alter the very justification for the bureau's existence in the first place. It is almost axiomatic to assert that if operational efficiencies are to be maintained within an expanding organizational environment, the goals or responsibilities of the organization must expand as well. Conversely, without expanded responsibilities, be they defined in terms of a greater number of organizational goals or in the application of identical goals to a larger domain, increases in the physical size of a bureaucracy could occur only at the cost of decreased operational efficiency.

Unfortunately, such a decline in the operational efficiency in larger organizations may be even more difficult to avoid. This is true for at least two basic reasons. First, by and large, smaller organizations accommodate change and innovation better than do larger ones. In an organizational sense, smaller bureaucracies are more nimble than larger ones by virtue of the fact that by definition they are less complex with respect to their range of functions and the size of their staffs. Smaller personnel chains are more amenable to change because line officials, in particular, and all subordinates, more generally, are not required, as they are in larger organizations, to institute or adopt a series of discretionary, ad hoc, procedures to fulfill their official duties. To the degree that lower officials are reliant on informal procedures, they are less likely to respond efficiently to commands from higher hierarchical levels. Put simply, smaller organizations are organizationally and functionally more parsimonious and, thus, are more amenable to shifts and changes in their operational procedures.

Second, as organizations grow larger, the amount of individual discretion that accrues to the lower officials increases. The more complex the organization becomes as a result of increased size, the more difficult it is to maintain that level of accurate and timely coordination that is necessary for optimal efficiency. Size alone can complicate and retard the flow of information up and down the hierarchy. Increased complexity in an organization places a high level of authority and decision-making discretion on lower officials who may not be in a position to make what are in the opinion of their superiors the best decisions.

It is important to note that the literature on bureaucracy looks upon the growth of these informal roles and practices within bureaucratic organizations, and the increased discretionary power of lower officials that supports them, as relatively functional developments. Such operational maneuverability on the part of lower officials can often contribute to the efficient functioning of the organization. Frequently, lower officials who enjoy discretionary powers within the normal range of their official responsibilities are thus able to utilize their own informal relationships with individuals both inside and outside the organization to rationalize the behavior of the bureaucracy at that particular level of its operation. Lower officials are more often than not in a better position, so the logic goes, to make improvements in the efficiency of the organization's operations, even if the informal procedures that are employed to do so fall outside the knowledge of that official's superiors. Put another way, organizational superiors with the formal responsibility and authority to institutionalize or formalize new procedures are often bereft of information regarding the activities of lower-level officials; in such circumstances, the formal changes from organizational superiors with real organizational authority are less desirable, from a strict efficiency perspective, than those enacted informally by lower officials with no real authority to do so. As shall be explored below, such a situation has profound affects on the ability of superiors to control the individual activities of their lower officials.

Finally, the literature on bureaucracy goes a long way in explaining what for the Soviet example was a noteworthy aspect of the political system in the Brezhnev period. Downs refers to the "rigidity cycle" or the "ossification syndrome" to explain a significant problem associated with extensive growth in a large bureaucratic organization. While observers of the Soviet Union have used such terms as "petrification" and "ossification" to explain the advanced aging of the Soviet political elite, the Downsian concept refers more to the rigidity of the operation of the bureaucracy itself. Briefly, he describes the increasing demands of paperwork, unnecessary procedures, and elaborate justifications that must be prepared and sent up the hierarchy before any action can be taken. Procedurally, the bureaucracy ossifies. The opportunity costs involved in innovation become quite immense and serve as formidable disincentives to innovation. According to Downs,

> The rigidity cycle is much more likely to occur in communist countries than in most western nations for two reasons. First, most bureaus in non-democratic societies receive weaker feedbacks. Second, the bureaucracies in at least two communist nations—China and Russia—are vastly larger in absolute size. Faced by enormous hierarchies with dozens of levels, top-ranking officials are compelled to establish giant monitoring bureaus that develop complex hierarchies of their own (such as the Communist Party).[5]

Because the organizational apparatus of the state becomes so unsympathetic to change, political leaders are forced to utilize different techniques to effect changes in policy direction or emphasis. This accounts for the typical Soviet practice of "campaigning," or "storming"—the phenomenon occurring most regularly at the end of the economic plan period marked by the accelerated and frenzied work pace aimed at fulfilling the production quotas set by superiors. Such high-profile measures can be seen as either an attempt on the part of the leadership to solve problems outside the normal administrative structure of the state or to prod the existing structures to operate in unconventional ways. Almost inevitably, of course, such campaigns wither away as the ossified bureaucracy again reverts to its normal mode of operation.

Factors Related to the Age of Bureaus

At a certain stage in the growth cycle of a bureaucratic organization, a point is passed beyond which the relative strength of organizational stasis tends increasingly to outweigh the relative strength of organizational change. By virtue of what Downs refers to as the greater "sunk costs" involved in large bureaucratic organizations when compared to smaller ones, there tends to develop in the former an individual, collective, and thus structural bias against innovation.

Innovation, by its very nature, threatens the older bureaucratic cadres whose self-interest is better served by the maintenance of the old methods of operation that are well known to them. New procedures that entail the repudiation of older operational practices will not be welcomed by bureaucratic officials whose power within the organization is based on their intimate knowledge of, and acquired skills relative to, the old. Because bureaucratic organizations reward this acquired competence, it is likely to be the case that these older officials, who are by this stage of their careers at the upper levels of the command hierarchy, will be able to delay or stall any innovation that they perceive as undermining their own self-interest. The picture of younger bureaucratic staff elements pushing for innovation and change within an organization, only to be thwarted by their more powerful superiors, is certainly not uncommon and is in large part due to the factors connected with age of the bureaucracy and its leading cadres. This conservative phenomenon is especially nettlesome in organizations that have traditionally experienced relatively low personnel turnover.[6]

Similarly, as the age of the bureaucratic staff increases, the behavioral tendencies of these cadres shift as well. Their psychological orientation toward their work assumes the character of what has been referred to as a "conserver." Conservers as bureaucratic officials do not necessarily seek additional power, prestige, income, or any other such perquisites, but they are determined to maintain those that they have already attained. Given that they do not expect to experience any further significant upward mobility in the bureau's hierarchy, conservers are biased in favor of maintaining the organizational status quo and thereby resist change. In their view, change has a great potential downside with very little possibility for positive gains.

Factors Related to the Control of Bureaus

Another set of problems related to both the size and age of bureaucratic organizations merits separate treatment here in that it impacts critically on the issue of corruption. These problems revolve around the difficulties within large bureaucracies in the control of lower officials by their superiors. At a general level, students of bureaucracy have noted the "leakage" of authority in large hierarchical organizations. The extreme specialization of functions in large organizations structured along bureaucratic lines permits, and indeed encourages, the development among lower officials of a certain degree of organizational freedom that may be both desirable and regrettable to those at the upper end of the hierarchy.

As mentioned above, the development of informal relationships and informal structures among interrelated, interdependent lower-level officials has been seen as a positive development in at least one sense: such relationships have helped increase the rationality and efficiency of the administrative system. The officials charged with the actual duty of implementing the minutiae of organizational policy are logically those with the best information as to how the formal system for doing so should be altered so as to increase the efficiency of the operation. Such tinkering can originate with no other segment of the bureaucracy's staff.

In this sense, all the benefits that normally accompany increases in the efficiency of the organization accrue to those at the top of the organization who are ultimately responsible for administration on a broad scale. In heavily socialized systems such as existed in the Soviet

Union, organizational or bureaucratic efficiency impacts on much more than the annual bonus of the organization's chief operating officer or the size of the stockholder's dividend. Rather, inasmuch as the legitimacy of such political systems is in large part defined by the level of efficiency of the pervasive public organs, increases in the latter can portend gigantic political gains. In this sense, then, the development of informal modes of behavior by bureaucratic officials may be encouraged by those very superiors who are unable to control the professional activities of their subordinates. Of course, in many if not most cases, the superiors have little information about the nature of these informal structures created over time by lower officials. These practices may nevertheless be unwittingly encouraged by superiors who assign to their subordinates the series of tasks that cannot be satisfied through normal means.

Unfortunately for these key organizational superiors, the very freedom on the part of lower officials to engage in such informal activities, to create informal associations with their peers in other organizations, and to develop creative procurement procedures, for example, entails some quite undesirable costs as well. While these activities may benefit the organization in some ways, it is doubtful that they were originated by the lower officials for that reason alone. Here is where the rub lies. Bureaucrats, be they American or Soviet, Chinese or German, are motivated significantly by self-interest. As discussed above, there are often positive side effects for the organization when its officials engage in self-interested activities beyond the view and control of their superiors. With these benefits, however, also comes some rather worrisome costs.

The extensions and adaptations of the formal rules that are utilized in large organizations will be put to use by officials to benefit themselves. The level of discretion that develops for these officials allows them to behave in ways that are in contradiction to the formal goals of the organization for which they work. As Downs puts it, "whenever officials have any discretion, they will use at least some of it to advance their own interests rather than the formal interests of the organization."[7] In a word, a bureaucracy's higher-ups will be unable in many cases to control the self-aggrandizing activities of their subordinates. What is more, they may not wish to do so, even if they could, for fear of losing the gains that accrue to the organization itself as a result of these activities.

Large organizations, then, have significant problems, both in a practical sense and in terms of organizational efficiency, in controlling the self-interested activities of staff. Since the phenomenon in question is known by the superiors to provide both credits and debits to the organization, leaders are inevitably forced to enter into some sort of calculus that revolves around the question of just what level of informal, self-interested activity on the part of the official staff is optimal. In systems such as that which operated in the Soviet Union, where both the potential selfish abuse on the part of officials is highest and where the efficiency of the public organs is so clearly tied to regime legitimacy, the stakes involved in such calculations are highest.

Historical Influences

This chapter started with the assertion that hierarchical, bureaucratic organization has been a tradition in Russia, both under tsarist and Soviet rule. Given the tendencies identified above, which inhere in large bureaucratic organizations by sheer virtue of their particular structure, it should not be surprising to find a historical legacy of administrative corruption in pre-1917 Russia. Indeed, a cursory look at the manner of public administration dating back to the late seventeenth century reveals striking similarities in this respect to the problems of Soviet official corruption. That is, despite rather marked differences in the types of individuals that comprised the administrative organs, the amount and type of training these officials enjoyed, and the ideology of administration under the two systems, to name only the most obvious factors, certain weaknesses of the tsarist system of administration have not been solved by the communists.

Historians seem to agree that Russian tsarist officialdom was of a generally poor quality. Marc Raeff has argued that the Russian civil service was noteworthy, until perhaps the middle of the 1800s, for its lack of formal education, its inadequate training, and mediocre performance.[8] These traits applied to central officials in Moscow and St. Petersburg, but especially to the provincial nobility. The motley character of the Russian civil service has been explained primarily by the inadequate economic conditions that governed its existence.

According to one student of the Russian civil service, the critical psychological distinction between private activity and public office, so crucial in the development of a professional administrative structure, came late to Russia, only in the second half of the nineteenth century.[9] Prior to this time, the notion that the appointment to public office was in large part a kind of personal sinecure, and that a living could be maintained only by extracting measures of wealth from the local population, was widely accepted and encouraged to a degree by the central authorities. As a result of the rather paltry salaries provided to officials and the ample opportunities to engage in corruption, the tsar and his ministers received frequent complaints about the illicit behavior of his officials.

Seventeenth-century Muscovy suffered under endemic corruption rooted in the *voevoda* system, in which the officials sent by the center to administer the various provinces would alleviate what for many of them was actual impoverishment by feeding off the local inhabitants.[10] For many years, the Russian provinces were administered by retired military officials, generally of noble rank, and their families who could not live off the rather paltry pensions provided by the state. The other provincial officials were likewise not provided adequate salaries and the center thereby encouraged the continuation of this practice of expropriation long after it was legally proscribed. Various types of bribery took place, despite prohibitions and exhortations from the center. "Tokens of respect" *(pochesti)* were paid to provincial officials, as were "name-day" gifts *(pominki)* given to officials on the holy feasts of their patron saints. Provisions or payments in kind *(korm)*, such as food from the harvest or the rendering of services, were also very frequent.

The state actually adopted a kind of schizophrenic policy with respect to the pervasive corruption of this period. On the one hand, the government issued strongly worded threats outlining the punishments that would fall on the heads of those officials abusing their positions while, on the other hand, consciously dispensing provincial positions as *satrapies*. The roots of this contradictory policy lay in the fact that the state budgets of the 1600s could not support these officials with adequate salaries. The Russian state was much better at conferring status on officials than it was in providing sufficient salaries. Over the years, the local populations came to see such behavior as relatively normal and accepted within bounds the existence of bribery and other such proscribed activities on the part of their provincial officials. As a popular Russian saying of the seventeenth century put it, "The horse loves oats, the soil manure, and the *voevoda* the bearing."[11]

Generally speaking, central authorities were patently unable to control the activities of their line officials in the provinces. The technology of the day was not conducive to the uniform administration of a vast territory. Complaints from Siberia, for instance, would take many months to reach Moscow, if they arrived at all. Inspectors were sent occasionally from Moscow to check up on the activities of the provincial officials, but these controllers were not infrequently bribed themselves to keep from reporting the real nature of the local governance. Given that provincial postings were by far the worst possible duties one could be assigned, it was difficult to find trustworthy individuals anxious to be sent to replace the incompetent and corrupt provincial noble. The center was thus forced to rely on an incomplete set of deterrents such as the replacement of officials and threats of punishment. Even in such cases where fresh faces were sent to the regions, the structure of the situation within which these individuals found themselves compelled them to engage in these activities, threats or no threats. Indeed, the political police considered service in the Russian provinces to be such a corrupting experience that under Nicholas I they requested for their officials the tsar's exemption from the normal requirement that they serve three years in the provinces before becoming eligible for posts in St. Petersburg.[12]

Such activities were not relegated solely to the backwoods of the Russian empire. Foreign visitors often complained of the rampant and open bribery necessary to do business in Moscow and St. Petersburg. Gioe, the Danish ambassador to Russia, issued a complaint in 1672 that is often heard in Moscow today, when he declared that "everything is for sale here."[13] The high organs of the tsarist state did indeed pass laws aimed at uprooting such activities, but the enforcement of such statutes tended to be rather sporadic. In explaining the pervasiveness of bribery in particular and corruption more generally, and their clear inability to stamp it out, the authorities often cited the traditional willingness and acceptance on the part of the local population to tolerate it. In the eyes of the empire's subjects, the corruption of state officials had become, as far back as the 1600s, axiomatic.

Peter the Great is generally given credit for setting in motion a series of reforms that eventually improved the quality of the Russian civil service.[14] For the purposes of the present topic, Peter's reign (1689–1725) is noteworthy for the development within the civil service of a well-defined and uniform ranking of career development, *chinoproizvodstvo*. As has been well documented, the structure of the imperial bureaucracy was established by the famous 1722 Petrine Table of Ranks. The 1722 decree entailed the creation of a set of parallel, fourteen-step hierarchies for civil, military, and court service. In such manner, Peter was the first to make a strong distinction between civil and military service. Each official was obliged to work his way through the service ranks *(chin)*, which ranged from the fourteenth, at the low end, to the first rank, at the very top. Noblemen and non-nobles alike were subject to the rigid structure of the civil service hierarchy; instances of officials within the civil service skipping a rank were almost non-existent. All officials who attained the eighth rank or higher automatically became hereditary nobles. In this manner Peter I introduced for the first time in Russia the possibility of officials attaining noble status through quality service to the state.

However, qualitative improvements in the Russian bureaucracy did not occur rapidly. Hereditary nobles frequently looked for ways to avoid their service obligation to the state. Moreover, the sons of the high nobility continued well into the second half of the eighteenth century to eschew civil posts for the more prestigious military career path. As a result, it was precisely the section of Russian society that, by virtue of its better educational backgrounds and other accrued advantages, was best suited to the tasks of civil administration that only reluctantly accepted such responsibilities for the state.

Catherine II (reign 1762–1796) is also credited with administrative reform that improved the internal management of the Russian state.[15] She sought to increase the efficiency of state management by improving the communication between the center and the periphery of the empire. Her reform of 1775 entailed the institution of elections to be held in the provinces whereby the local nobility would select officials for service in the provinces. Each provincial government *(guberniia)* would be staffed, then, by the governor *(gubernator)*, who was responsible for overseeing numerous staff members appointed by Moscow, as well as an official cadre elected by the local provincial nobility. In this way, Catherine and later autocrats were able simultaneously to incorporate the local nobility into the affairs of the Russian locales without providing them a totally autonomous sphere of influence. The officials elected for service would be held accountable to the dictates of the *gubernator* and the remaining center-appointed *guberniia* staff. The potential impact of these new election mechanisms was lessened further by the fact that there never developed more than a passing interest among the nobiliary class, or the *dvorianstvo,* in the actual holding of elective office.

Such reforms, however, failed to address the root cause of official misconduct in the regions as well as the center: insufficient rewards from the state treasury for officials. Pensions for the frequent retired military officers who assumed provincial posts were almost non-existent until 1764, and after this time pensions of half-pay were issued only to officers who had served a military term of at least thirty-five years. Given the decidedly low salaries provided to the civil servants of this period, and the general flavor of the pension system, it is not surprising, again, that official corruption in the provinces remained ubiquitous. Moreover, given the state's inability to find sufficient funds from the treasury to pay provincial officials, it is not surprising either that the legal punishments for official corruption were never uniformly applied. Indeed, one is drawn to the conclusion that the Russian imperial court viewed the corruption of its officials, especially those in the provinces, in functional terms. As Marc Raeff has put it,

> Status conferred by state service was crucial in the Russian case, for the government was quite parsimonious about material compensation while very generous in providing outward signs of authority that, incidentally, could in turn provide opportunities for graft—a significant item in view of the low salaries. This consideration justifies the inclusion in official-dom of clerks and other officials below those who comprised the hierarchy in the Table of Ranks; for these more lowly servants of the state shared with their superiors an authority and the extralegal sources of revenue denied anyone outside of officialdom. . . .[16]

If the state was unable to provide sufficient remuneration directly to these officials, it could do so indirectly by providing the status required by these individuals to extract graft from the populations with which they dealt. If such a calculus was entertained in St. Petersburg, the enforcement of anti-corruption decrees would of necessity be applied only to those cases where the offending official went beyond what was considered by his superiors to be a "normal" level of corruption. This theory may partially explain the rare (given the pervasiveness of corruption) instances when officials actually were severely punished.

Tsar Aleksandr I (reign 1801–1825) adopted a liberal domestic policy. He released many political prisoners, relaxed censorship, and loosened the strictures against the importation of foreign literature. Aleksandr replaced many bureaucrats with better qualified individuals and also is credited with structural reform of the Russian administrative state. He instituted the uniform ministerial structure in 1802, a structure that has persisted in its basics up to the present time. His reorientation of the Cabinet placed individual responsibility in heads of newly established ministries. By virtue of his decree of September 1802, the old administrative system was abolished and several ministries, each headed by a responsible minister, were established: Interior, Foreign Affairs, War, Navy, Finance, Justice, and Education.[17] While each minister was responsible to the crown alone, Aleksandr's reform further rationalized the Russian state apparatus. In 1810, Aleksandr I created the Council of State, which was based on the model of Napoleon's *Conseil d'État*, and appointed Count Mikhail Speransky to the position of Secretary of State. The Council of State was composed of a number of experts whose purpose was to aid the Tsar in legislative matters. According to one noted historian of the period, the Council "reflected the emphasis on legality, competence, and correct procedure. . . ."[18]

Speransky also restructured the ministerial system, focusing especially on the adoption of sound financial and budgetary procedures. Finally, in yet another positive step for Russian officialdom under Aleksandr I, the secretary of state introduced a rudimentary civil service examination for the bureaucracy and thereby strengthened the more meritocratic elements of internal administrative procedure.

According to Pintner, the development of Russian officialdom during the century ending with the death of Nicholas I in 1855 involved two major developments: (1) the great increase in the size of officialdom, and (2) the significant further development of functional specialization, which allowed for a greater differentiation of the nobility and other groups from the cadres of the administrative apparatus. Russian civil officialdom witnessed an increase in size during this period on the order of ten to one, from approximately 10,500 in 1755 to 113,990 in 1856.[19] Such a growth in the number of officials clearly outpaced the growth of the Russian population during this time and thus represented an increase in the social role of Russian officialdom. With respect to the specialization and growing professionalization of the state officials, Pintner argues that

> Major and rapid changes occurred not in the pedigree and economic background of officialdom, but in the nature of their service experience and in the training officials underwent as preparation for it. Put very

briefly, what happened was that in the course of the first fifty years of the nineteenth century civil service became a distinct professional career requiring specialized training prior to entry. The life patterns and experience of officials came to be essentially the same as those of the bureaucrats of contemporary Western European states.[20]

Under Nicholas, greater emphasis was placed on the strict hierarchical nature of the administrative structures, even to the point of his introduction of official uniforms, complete with symbols of rank, for members of the bureaucracy. Centralization increased as many of the prerogatives of the local governmental bodies established under Catherine were emasculated and the provincial authorities were subject to a greater degree to central control, particularly to the Ministry of the Interior. The Russian bureaucracy during the reign of Nicholas I, then, became more hierarchical, disciplined, centralized, and orderly—but remained, especially at the lower levels, a corrupted officialdom.

Despite the increases in formal bureaucratic tendencies, Nicholas I also relied heavily on a number of ad hoc committees that allowed him to bypass the conventional state bureaucracy. As a result, the importance of these institutions (e.g., the State Council, the Senate, the Committee of Ministers) declined somewhat during his reign. Furthermore, the increased specialization of his own Imperial Chancery, especially its famous Third Department—the political police—provided the tsar with a number of personal bureaucratic weapons outside the regular state channels. His Majesty's Own Private Imperial Chancery, its official name, was eventually to become organized into six sections or departments, each with a specialized area of responsibility.[21] The First Department managed the imperial family's estates. The Second Department, headed by Speransky, was involved in the codification of Russian law. The Third Department, the political police, enjoyed an almost unlimited sphere of action and often overlapped other public and social institutions. In addition to the predictable duties associated with political police, the Third Department prepared for the tsar a survey of public opinion on various issues for his use in preparing legislation. The Fourth Department handled imperial charities and the Fifth was involved in planning with respect to the emancipation of the serfs. Finally, the Sixth Department of His Majesty's Own Private Imperial Chancery was created to oversee the administration of certain territories in the Caucasus.

Despite the increases in the prior training required of the official-dom,[22] the functional specialization of the administrative apparatus, and other trends that can generally be considered to have increased the professionalization of the bureaucracy, the level of remuneration made available to state officials, especially in the provinces, where "a truly Gogolian picture of backwardness and neglect"[23] obtained, proved inadequate to solve the still persistent level of official corruption in the system.

Little changed in this respect during the reigns of the final three tsars of the Romanov dynasty, Aleksandr II, Aleksandr III, and Nicholas II. Of course, some significant administrative and other reforms occurred during the early years of Aleksandr II (reign 1855–1881). He emancipated the serfs in 1861, initiated changes in local governance which distributed power over some local matters to the *zemstva,* and instituted some notable reforms in the judiciary. However, this period of rather liberal rule ended with the attempted assassination of Aleksandr II by Dmitrii Karakozov in April 1866. Centralization increased, and his actual assassination in 1881 set the tone for the last years of the imperial period.

Such were the general feelings about the power, pervasiveness, and corruption of the bureaucratic apparatus in Russia by the ascendancy of Nicholas II in 1894 that officials from the *zemstva,* comprised mostly of members of the nobility, declared in an open letter to the new tsar that

> if autocracy in word and deed proclaims itself identical with the omnipotence of bureaucracy, if it can exist only so long as society is voiceless, its cause is lost. It digs its own grave.[24]

Russian society during this period underwent rapid changes to be sure, but the role of the state was always preeminent. Rapid industrialization and the resultant urban migration[25] did not alter the pervasiveness of state organs. In language to be used often by students of the Soviet period, historians of this final period of imperial rule in Russia argued that

> the Russian empire stood alone as a society in which a great many aspects of human activity were to a large extent administered or at least regulated by the state.... There were few phases of Russian life in

which it was not directly interested, and over many of the most important it had a virtual monopoly through direct administration and a deci-
sive influence in policy-making.[26]

As this brief review has highlighted, the historical legacy of bureaucratization and rampant official corruption was one of the most salient
features of a system inherited by the Bolsheviks with their seizure and
consolidation of power between 1917 and 1920. While the Soviet period certainly added its particular flavor to these problems, and in the
process elevated both to unprecedented levels of influence, the roots of
official corruption extend back into Russian history. In Russia as well
as the Soviet Union, government meant officialdom, its progressive
bureaucratization, and its pervasive corruption.

The 1917 Bolshevik Revolution marked the demise of the nobility
as a significant social group and as the major feeder of individuals into
state officialdom. It did not, however, arrest the inherited trends toward
the increasing bureaucratization of public institutions in Russian society. In that year Lenin proclaimed to his followers: "We have con-
quered Russia, now we must govern it." In governing Soviet Russia,
the Bolshevik method of public administration was firmly rooted in the
tradition of its tsarist predecessors. Indeed, in many respects, it can be
argued that the Soviet state structure was built on the existing founda-
tion inherited from the imperial period. To be sure, the Soviet period of
history witnessed the extreme exaggeration of the state, the bureaucratization of public life, and the corruption of officialdom, all to a degree
unparalleled by anything in the historical record of Russia. In addition,
certain distinct elements of the Bolshevik scheme of public administration exacerbated these characteristics and thereby guaranteed the development of corruption from a social problem to a system requisite.

Soviet-Specific Influences

As I have attempted to demonstrate in the previous two sections, the
Bolshevik leadership that inherited the Russian state also inherited an
endemic problem of official corruption. Moreover, the eradication or
control of these corrupt practices would not be facilitated by the strict
hierarchical and bureaucratic schemes for the administration of society
that the Soviets eventually adopted. In fact, as the brief discussion of
organizational theory with respect to corruption highlighted, the

schemes that the Soviet leadership did adopt for the running of the Soviet state accomplished little more in this regard than to exacerbate the inherited problem of corruption. It was partially for these reasons that contemporary commentators during the rapid rise of bureaucratization in Soviet Russia raised such serious and vociferous warnings against the Bolshevik state.

Again, at the risk of making artificial distinctions, what follows attempts to explicate those aspects of political corruption in the USSR that can be traced to policies, structures, and institutions of a particularly Soviet nature. With this goal in mind, this section of the chapter is divided under five headings which seek to highlight separate considerations of the phenomenon of Soviet-inspired corruption. Briefly, the treatment focuses on corruption as related to (1) the ideology of Soviet administration, (2) organizational structure, (3) economic planning, (4) Soviet law, and (5) institutional weakness. While each theme to be developed is certainly related to each of the others in important ways, they have been separated for purely analytic reasons. It is hoped that in so doing, a clearer and more objective view of corruption in the Soviet Union may be approached.

Factors Related to the Ideology of Soviet Administration

It is a bit unusual to speak of an "ideology of administration" or an "administrative ideology" if by that is meant anything other than the notions of how bureaucrats behave in an idealized Weberian sense. That is, ideology is normally considered to reside in the realm of politics, not in the realm of administration, which is seen as more or less operationally devoid of an "ideology." Bureaucracy is said to be pragmatic, empirical, dispassionate or impersonal, even clinical in its approach to tasks—all seeming antonyms to normal understandings of the concept "ideology." This is not to say, of course, that members of the bureaucracy have no political or ideological positions or that political debates do not exist within the bureaucratic apparatuses of a state. But there is assumed to be a separation between the personal political leanings of individuals who comprise the administrative organs of a state and an *operational ethos* that conditions how administrative units go about fulfilling their duties.

However, an ideology of administration with respect to the issue of official corruption certainly did exist in the Soviet Union. In discussing this concept, Michael E. Urban has argued that "contradictions inherent within the practice of administration find expression and resolution at the level of symbols (ideology) which, as mediators between the world of action and the realm of reflection, serve to stabilize the administrative role."[27] The behavior of bureaucrats (the "world of action") is conditioned by a set of ideological principles that lend the stability to their professional roles and that is not provided my their mere "speculations" or thoughts about their roles. In some sense, then, this ideology of administration intervenes between the theoretical role of bureaucrats, on the one hand, and the way they actually behave in their official capacities, on the other. As Urban puts it, "administrative ideology understands its object, administration, as a technical project emanating from technical needs."[28] Understanding the major elements of this administrative ideology sheds a significant amount of light on the phenomenon of official corruption in the Soviet Union.

The particular history of how Stalin reversed most aspects of the mixed economy of the "New Economic Policy" and introduced in late 1927 the command economy based on five-year economic planning is well known and need not be reviewed in any great detail here. It is worth noting, however, that perhaps from the very beginning of First Five-Year Plan (1928–1933) in the Soviet Union, an ideology of economic and political administration was introduced which established the tone of managerial behavior for decades to come. Stalin adopted as the official slogan of the First Five-Year Plan the dictum: "Victors of production are not judged." While it is certainly true that many hundreds of thousands of Soviet officials *were* "judged" during Stalin's rule in the Soviet Union, the political rules that governed their behavior and established official expectations were, as stated in the previous pages, mainly informal. Despite the fact that these rules were never written down, codified, and promulgated as such, Soviet officials quickly understood the prevailing ideology of administration.

Charles A. Schwartz has highlighted six informal operational rules of behavior that speak to the content of an ideology of administration in the USSR.[29] The first operational rule to be honored states that *party interests have supremacy over legal ones.* This axiom of the informal ideology reveals the political bias that existed with respect to questions of official misconduct and corruption in office. The party's interests had primacy over those of the law and were as a matter of course to be defended over mere legal statutes. As an appropriate indication of the strength of this axiom, it is worth noting that members of the Communist Party in the USSR could have legal charges leveled against them only with the permission of the relevant party committee. Without the approval of the party apparatus itself, criminal charges against party members had no effect. The second rule states that *nothing succeeds like plan success.* This tenet of the informal ideology is certainly reflected in the above-cited 1928 slogan of Stalin, which states that good producers will not have their methods scrutinized. So long as the production goals of the regime are being facilitated, unsavory and illegal tactics may be tolerated. As Schwartz states, "the *nomenklatura* and courts tend to weigh corruption on the scale of public usefulness and political expediency."[30] The more closely the transgressions dovetail with state interests, the less "criminal" they are considered by the authorities and the less likely they are to be punished by the authorities.

A third informal political rule posits that *state money likes to be counted.* Here Schwartz argues that Soviet authorities made a sharp distinction between state property and personal property when it came to evaluating various shades of illicit behavior. Managers who crossed the line and involved themselves in blatant theft of state property risked extremely severe penalties, while those who were involved in the theft or embezzlement of personal property received significantly less serious sentences. This distinction between state and personal property in the eyes of the enforcement organs was partially erased in the early 1960s. Khrushchev's reinvigoration of the anti-corruption penalties in 1961 and 1962 certainly raised the stakes for official transgressions. In May of 1961, the death penalty was reimposed for large-scale theft of state property (it had been abolished by Stalin in 1947). Two months later, the list of crimes punishable by death was extended to speculation in foreign currency. Finally, in February 1962, Khrushchev extended the death penalty as a possible punishment for serious cases of bribe-taking. It should be noted, however, that Brezhnev reestablished rather quickly the distinction blurred by Khrushchev. The axiomatic status of this informal rule reached new heights under the Brezhnev regime and, in fact, one need look no further than the Brezhnev family itself[31] for prime examples of illicit personal aggrandizement. The message to Soviet political and economic officials was quite clear.[32]

A fourth tenet of the ideology of administration in the Soviet Union stated that *benign or "white" forms of corruption will be tolerated.* "White" corruption does not involve material gain for individuals beyond the *premia* they would have received anyway if the quota would have been filled. If managers engaged in report padding to make it appear that they have performed their duties well, and if bonuses are secured, this form of corruption was considered to be of a more benign nature and was not to be met with severe punishment. One scholar who analyzed the penalties meted out on various levels of corruption cited a case of report padding at a power plant in Siberia where the plant director was convicted of what amounted to a 300,000 ruble transgression. In another case, managers at an automobile factory in the Caucasus were also convicted of report padding. Their punishment did not entail any deprivation of freedom or fines, but came to nothing more than dismissal from their positions in their respective enterprises.[33]

A fifth aspect of the informal administrative ideology states that *marginal or "gray" forms of corruption will be evaluated with respect to a set of economic performance criteria.* Instances of "gray" corruption included the sometimes significant material gains of those involved. Into this category one could place cases involving graft, influence peddling, and certain activities of procurement agents *(tolkachi).* If it could be demonstrated to enforcement agencies that such activities, while involving modest and almost incidental material gains to individuals, were predicated on the desire to perform official duties successfully and that both the amount and type of corruption engaged in were necessary and sufficient for the attainment of such success, then punishment was minimal. Such considerations as to intent, scale, and type of illicit activities on the part of Soviet officials highlight the ambiguous status, or large "gray areas," that required a case-by-case analysis by enforcement officials.

A final informal rule that helps comprise the ideology of administration and govern the behavior of Soviet officials states that *"black" forms of corruption will not be tolerated.* In this case, "black" corruption was seen by the authorities as the most dangerous and threatening to the system. It involved large and boldly conspicuous material gains, high living, and a blatant disrespect for Soviet law. Again, the scale of the corrupt activities is important here. Small-scale corruption within limits set by the authorities would be tolerated. Large-scale corruption and sizable accumulation of wealth would bring severe criminal penalties. Bribery for personal gain was a serious criminal offense in the Soviet Union, and officials who abused their position to accumulate vast stores of wealth were subject to the death penalty.

For example, several high government and Communist Party officials of the so-called "Uzbek Mafia" were sentenced to death in the
1980s for a variety of crimes, including issuing false statistics, bribery,
nepotism, and misallocation of funds. Several regional bosses had even
assembled secret private armies. Coming on the heels of revelations
concerning Uzbekistan's habit of charging Moscow for almost a million tons of non-existent cotton annually, the entire upper echelons of
Uzbekistan's state and party apparatuses were purged. The scam was
allegedly uncovered by Yuri Andropov, who, as chairman of the KGB,
ordered the Uzbek cotton field harvests to be photographed with recon-
naissance satellites.

In summarizing these aspects of the informal Soviet administrative
ideology, Schwartz argues that

> what makes the Soviet system relatively distinctive in this respect are
> its two basic features: (1) party supremacy over the society, and thus "a
> differential approach to lawbreakers," and (2) the contradiction between
> the exaggerated ambitions of the development plans and the severe
> limitations that scarce resources and shoddy institutions impose. It is
> this basic combination—party supremacy and system shoddiness—that
> demands and rewards risk taking for the good of the cause.[34]

Factors Related to Organizational Structure

The first section of this chapter focuses directly on the generic problem
of bureaucratic organization with special attention paid to the issues of
the size, age, and control of bureaus. Without doubt, many of the
problems that seemingly inhere in all large hierarchical bureaucracies
were present in the Soviet case. Of particular relevance to the USSR,
however, were a number of dysfunctions that had their roots in the
specifics of the Soviet organizational structure.

It is important at the outset to state that the *modus operandi* of the
Soviet economy presented a series of selective material incentives to
economic actors that collectively guaranteed a significant level of corruption both among the general population and among those officials
charged with the duty of running the Soviet state. Montias and Rose-
Ackerman have provided a very fine review of organizational factors
and the incentives they produce as they related to the flourishing Soviet second economy.[35] They cite several organizational problems that
facilitated corruption in the Soviet Union.

First, any social system organized in such a decidedly hierarchical manner will experience a large degree of authority "leakage," which entails in the present context the creation of a set of incentives not fully compatible with the stated interests of those at the top of the decision-making pyramid. As a result, the very officials interested in controlling the actions of their subordinates will be largely unable to do so. Given that lower-level officials in the Soviet Union were frequently confronted by a different set of pressures than those conceived of by superiors, the leakage of authority was significant, as was the deviation of subordinates' actions from those expected and desired by superiors.

Second, given the set of challenges faced by Soviet managers, the characteristics developed by "successful" managers included behaviors that were technically illegal. That this is the case was almost axiomatic in the Soviet Union. Nicholas Lampert explains:

> [T]he Soviet form of political management itself helps to create an environment in which illegal practices flourish. . . . In the first place, because the mechanism of directive planning is highly imperfect, the managers of economic units feel obliged regularly to break the law in order to meet their targets in the face of constant difficulties with the supply of needed goods and materials. In this way "unofficial" practices become part and parcel of "official" production and exchange.[36]

Given the organization of the Soviet system, there was a significant disincentive for the authorities to apply the law against officials who relied on "corrupt" activities to perform their official duties successfully. As Montias and Rose-Ackerman put it, "agents capable of managing subhierarchies (ministries, chief administrations, enterprises) and of exercising initiative are scarce. Therefore, they cannot be dismissed or imprisoned without causing some loss to the organization to which they belong."[37] Both superiors and subordinates, then, come to have their decisions governed less by the official code of behavior than by a set of informal and unofficial rules.

Third, because the Soviets adopted an economic and political schema that tended toward the creation of large and extremely well-integrated (or interdependent) organizations, each controlled through the central hierarchy, it facilitated an almost perfect environment for the proliferation of corruption. Once corruption became a mode of behavior in one unit of the hierarchy, the organizational structure of Soviet society immediately and rather easily elevated such practices to an organizational *ethos*. Put conversely, in a hierarchical organizational structure such as existed in the Soviet Union, where strong vertical forces (formal) facilitated the development of strong mutual-assistance horizontal forces (informal), controlling the spread of such informal (and illegal) activities becomes quite problematic—even to the degree that superiors wish to control them.

A fourth force extant in the Soviet case further exacerbated the problem of corruption. In what has been called a mono-organization society, individuals acting either as *homo economicus* or *homo politicus* are presented with very few options in resolving their problems. The system creates a series of near-monopolies (producers, ministries, agencies) with which one must interact in order to get things done. In such a system, all individuals must get various permissions, licenses, and other documents from official state organizations. Persons seeking benefits legally must compete in this setting with persons seeking benefits illegally. If two claimants seek needed documents from a government official, the claimant providing a bribe to that official tends to receive preferential treatment from that official. This practice leads to the corruption of all parties involved: the official, through whom every claimant must pass, receives illegal bribes for the performance (or non-performance) of his official duties; the claimant seeking benefits illegally is rewarded for the use of his bribe; and the claimant seeking benefits legally quickly learns that doing so severely hinders the chances of attaining that benefit—he or she will just as quickly be forced to offer bribes in order to compete in the system.

Fifth, because such an organizational system creates mutual-support networks of official across organizational lines (party, state, government, and so on), "whistleblowing" is extremely discouraged. If the informal system in the Soviet Union involved networks, friends, factions, followers, patrons, and clients, it created a structure of uncertainty for the whistleblower with respect to his activities as complainant. To whom could the whistleblower complain? How could the response of officials be predicted? Would rewards or punishments be forthcoming for whistleblowing? The existence of official agencies for such purposes, for example the Interior Ministry's Administration for Combating the Embezzlement of Socialist Property and Speculation (OBKhSS), did lessen the uncertainty a bit, but whistleblowers in the Soviet Union tended to be treated worse than those in the United States, hardly an encouraging situation.[38]

Finally, the issue of organizational secrecy must be addressed. One of the hallmarks of bureaucratization is that decision making within the organization is kept out of the public eye. Robert Merton states that "bureaucracy is administration which almost completely avoids public discussion of its techniques, although there may occur public discussions of its policies. This secrecy is confined neither to public nor to private bureaucracies."[39] Given the status and power of public bureaucracy in the Soviet Union, as well as the patent lack of private pressure groups in society which could act as a counter-balance to the governmental machinery, bureaucracies in the Soviet Union were much more secretive than those in the West. Such an environment, of course, provides fertile ground for the development of illicit administrative techniques. The extreme extent to which the Soviets traditionally ran public affairs through exclusive and secretive public bureaucracies provided yet another organizational impetus to official corruption.

In the organization of the Soviet economy, another set of incentives tended to support the proliferation of illegal activities. The formal incentive structure, informed as it was by the failed attempts on the part of the Soviet leadership to instill in both the producers and the consumers the ideological precepts of state socialism of the Soviet type, was a demonstrable failure. David Conn has expressed what a formal incentive structure would have to do to be considered a success:

> An incentive structure is effective if it (ultimately) ensures that an economy behaves in an appropriate manner. A more usual way of expressing this is to present a set of behavioral rules, one for each agent of the economy, that collectively guarantee that the economy performs optimally (or efficiently) and then ask that an incentive structure render it in each agent's self-interest to follow his prescribed behavioral rule. An economic system with an incentive structure of this nature is called incentive-compatible.[40]

Clearly, by these criteria, the official or formal Soviet economic system was not "incentive-compatible." However, it is the opinion of a large number of observers that the Soviet second economy and the illegal activities at its core did provide a different and relatively efficient set of incentives to Soviet economic actors. The Soviet mode of organization produced an official incentive structure that, according to one analyst, under-appreciated individuals "capable of managing and innovating in the workplace" and rewarded economic managers "more for their political reliability than for their skills in running a complex economy."[41] Compare this view with the following assessment of the informal incentive structure in the Soviet second economy:

> The second economy also helps dispel the not uncommon view that generations of Soviet rule have extirpated nearly all private initiative and enterprisingness. An observer of the second economy cannot but be impressed by the constant evidence of widespread enterprise, ingenuity, flexibility, and speed in pursuit of private gain, despite formidable obstacle and great personal risk. Illegality does not, of course, necessarily make enterprise or initiative any less such.[42]

Such a state of affairs entails an organizational structure that encourages corruption, the abuse of office, and other related illegalities. On this specific point, Nicholas Lampert perhaps put it most succinctly when he argued that

> one can argue that the form of Soviet centralised management is itself a major source of widespread shortages of goods and services, which encourage people to use their public positions for private gain. It assists theft, and allows people who control the distribution and allocation of goods and services to reward favourites and to extract extra benefits by taking gifts and bribes. If these assertions are true, or partly true, then the problem is that the political structure itself helps to generate the illegalities that regularly preoccupy Soviet political party leaders and law enforcement agencies.[43]

At the root of the Soviet incentive system, of course, is the nature of centralized planning. It is of such a particular importance and carries with it its own set of considerations, quite apart from the above treatment, that it merits the following separate consideration.

Factors Related to the Plan

It has been well established for many decades that the Soviet command economy and the political system that supported it operated in large part through a series of informal practices that owe their creation to the particular nature of the formal structure adopted by the Soviet leadership. Many analysts have noted the development of this informal system. Foremost among the early treatments of this topic are those of Joseph Berliner and David Granick. Discussing in 1952 the "informal organization of the Soviet firm," Berliner was among the first Western scholars to highlight what in effect could be called the operational code of industrial management in the Soviet Union.[44] The ambitious attempt at centralized economic planning adopted by the Stalin with the promulgation of the First Five-Year Plan in 1928 created a specific informal incentive structure that determined in large part the behavior of individual enterprise managers. Early Soviet émigrés who came to the West in the aftermath of the Second World War were interviewed by Berliner and others and spoke of these specific forces that affected the economic behavior of workers and management.

Since the performance of economic and political cadres in the Soviet Union was traditionally evaluated in terms of the quantitative output of enterprises over which they have authority, managerial behavior of both an economic and political nature was aimed at the maximization of industrial and agricultural output. At lower levels, the salaries of workers had also been tied to the amount of output achieved, or, put another way, by the degree of success achieved in fulfilling the enterprise's quantitative production quotas—the Plan. As much as one-third or more of salaries of economic managers was accounted for by the bonuses, or *premia*, awarded with the fulfillment or over-fulfillment of the Plan quotas. As Berliner points out, the difference in salaries for managers whose enterprise produced 99 percent of Plan quotas and those whose enterprise produced 100 percent of the Plan could be as much as 30 percent. This logic of salaries and *premia* based on quantitative Plan fulfillment led to a number of other problems and, in Berliner's words, "place[d] a great strain upon the honesty of plant accounting."[45]

One of the most obvious consequences of the practice of basing worker and management salaries and bonuses on Plan fulfillment was the illegal falsification of production level reports sent by managers to their organizational superiors. If the Plan quota could not be attained through normal means, then significant economic incentives compelled the managers to produce at least the appearance of Plan fulfillment. Traditionally that has been accomplished through the over-reporting or falsification *(pripiski)* of production figures.[46] Since almost every individual involved in the running of the enterprise—the workers themselves, the managers, the local and regional party officials who provide oversight for the enterprise—had a personal and professional vested interest in seeing that their segment of the Plan was fulfilled (or appeared to have been fulfilled), there was little likelihood that such falsifications would be punished. Of course, false reporting of production figures was a crime in the Soviet Union, played havoc with economic planning, and exaggerated the true level of supplies and stocks. However, the Plan also had the force of law, and careers were cut short by poor economic performance. Given that all those capable of ascertaining the truth about real production levels in enterprises were compelled by economic reasons to engage in falsification, a network of corruption existed at almost every level of the Soviet economic system and involved workers, managers, and responsible cadres from the Communist Party apparatus and the respective economic ministries.

A second relevant consequence of central planning in the Soviet Union involved the maintenance at the enterprise level of the so-called safety factor, or *strakhova*. Because most production facilities in the USSR were at various points in time required to engage in the falsification of production, planners at high levels often allocated non-existent or "paper" resources to enterprises. Because these resources (raw materials, spare parts, and so on) may not have been available from the suppliers, and could force down time in an enterprise's production activities (thus endangering its chances of fulfilling its own production Plan quotas), enterprise managers regularly sought to create a safety factor that allowed them to continue on in spite of supply irregularities.

Principally, managers were forced again to engage in over-reporting, this time in padding statements of their own material requirements *(zaiavki)* for production. If they anticipated a 10 percent shortfall in their supplies of necessary production materials, for example, enterprise managers simply inflated their requests for materials to compensate for this eventuality. If the planners who were authorized to allocate production materials and supplies then adjusted these requests downward according to their own calculations of what an enterprise needed to produce its allotted quota (referred to as the materials utilization norm, or *norma)*, this padding, or material requests, then provided a comfort zone for the enterprises and thus increased the likelihood of Plan fulfillment, the distribution of *premia,* and so on.

Also related to the creation and maintenance of this *strakhova* was the hoarding of production materials by enterprises. Because the Soviet system did not support a large number of alternative sources for production resources,[47] and because suppliers, themselves subject to the vicissitudes of the planning system, were frequently unable to provide the required materials, enterprise management hoarded materials "for a rainy day." In fact, enterprises occasionally received materials that were not needed for their specific production tasks. Rather than notifying the planning organs of the mistake, managers kept whatever materials came their way, the better to use in future and inevitable barter deals over scarce *(deficitny)* goods with other enterprises.

Finally, the safety factor was also ensured by the standard practice of plant managers of underestimating to superiors the production capacity of their enterprise. By lowering the expectations of superiors with respect to the goals set for plant production, enterprises were thus more likely to fulfill or over-fulfill their Plan quotas. However, as shall be seen, economic planners were fully aware of this and other informal practices of Soviet firms and attempted to counteract them.

A third consequence of the Plan and its impact on the behavior of economic actors in the Soviet Union involved the ubiquitous charge of "eye-washing" *(ochkovtiratel'stvo)*. In the Soviet context this involved a series of steps aimed at simulating successful economic performance through the use of deception, again with the goal of satisfying Plan quotas and ensuring *premia* and related benefits.[48] Taken as a whole, *ochkovtiratel'stvo* entailed a variety of semi-legal and illegal acts aimed at satisfying the structural demands of the Soviet command economy. Berliner cites four major examples of behavior, or techniques, adopted by enterprise managers that fall into this category of "eye-washing," or deception.

Enterprise managers were obligated to fulfill economic plans or production quotas designated by planning officials connected to one or another of the Soviet ministries. These plans designated gross production quotas, defined according to the total value of the output during the plan period, as well as quotas on individual products. Enterprise managers realized, however, that the quota setting the overall value of production had primacy over the individual quotas related to categories of products or individual products, per se. That is, *premia* and other methods of evaluating their performance were based more directly on the gross quotas related to the Plan than on the actual mix of products produced. As a result, enterprise managers, faced with uneven resources from suppliers, uneven production costs associated with specific product lines, and similar factors, frequently satisfied the gross planning quotas by producing either the goods that they were able to produce (i.e., for which they had ample materials) or goods that entailed the lowest production costs. This practice resulted in the production of what was for the national economy the wrong assortment of goods. While ministerial economic planners sought the production of a specific mix of products, enterprises produced a mix that satisfied their own drive to fulfill the gross quota, not the needs of the rest of the industrial enterprises or those of the economy as a whole.

Stories are legend in the Soviet Union of manipulations of production output to meet gross quantitative quotas for the production of certain goods. For example, such quotas for the production of household furniture in the Soviet Union (designated by gross weight of furniture produced) were met simply by producing fewer pieces that weighed more. In like fashion, jokes are told of the Soviet ball-bearing or tack enterprise (the stories vary among several targets), which satisfied its yearly gross quantitative production quota by producing a single giant ball bearing or a gargantuan tack. The Plan is fulfilled, *premia* are awarded, but nothing of value to the economy is produced.

An obvious second manifestation of *ochkovtiratel'stvo* in the simulation of higher quantitative levels of production involved the sacrifice of qualitative standards for quantitative ones. If your production activity is evaluated first and foremost on the *number* of commodities produced, and such numbers can only be produced via rapid, shoddy, or incomplete production techniques, then so be it. It was not at all unusual for Soviet goods of almost every type, from consumer goods to heavy industrial machine tools, to be shipped out of the enterprise with crucial parts missing. Such a state of affairs logically fueled both the hoarding of spare parts by recipient factory managers who then had to complete the production of these needed items, and the thriving spare parts exchanges on the black market. But enterprise accounting described these products as finished goods, in fulfillment of the Plan.

Yet another example of deceptive "eye-washing" by Soviet managers intent on satisfying their quotas entailed the misappropriation of earmarked funds to purposes more directly tied to production processes. If special in-house bonuses had to be paid to get workers to exert extra effort to complete the Plan, or if additional labor had to be hired to do so, wage funds had to be acquired from other sources. Frequent losers in this financial shuffling were funds dedicated to needed repairs, overhead costs, and so on. Neglecting repairs, for example, in order to hire extra workers may indeed solve the production problem for the specific economic planning period, but in the long run production will suffer stoppages, thus requiring managerial creativity of a second-order magnitude. At some point, enterprises built of such a house of cards confront an economic and political crisis requiring the intervention of higher state and party authorities, who in most cases also have a vested interest in covering up the malfeasance.

A third major consequence of centralized planning in the Soviet Union involved the development of informal mechanisms of what might be called "influence peddling." The well-known Soviet expression of *ZIS,* which is the acronym for *znakomstvo i sviazy,* or "acquaintantship and connections," describes the method by which many needed goods and services were acquired. A related term that goes a long way in describing the informal system of exchange and barter is *blat,* usually translated as "pull" or "influence." Hedrick Smith has described this everyday phenomenon as follows:

> In an economy of chronic shortages and carefully parceled out privileges, *blat* is an essential lubricant of life. The more rank and power one has, the more *blat* one normally has. But almost everyone can bestow the benefits of *blat* on someone else ... because each has access to things or services that are hard to get and that other people want or need.[49]

Thus, both critical goods for the everyday consumer as well as the procurement needs of Soviet enterprises were gotten *po blatu* (through pull) or *po znakomstvu* (through acquaintances). This phenomenon of barter and influence peddling was no less important for enterprise managers acting in their professional capacities than it was for regular citizens in their private capacities as consumers. Given, of course, that the Soviet Union was both economically and politically very hierarchical and supported a very limited private sphere, the points at which the system required the formal approval of one official or another were extremely numerous. Equally numerous were the points at which the corruption of these officials, and the development of this type of informal process, were possible.

As a result of these extant pressures on procurement for Soviet enterprises, many managers sought the services of a special breed of procurement officers called *tolkachi,* or "pushers."[50] Often these innovative procurement specialists operated as free-lance expediters, and in other instances they were regular employees of specific enterprises.

The tactics they employed in the search for the needed materials for enterprises were legally questionable, to say the least. In many instances outright bribes were tendered, favors promised, and barter deals completed entirely off the books. At the crux of their specialized abilities was a long and reliable network of friends and contacts in a vast array of offices in a given geographical location.

The legal status of the *tolkachi* was debated in Soviet circles, but generally these agents were able to operate rather freely because they served useful functions for the running of the Soviet economy. Even in cases where these agents violated the informal norms governing their behavior, enforcement officials were disinclined to punish them severely. The Soviet authorities were well aware of the exigencies under which enterprise managers operated and sympathized with their efforts to procure the needed materials to perform their official duties. The treatment of *tolkachi* reinforced the notion that the coercive organs of the Soviet state allowed a significant amount of illegal activity, especially if in their opinion these violations were perpetrated primarily for system goals (e.g., to satisfy production quotas) as opposed to self-aggrandizing ones. Of course, inasmuch as these two forces were intermingled—job security and *premia* were the individual fruits of fulfilling the Plan—very often the dichotomy could not stand up to serious scrutiny.

A final ramification of the nature of Soviet economic practices and the impact of the Plan on enterprise activity was the Soviet practice of "storming." *Shturmovshchina* refers to the period of accelerated work activity near the end of the Plan reporting period. Storming took place as the enterprises sought to satisfy their quotas; extraordinary activity was required in most cases because labor and enterprise productivity were not spread evenly throughout the Plan period.

What typically occurred in the early portions of the year was that much of the padding associated with the previous period's reporting had to be made up for in an attempt, so to speak, to cover the tracks of deceptive reporting. In addition, without the imminent pressure of the end of the Plan period, worker productivity declined. As a result, at the end of the year, a frantic rush was required to meet production quotas. It has been shown repeatedly by Western analysts of the Soviet economy that a vastly disproportionate amount of the gross production of Soviet enterprises took place during the last quarter of the year, and especially during the last few weeks of the year. One such study showed that 35 percent of all housing starts in the Soviet Union took place during the last three months of the Plan year. Seventy percent of that amount, it noted, occurred in the last week of December. In effect, then, if these numbers are accurate, roughly a quarter of all housing starts took place during the last seven days of December—hardly the most opportune time to pour cement in the USSR. In like fashion, one can venture educated guesses about the level of quality control being exercised on enterprise production during *shturmovshchina*. But, again, quantitative criteria consistently held primacy over qualitative ones. Indeed, this was a critical problem in Soviet economic planning. As one western economist has put it,

> there is a strong presumption . . . that Soviet managers, maximizing the *quantity* of their output, choose a quality level which is not only below plan but inefficiently low. Taking into account its secondary repercussions, from one sector to another, quality deterioration is probably the most serious flaw in the mechanisms of plan execution.[51]

From the evidence of these informal—and in many cases illegal—practices relevant to the operation of Soviet enterprises, it is clear that many of the most important decisions made by managers in the USSR were not made in accordance with official policies and procedures. As Anthony Downs has stated it,

> bureaucracies in communist nations are undoubtedly subject to at least some high-level control. But the leakage of authority in the whole structure is so great that the pressures felt by low-level officials are often almost totally unrelated to the objectives of those at the top of the pyramid.[52]

In fact, to a considerable degree, managers were forced to make decisions about the pace of production, the product mix, the procurement process, the use and misuse of enterprise finances, the bonuses paid to employees, and even the hours and pace of operation on the basis of what from a planning and legal perspective would have to be considered illegitimate, dysfunctional, and illegal activities. But such was the structure of the situation facing Soviet managerial officials that it was well near impossible to satisfy the expectations of their superiors without regular resort to what was technically criminal activity as defined by Soviet law. One observer has stated that since the condition of success was to meet Plan targets, "many forms of managerial illegality in the Soviet Union are conditioned by the particular pressures faced by Soviet organisations. . . . The requirements of the ever-looming plan confront Soviet managers with a struggle for survival that cannot be fought without regular breaches of the law."[53] It is in this sense that David Granick, one of the preeminent Western scholars of Soviet industrial management, argues that "all Soviet managers are, ipso facto, criminals according to Soviet law."[54]

Factors Related to Soviet Law

In *The Wealth of Nations,* Adam Smith wrote that the English smuggler "would have been, in all respects, an excellent citizen, had not the laws of his country made that a crime which nature never meant to be so."[55] A more generalized charge of this type may, of course, be applied to the Soviet Union. Many of the activities that were criminal offenses in the Soviet Union were perfectly legal (and encouraged) elsewhere. On one level, one can argue that, by virtue of the extreme level of regulation of public and private life (to the point where the sphere of the latter tended to be overwhelmed by that of the former), there were just that many more laws to be violated in the Soviet Union than in other states. Furthermore, because the size of the state or public sector was so large in the USSR—and therefore the size of the governmental bureaucracy was exaggerated in like fashion—the arithmetic potential for "official" crimes was that much higher as well. Given the related phenomena of an extremely regulated society and its concomitantly large officialdom, it could be anticipated that in comparison to more privatized, *laissez-faire* states, the level of illicit official behavior in the Soviet Union would be higher.

The laws governing the behavior of Soviet officials were quite specific with regard to both the types of behavior proscribed and the penalties applied for transgressions. Soviet law adopted a very inclusive view of officialdom, and, as stated above, this accounted in some measure for the large amount of "official" corruption in the Soviet Union. According to Chapter Seven of the Special Part of the RSFSR Criminal Code, "official persons" are

> persons who are permanently or temporarily effectuating the functions of representatives of authority, and also who are permanently or temporarily occupying offices in state or social organizations connected with

the fulfillment of organizational-executive or administrative-economic duties, or who are fulfilling such duties in the said institutions, organizations, and enterprises in accordance with a special authorization.[56]

In addition to individuals holding various responsible government and other public positions, such a definition technically would include regular policemen, soldiers on guard duty, members of voluntary people's guards, and other similar figures not usually treated in a strict sense as state or government "officials."[57]

Official corruption usually fell into one of a small number of Soviet legal categories. "Official Crime" was defined in Chapter Seven of the Special Part of the Criminal Code. Briefly, the Articles comprising this Chapter outlawed the abuse of authority or official position (Article 170), the exceeding of authority or of official powers (Article 171), neglect of official duties (Article 172), the taking of a bribe (Article 173), the giving of a bribe (or acting as an intermediary in the giving of a bribe) (Article 174), and official forgery (Article 175). However, many of the acts of corruption engaged in by officials as part of their informal governing activities were dealt with in other sections of the Code. For example, the ever-present problem of report padding *(pripiska)* was dealt with under the Chapter that focuses on "economic crimes" (Chapter Six). Here, Article 152 Paragraph 1 proscribed "additions to and other distortions of accounts concerning the fulfillment of plans." Acts of report padding were considered under Soviet law "anti-state actions inflicting harm on the national economy of the USSR"; the maximum sentence for conviction of this crime was three years' deprivation of freedom.

Other economic crimes relevant to officials were prohibited explicitly in the Code: the issuance of poor-quality, non-standard, or incomplete products (Article 152), private entrepreneurial activity (Article 153), and speculation (Article 154). Each entailed significant penalties, at least theoretically. Finally, other aspects of the informal rules of official behavior were prohibited under Chapter Two of the Special Part of the Criminal Code. This Chapter detailed "crimes against socialist ownership" and proscribed primarily acts of theft of socialist property. Among the Articles of interest here, Article 92 prohibited the stealing of state or socialist property through misappropriation or embezzlement or by the abuse of an official position. Each Article of the Code meted out specific and weighty penalties, including extended prison sentences, fines, and a series of administrative penalties.

Technically, then, Soviet law was empowered to deal with the vast majority of the acts that could be considered acts of official corruption. However, as has been shown, strong social forces were at work which militated against the objective application of formal law to the behavior of Soviet officials. One scholar who analyzed the type and frequency of criminal prosecution in the USSR concluded with respect to official crimes that the number of prosecutions was declining in relative terms. Ger P. Van Den Berg cited a decline in the prosecution of official crimes, especially during the Brezhnev era. As to the reasons for this decline in the vigilance against official corruption, he concluded that "apparently, it was not the courts which downgraded the social dangerousness of official crime, but rather the political leadership itself."[58]

It may be useful, in light of the above, to emphasize a distinction in official "crime" that the Soviet enforcement agencies seemed to make themselves. David Granick separates "technical" crimes from "real" crimes with respect to the actions of Soviet officials.[59] As chronicled in previous sections of this chapter, officials had to work within a complex web of rules and regulations, most of which were reinforced by legal statute. For example, Soviet managers in the pre-perestroika days were forced to adopt a series of informal procedures, many if not most in violation of Soviet law, in order to fulfill the Plan. Why? Because the Plan was law as well. As has been argued, satisfying one legal imperative (fulfilling the Plan) has always had precedence over satisfying others (the day-to-day methods by which the Plan is fulfilled). Violating Soviet law with respect to these methods and procedures would, for Granick (and the Soviet authorities) constitute "technical" crimes—violations, to be sure, but violations of a decidedly lower magnitude and for the good of the state, as it were. These "technical" crimes would not carry stiff penalties, if they were targeted for punishment at all. Failure to fulfill the orders from your superiors with respect to production quotas, for example, usually landed an official in more difficulty and was to be avoided at all costs. Unfortunately for Soviet officials, it was difficult to resist the temptation to escalate from petty "technical" crimes to larger "real" crimes when, by virtue of the official position in society occupied, one has almost unlimited opportunities for self-aggrandizement.

Implicit in this explanation is the fact that supervisory and oversight officials were fully aware of the situation confronting managers, were sympathetic to them, and were constantly filtering their evaluations of managerial behavior through the appropriate lenses. For example, party officials, charged with the duty of supplying policy "guidance" to state officials, were fully aware of the methods adopted by economic managers. Indeed, it was also in the party officials' vested interests to see that the manager was successful. Nicholas Lampert puts it this way:

> In the first place, the party people know that certain forms of law-breaking are unavoidable if plans are to be met, and that some leeway must therefore be given to managers in this respect. The position and prospects of party officials depend heavily on the economic success of the enterprises within their domain, and success is measured in terms of plan fulfillment.[60]

As a result, party officials tended to protect other officials in their domain from overzealous legal authorities. Again, party members could not have criminal charges brought against them without the approval of the relevant party committee, and in many cases this permission would not be granted. Even in cases where significant crimes of self-aggrandizement occurred, whether by enterprise managers or by responsible party cadres, there was an inherent proclivity on the part of the party apparatus to keep the transgressions under wraps. In the first case, as stated above, the career prospects of party officials were also tied to the performance of economic entities over which they exercised authority. Second, party officials feared the publicity of criminal proceedings within their domain in that such developments tended to present the picture to their superiors that party oversight in the region or locality was lax. Finally, very few lower- or middle-level party *apparatchiki* made successful careers in the Soviet Union by aiding in the prosecution of other party or state officials.[61]

The above is not meant to imply that criminal prosecutions of party and state officials did not occur, but merely that the vast majority of official corruption went unpunished. These crimes went unpunished, in sum, because many of them served useful functions for the operation of the political system. Other crimes were ignored for political reasons, a theme that will be picked up in chapter 5. What emerges from an examination of Soviet law with respect to official corruption in the

Soviet Union, then, is the understanding that the technical force of law was weakened in the USSR by a powerful array of informal rules and regulations that tended to condition the ways in which law was applied. In many if not most cases, these informal rules were more relevant for Soviet officials than was the letter of the formal criminal code. As one student of corruption puts it, "the Soviet meaning of corruption is best described as an alliance of law and informal political rules. Law is by all odds the weaker ally."[62]

Factors Related to General Institutional Weakness

As was discussed in chapter 1, many scholars who have focused their attention on the process of political development have noted that corruption, both as manifested by thriving black markets in the private sphere and by what one observer has called "black market bureaucracy"[63] in the public sphere, is at least partially the result of the general institutional weakness of the system. Specifically, in such situations emergent societal groups are bereft of effective institutions, such as political parties, for the aggregation and articulation of their political interests. In addition, legitimate opportunities for societal mobility are few, thus forcing individuals into developing and adopting alternative methods to satisfy their demands. Conditions such as these are prevalent in modernizing states, in states where demands for active political participation outpace those formal institutions created to accommodate them, and in states where traditional modes of behavior lag behind the adoption of a new set of official societal norms and expectations.[64] In such cases, institutions of the state are not able to accommodate the demands of the population, are considered by the population to be more or less illegitimate, or prove ineffective in resolving any number of societal needs. For Huntington,

> Like machine politics or clientelistic politics in general [also quite prevalent in the USSR], corruption provides immediate, specific, and concrete benefits to groups which might otherwise be thoroughly alienated from a society. Corruption might thus be functional to the maintenance of a political system in the same way that reform is. Corruption itself may be a substitute for reform and both corruption and reform may be substitutes for revolution.[65]

Of course, one can argue that most of these conditions existed in the Soviet Union, providing another clue as to the institutional roots of systemic corruption in that system.

Many scholars have put forth the argument that in many cases, political corruption can serve useful functions in developing societies, providing alternative methods by which goods and services can be distributed; in this way, then, certain kinds of corruption can actually facilitate political development.[66] This issue of the functionality of corruption for the Soviet Union is taken up in greater depth in a later chapter of this book, but it is worth noting here that the evidence is quite clear that the Soviet authorities accepted and encouraged certain types of official corruption for precisely these reasons. Certain forms of corruption in the Soviet Union performed beneficial system functions, rationalizing the overly rigid and inflexible rules and regulations that marked the Soviet mode of administration.

These themes have been evident in the work of those looking at the Soviet case in particular. Charles Schwartz, for example, in his analysis of corruption in the USSR, states that "corruption tends to flourish, and to be functional, where institutions are weak and inflexible."[67] Similarly, John M. Kramer has concluded that "undeniably, corruption [in the Soviet system] has made important contributions to its efficient functioning. . . . The Soviets in fact realize that some types of corruption may be functional while others may not, for they have often extended a *de facto* toleration to the former while combating the latter."[68]

Formal Soviet public institutions patently failed to fulfill the functions for which they were created, and Soviet officials behaved in their official capacities in a manner quite at odds with what one would expect from an understanding of their formal duties. The performance of these formal institutions was demonstrated to be inadequate, and had to be buttressed through the development of a wide array of informal institutions, many of which were specifically proscribed by the rules of the formal system. Such a state of affairs clearly describes an inherent weakness in the Soviet institutions charged with the responsibility of administering public affairs. On this general point, Robert Merton has described what weak bureaucratic institutions and their personnel look like. He writes:

> the bureaucratic structure exerts a constant pressure upon the individual
> to be "methodical, prudent, disciplined." If the bureaucracy is to operate

successfully, it must attain a high degree of reliability of behavior, an unusual degree of conformity with prescribed patterns of behavior. . . . Discipline can be effective only if the ideal patterns are buttressed by strong sentiments which entail devotion to one's duties, a keen sense of the limitations of one's authority and competence, and methodical performance of routine activities. The efficacy of social structure depends ultimately upon infusing group participants with appropriate attitudes and sentiments.[69]

Such a description of the *desiderata* of efficient bureaucracy, including the individual *ethos* of efficient bureaucrats, certainly highlights the problems that inhered in Soviet institutions. In the final years of the Soviet Union, public institutions no longer exerted a pressure sufficient to create "methodical, prudent, disciplined" officials. Bureaucratic behavior was, further, highly unreliable and, in fact, seemed at times to display an unusual degree of conformity not to *pre*scribed behavior, but to *pro*scribed behavior. If, as Merton says, structural efficacy rests "ultimately" upon the ability of those structures to infuse participants with "appropriate attitudes and sentiments," then the efficacy of Soviet public institutions was extremely low. In fact, juxtaposing this short list of the traits desirable in public officials with the behavior of Soviet officials highlights not only the legal sense of "corruption," but also its moral sense.

In a sense, then, the formal system in the Soviet Union was being rationalized by the very types of informal institutions it had proscribed. That such a situation existed was, as will be argued consistently through this book, accepted by those individuals who were in positions of authority within the formal structure, speaks volumes to the issue of institutional strengths and weaknesses. David Granick, writing at a time when Soviet economic performance was considered relatively robust, anticipated just what developed in the USSR of the 1970s and 1980s:

When a huge organization is this highly centralized, two possibilities exist. The organization may founder in its own bureaucracy, or it may ignore its own rules. No one can say that Soviet industry has foundered during the past thirty years. The evidence is conclusive that formal decision-making regulations have been consistently violated. Plant managements have had to make their own decisions if they were to produce the results demanded of them. Top authorities have had to wink at violations of rules if they wished industrial production to grind ahead. Both groups have recognized reality.[70]

What Granick failed to imagine in 1960 was the development of a third, and perhaps the worst, possibility: that the organization may founder in its own bureaucracy *and* it may ignore its own rules. Unfortunately for the future of the former Soviet Union, just such a development had come to dominate public life. That this reality finally set in among the Soviet leadership is well established by the radical restructuring of the political and economic systems advocated by Gorbachev and other reformers since the second half of the 1980s.

One of the major reasons that corruption came to be so readily accepted and in a certain sense encouraged by the upper echelons of the political elite during the Brezhnev period is closely tied to the issue of structural reform. Gorbachev is noteworthy in Soviet history not because he was the first to recognize the critical weaknesses of Soviet institutions and their need for a thoroughgoing restructuring. Leonid Brezhnev, for all his mediocrity and petty materialism, recognized just such a need well over two decades ago. Others in positions of political power during the late 1960s and the rest of the Brezhnev period certainly recognized the state of affairs long before it became known to the rest of Soviet society and the outside world. Certainly one can view the early attempts at tinkering with the system, such as the 1957 *sovnarkhozy* reforms that attempted to decentralize economic decision making, and the Liberman and Kosygin "reforms" of the 1960s, as signs that the authorities were aware of the significant problems that existed. What makes Gorbachev important in this regard is that he decided to embark on what Brezhnev and his colleagues lacked the nerve to attempt: radical reform of the inadequate public institutions of the Soviet state.

Brezhnev's leadership will be remarked upon historically as one that displayed a lack of imagination and, above all, a lack of courage in addressing the structural problems of the Soviet Union. Instead of attempting real reform of the system, which perhaps even he recognized was needed, Brezhnev and his leadership cohort instead relied upon a series of measures the aim of which was to provide short-term palliatives to the system. These steps were taken in order to avoid fundamental reform of the system that allowed them to live as the new tsars of Soviet Russia. One such reform-avoiding policy was

Brezhnev's famous détente initiative. Another was his encouragement of petty illegal corruption among both the general population and his officialdom.

On this point, James Millar has argued that the Brezhnev years were mainly devoid of large-scale institutional reform. Rather, Brezhnev entered into an implicit arrangement with the Soviet population which entailed the "expansion of petty marketing" as a means "to offset to some degree the inefficiency and maldistributions caused by the cumbersome Soviet retail distribution system."[71] Rather than reform these weak institutions,

> The Brezhnev leadership struck a new but tacit bargain with the urban population: to tolerate the expansion of a wide range of petty private economic activities, some legal, some in the penumbra of the legal, and some clearly and obviously illegal, the primary aim of which was the reallocation by private means of a significant fraction of Soviet national income according to private preferences.[72]

Since the system of discipline and punishment of the Stalin period could not be recreated in the 1960s and 1970s, and since the Brezhnev leadership was unwilling to engage in real structural reform, the institutional structure was no longer appropriate to the rules of the game in the Soviet Union. Corruption flourished in the USSR during this period precisely because of the inappropriateness of this marriage of 1940s institutions and 1970s informal ideology. In Millar's words, the "Little Deal" was "an accommodation that required neither major reform nor a significant reallocation of resources, only ideological retrenchment."[73]

As has just been touched on, many commentators have pointed out that certain types of corruption can serve as palatable alternatives to institutional reform.[74] While the détente policy enabled Brezhnev to acquire Western technology, agricultural goods, and other much-needed resources that the Soviet economy itself was unable to produce, it also thereby permitted Brezhnev to delay or ultimately to ignore the need to restructure the Soviet economic system. In this particular sense, détente with the West allowed the facade of Soviet economic stability to be maintained a few more years. Faced with the choice of championing a serious and politically dangerous reform agenda (a long-term solution to institutional weakness) or acquiring needed resources from outside sources (a decidedly short-term solution to institutional weakness), Brezhnev took the path of least resistance. At the time, Brezhnev had some difficulty convincing some of his Politburo colleagues, especially Ukrainian party chief Petr Shelest, of the correctness of even this less ambitious policy. In such an environment, Brezhnev would have been unwilling to press for serious institutional reform, even if he were convinced of its necessity. Given his level of talent, energy, and desire to maintain his own elite life-style, Brezhnev was perhaps the last person in the Soviet Union capable of such boldness.

Applying the same logic, corruption developed for functional reasons having to do with the weakness of Soviet economic and social institutions and was selectively encouraged because it allowed for ad hoc, incremental, and informal alterations of the institutional structure in a way that benefited the Soviet leadership. Kramer remarks that the fact that Soviet authorities discouraged the combating of such "functional" illegalities as the activities of *tolkachi* or the use of *blat* reflects "elite perceptions that these forms of corruption often perform vital systemic functions."[75] Such a cynical attitude on the part of the Soviet leadership toward official crime and black market activities might, if given the benefit of the doubt, be considered some perverse form of "passive reform." That is, the Soviet leadership, in allowing the proliferation of criminal activities within both the public and private spheres of life, were admitting the obvious failures of the formal institutions of the state and allowing for the existence of social forces that sought to address them. Objectively, though, just as the development of black market bureaucracy in the Soviet Union spoke to the weaknesses of formal institutions, its expansion within Soviet life during the past three decades—with the full knowledge and in many cases the encouragement of the leadership—speaks to the utter lack of integrity of those charged with the responsibility of administering the Soviet state.

Conclusion

The implications for the Soviet system associated with these bureaucratic characteristics were many. Like bureaucratic actors in all systems, Soviet officials, whether associated with the Communist Party apparatus, the government ministries, or any other such institution, responded rationally to the organizational structure of their social environment. That the Soviet bureaucratic system failed to achieve a measure of efficiency or professionalism expected in the West is not an indictment of the bureaucratic irrationality of the individual administrators. Rather, the problems associated with the individual behavior of Soviet officials—corruption, bribe taking, patronage, false reporting to superiors, and so on—more closely reflected the *rational* responses of these officials to a bureaucratic structure that logically encouraged such behavior. In this way, the aggregation of a vast number of individual rational actions by Soviet officials led to the manifestation and dominance of extremely dysfunctional system traits. Alternatively, the logic or ideology of Soviet administration, as it was traditionally structured, compelled the rational bureaucratic actor to behave in ways that violated norms of personal integrity, party rules, and the state legal codes themselves. The failure of bureaucratic actors in the Soviet Union to behave according to the "logic" of the system as it itself operated facilitated the rapid ruination of that system. In a word, system maintenance in the USSR required the acceptance and indeed the encouragement by the political elite of extremely high levels of individual illicit behavior by rank and file *apparatchiki*.

To be sure, these corrupt behaviors fit the strict definition of "dysfunctions," which on the structural level imply the concepts of strain, stress, and tension. However, as has been argued throughout this chapter, these "dysfunctions" often tendered rationalizing and efficiency-increasing effects to the Soviet economic and political system. That such was the case has been acknowledged for some time by both Western and Soviet authorities. In effect, then, many of these strains, stresses, and tensions were considered essential for the continued functioning of the Soviet system.

In searching for an appropriate label to use in describing this seemingly contradictory nature of corruption in the Soviet setting, it is perhaps useful to adopt some of the thinking put forth four decades ago by Robert Merton. In studying bureaucratic behavior from a structural perspective, Merton described an organizational phenomenon wherein individual officials experience rather marked role ambiguity due to the seeming divergence between system-level goals and the structure of the demands facing them as the individual actors of that system. Often these bureaucrats are forced by circumstances to behave in ways that could not be anticipated from the set of formal system goals—just as Soviet officials were forced by the structure of their official environment to engage in corruption in order to maintain macro-level system stability. What Merton seems to be referring to in his description of the illicit actions of bureaucratic agents might be labeled "functional dysfunctionalities."[76] Certain types of corruption in the USSR may have indeed possessed a similar role within the Soviet system. Formally, these practices were dysfunctionalities (stresses and strains on the official system), but ones that performed quite useful system functions.

Notes

1. David Granick (1960), *The Red Executive: A Study of the Organization Man in Soviet Industry* (New York: Doubleday): 43.

2. Paul R. Gregory (1980), *Restructuring the Soviet Economic Bureaucracy* (Cambridge: Cambridge University Press): 1.

3. Don Karl Rowney and Walter M. Pintner (1980), "Officialdom and Bureaucratization: An Introduction," in Walter McKenzie Pintner and Don Karl Rowney, eds. (1980), *Russian Officialdom: The Bureaucratization of Russian Society from the Seventeenth to the Twentieth Century* (Chapel Hill: The University of North Carolina Press): 9.

4. Anthony Downs (1967), *Inside Bureaucracy* (Boston: Little, Brown): 2.

5. Ibid., p. 164.

6. This development is referred to in the literature as the Law of Increasing Conservatism. See Downs (1967), ibid., pp. 19–20. It is worth noting in this regard that the four Communist Party Central Committees elected at the Party Congresses that took place during the Brezhnev years had very low rates of turnover; reelection rates for incumbent members of the Central Committee ran at 76 percent (1966), 81 percent (1971), 89 percent (1976), and 89 percent (1981).

7. Ibid., p. 65.

8. See, for example, Raeff: "The Russian Autocracy and Its Officials," pp. 77–91 in Hugh McLean et al., eds. (1957), *Russian Thought and Politics* (Cambridge, MA: Harvard University Press); "The Well-Ordered Police State and the Development of Modernity in Seventeenth and Eighteenth Century Europe: An Attempt at a Comparative Approach," *American Historical Review*, Vol. 80 (No. 5) (1975): 1221–1243; and *Understanding Imperial Russia: State and Society in the Old Regime* (New York: Columbia University Press, 1985),

9. Hans J. Torke (1988), "Crime and Punishment in the Pre-Petrine Civil Service," in Ezra Mendelsohn and Marshall S. Shatz, eds., *Imperial Russia, 1700–1917: State, Society, Opposition* (DeKalb: Northern Illinois University Press): 9.

10. Refer to Robert D. Givens (1980), "Eighteenth-Century Nobiliary Career Patterns and Provincial Government," pp. 106–129 in Walter McKenzie Pintner and Don Karl Rowney, eds., (1980), *Russian Officialdom*.

11. *"Loshad' liubit oves, zemlia navoz, a voevoda privoz,"* cited in Robert Givens (1980), "Eighteenth-Century Nobiliary Career Patterns and Provincial Government," p. 117.

12. Sidney Monas (1970), "Bureaucracy in Russia under Nicholas I," in Michael Cherniavsky, ed. (1970), *The Structure of Russian History: Interpretive Essays* (New York: Random House): 275.

13. Gioe, in other comments that highlight the traditional nature of current practices, castigated the Russian officials for procrastination and red tape and referred to them as formalists, blockheads, and procrastinators. Cited in Hans J. Torke (1988), "Crime and Punishment in the Pre-Petrine Civil Service," in Ezra Mendelsohn and Marshall S. Shatz, eds. (1980), *Imperial Russia, 1700–1917,* p. 7.

14. For a fine review of the Petrine Table of Ranks and the nature of Russian officialdom during and immediately after the reign of Peter I, see Brenda Meehan-Waters (1980), "Social and Career Characteristics of the Administrative Elite, 1689–1761," pp. 76–105 in Walter McKenzie Pintner and Don Karl Rowney, eds., (1980), *Russian Officialdom.*

15. See Robert D. Givens (1980), "Eighteenth-Century Nobiliary Career Patterns and Provincial Government."

16. Marc Raeff (1979), "The Bureaucratic Phenomena of Imperial Russia, 1700–1905," *American Historical Review,* Vol. 84 (No. 2): 403.

17. A Ministry of Commerce was added later.

18. Nicholas Riasanovsky (1977), *A History of Russia,* 3rd ed. (New York: Oxford University Press): 340.

19. Walter M. Pintner (1980), "The Evolution of Russian Officialdom 1755–1855," in Walter McKenzie Pintner and Don Karl Rowney, eds. (1980), *Russian Officialdom,* p. 192. According to P.A. Zaionchkovskii, that figure reached about 385,000 by 1903. Cited in Marc Raeff (1979), "The Bureaucratic Phenomena of Imperial Russia, 1700–1905," p. 401 fn.

20. Ibid., p. 209.

21. Sidney Monas (1970), "Bureaucracy in Russia under Nicholas I," pp. 274–275.

22. Three-quarters of the Russian civil service in 1755 had no formal education whatsoever. By 1855, over 80 percent of those individuals entering the civil service received a higher education. That such was the case in 1855 highlights the fact that the state civil service was still drawing its cadres from an elite segment of society.

23. Walter M. Pintner (1980), "Civil Officialdom and the Nobility in the 1850s," in Walter McKenzie Pintner and Don Karl Rowney, eds. (1980), *Russian Officialdom,* p. 228.

24. Cited in Anatole G. Mazour (1962), *Russia: Tsarist and Communist* (Toronto: D. Van Nostrand): 314.

25. The urban population grew from 7 to 20 million during the last half-century of the empire.

26. Cyril E. Black (1964), "The Nature of Imperial Russian Society," pp. 173–190 in Donald W. Treadgold, ed. (1964), *The Development of the USSR: An Exchange of Views* (Seattle: University of Washington Press): 175, 177.

27. Michael E. Urban (1982), *The Ideology of Administration: American and Soviet Cases* (Albany: State University of New York Press): xiii.

28. Ibid., p. 35.

29. Refer to his fine article, "Corruption and Political Development in the U.S.S.R.," *Comparative Politics,* Vol. 11 (July 1979): 425–442. For present purposes, pages 430–431 are especially relevant.

30. Ibid., p. 430.

31. See Sidney I. Ploss (1982), "Soviet Succession: Signs of Struggle," *Problems of Communism*, Vol. 31 (No. 5): 41–52.

32. For more on this implicit deal between the authorities and the Soviet population, refer to James R. Millar (1985), "The Little Deal: Brezhnev's Contribution to Acquisitive Socialism," *Slavic Review*, Vol. 44 (No. 4): 694–706.

33. F.J.M. Feldbrugge (1984), "Government and Shadow Economy in the Soviet Union," *Soviet Studies*, Vol. 36 (No. 4): 536.

34. Schwartz (1979), "Corruption and Political Development in the U.S.S.R.," p. 431.

35. J.M. Montias and Susan Rose-Ackerman (1980), *Corruption in a Soviet-Type Economy: Theoretical Considerations* (Washington, D.C.: Kennan Institute Occasional Paper No. 110).

36. Nicholas Lampert (1984), "Law and Order in the USSR: The Case of Economic and Official Crime," *Soviet Studies*, Vol. 36 (No. 3): 367.

37. Montias and Rose-Ackerman (1980), *Corruption in a Soviet-Type Economy*, p. 3.

38. For a fine analysis of the phenomenon of whistleblowing in the USSR, see Nicholas Lampert (1985), *Whistleblowing in the Soviet Union: Complaints and Abuses under State Socialism* (New York: Schoken Books).

39. Robert K. Merton (1957), *Social Theory and Social Structure* (Glencoe, IL: The Free Press): 197.

40. David Conn (1979), "A Comparison of Alternative Incentive Structures for Centrally Planned Economies," *Journal of Comparative Economics*, Vol. 3 (No. 3): 262.

41. Louise I. Shelley (1990), "The Second Economy in the Soviet Union," pp. 11–26 in Maria Los, ed. (1980), *The Second Economy in Marxist States* (New York: St. Martin's Press): 14.

42. Gregory Grossman (1987), "The Second Economy: Boon or Bane for the Reform of the First Economy?" *Berkeley-Duke Occasional Papers on the Second Economy in the USSR*, Vol. 11 (No. 2): 2.7.

43. Nicholas Lampert (1984), "Law and Order in the USSR: The Case of Economic and Official Crime," p. 367.

44. Joseph S. Berliner (1952), "The Informal Organization of the Soviet Firm," *Quarterly Journal of Economics*, Vol. 66: 342–356. See also Berliner's later work, *Factory and Manager in the USSR* (Cambridge: Harvard University Press, 1957).

45. Ibid., p. 349.

46. See Steven Shenfield (1983), "Pripiski: False Statistical Reporting in Soviet-Type Economies," pp. 239–258 in Michael Clarke, ed. (1983), *Corruption: Causes, Consequences and Control* (London: Francis Pinter).

47. According to David Granick, over 60 percent of certain key economic materials are produced in single factories. Thus, if for whatever reason production in these key factories stops or is reduced, the reverberations are felt throughout the economy as the key production resources cannot be delivered to other enterprises.

48. See Stanislav Pomorski (1978), "Crimes against the Central Planner 'Ochkovtiratel'stvo'," pp. 291–311 in Donald D. Barry, et al., eds. (1978), *Soviet Law after Stalin*, Vol. 2 (The Hague: Martinus Sijthoff).

49. Hedrick Smith (1976), *The Russians* (New York: Quadrangle): 88.

50. Perhaps still the best treatment of the Soviet *tolkach* is provided in chapter 12 of Joseph Berliner (1957), *Factory and Manager in the USSR* (Cambridge: Harvard University Press).

51. Raymond P. Powell (1977), "Plan Execution and the Workability of Soviet Planning," *Journal of Comparative Economics*, Vol. 1 (No. 1): 67.

52. Anthony Downs (1967), *Inside Bureaucracy*, p. 164.

53. Nicholas Lampert (1984), "Law and Order in the USSR: The Case of Economic and Official Crime," pp. 369, 370.

54. David Granick (1961), *The Red Executive*, p. 43.

55. Adam Smith (1937), *The Wealth of Nations* (Modern Library Series): 849.

56. William E. Butler, ed. (1983), *Basic Documents on the Soviet Legal System* (New York: Oceana Publications): 359.

57. See F.J.M. Feldbrugge, ed. (1973), *Encyclopedia of Soviet Law*, Vol. 2 (Dobbs Ferry, NY: Oceana Publications): 476.

58. Ger P. Van Den Berg (1985), *The Soviet System of Justice: Figures and Policy* (Dordrecht: Martinus Nijhoff): 60.

59. David Granick (1961), *The Red Executive*, pp. 30–31.

60. Nicholas Lampert, "Law and Order in the USSR," p. 379.

61. To the degree this is true, then, whenever anti-corruption campaigns are unveiled at any level of the system, there are likely to be a number of other motives for the drive, not merely the desire to root out illegal activities. This theme is developed further in a later chapter of this book.

62. Charles A. Schwartz (1979), "Corruption and Political Development in the U.S.S.R.," p. 429.

63. Robert O. Tilman (1968), "Emergence of Black-Market Bureaucracy: Administration, Development, and Corruption in the New States," *Public Administration Review*, Vol. 28 (No. 5): 437–444.

64. Huntington (1968) posits, on this final point, that "corruption in a modernizing society is not so much the result of deviance of behavior from accepted norms as it is the deviance of norms from the established pattern of behavior" (*Political Order in Changing Societies*, p. 60). This argument, as applied to the Soviet Union, gains support from an examination of corruption outside the Russian or Slavic areas of the Soviet Union. See Gerald Mars and Yochanan Altman (1983), "The Cultural Bases of Soviet Georgia's Second Economy," *Soviet Studies*, Vol. 35 (No. 4): 546–560. This topic is addressed more directly in chapter 3 of this book.

65. Samuel Huntington (1968), *Political Order in Changing Societies, op cit.*, p. 64.

66. See, for example, Nathaniel H. Leff (1964), "Economic Development through Bureaucratic Corruption," *American Behavioral Scientist*, Vol. 8 (No. 3): 8–15; Colin Leys (1965), "What Is the Problem about Corruption?" *Journal of Modern African Studies*, Vol. 3 (No. 2): 215–230; and John Waterbury (1973), "Endemic and Planned Corruption in a Monarchical Regime," *World Politics*, Vol. 25 (No. 4): 533–555.

67. Charles A. Schwartz (1979), "Corruption and Political Development in the U.S.S.R.," p. 427.

68. John M. Kramer (1977), "Political Corruption in the U.S.S.R.," *The Western Political Quarterly*, Vol. 30 (No. 2): 223, 224.

69. Robert K. Merton (1957), *Social Theory and Social Structure,* pp. 198–199.

70. David Granick (1961), *The Red Executive,* p. 157.

71. James R. Millar (1985), "The Little Deal: Brezhnev's Contribution to Acquisitive Socialism," *Slavic Review,* Vol. 44 (No. 4): 697.

72. Ibid.

73. Ibid., p. 705.

74. Schwartz, for example, argues that "functional patterns of corruption provide some remedy for institutional weakness and may endure as alternatives to institutional reform" ("Corruption and Political Development in the U.S.S.R.," p. 427). Huntington states that "corruption may thus be functional to the maintenance of a political system in the same way that reform is. Corruption itself may be a substitute for reform" *(Political Order in Changing Societies,* p. 64).

75. John M. Kramer (1977), "Political Corruption in the U.S.S.R.," p. 221.

76. Robert K. Merton (1952), "Bureaucratic Personality and Structure," in Robert Merton, et al., eds., *Reader in Bureaucracy* (Glencoe, IL: The Free Press): 368–371.

3

CORRUPTION IN THE POLITICAL ELITE, 1965–1990

The Soviet meaning of corruption is best described as an alliance of law and informal political rules. Law is by all accounts the weaker ally.
—Charles A. Schwartz[1]

It was during the Brezhnev period in Soviet political history that the structural irrationalities of the formal mechanisms of state rule became elevated to a critical stage. Despite a perception of increased Soviet strength throughout the 1970s, fueled primarily by a number of foreign policy and propaganda measures, it was the lack of real structural reform of the state's formal institutions that led to the dramatic reversal of Soviet fortunes in the 1980s. Since the disintegration of the Soviet state in 1991, many observers have made retrospective note of the internal problems inherent in Soviet institutions during the Soviet Union's last quarter-century. Indeed, based on the number of post-mortem analyses that have appeared in the short period of time since the demise of the USSR, as well as the clarity with which these analyses have been argued, it is presently quite easy to get the impression that sovietology as a field of study was consistently and acutely aware of the problems as they developed, and that our estimates of Soviet power and the stability of the regime always reflected an accurate appreciation of the true scale of their internal crises. Of course, such was not the case.

It is instructive at this point, then, to investigate the manner by which the Soviet state addressed the problems of its formal institutions. While it is true enough that Soviet leaders before Gorbachev refused to engage in the kind of serious reform of these institutions necessary to ensure the future stability of Soviet state power, it is not accurate to argue that the Soviet leadership was unaware of the problems, or that the leadership did not make changes in policy aimed at alleviating the irrationalities of its administrative state. It is fairer to say that the Brezhnev leadership and the weak leaders of the Andropov–Chernenko interregnum balked at the prospects of serious reform, but acquiesced to the creation of an entire series of implicit compromises, deals, and other unstated half-measures aimed at the maintenance of their rule.[2] In a word, while eschewing the reform of formal institutions, the Soviet leadership during the 1965–1990 period accommodated itself to the creation and operation of alternative, informal institutions which, in its estimation, tended to perform certain social functions in a more efficient manner. That these informal mechanisms tended to supplant the formal institutions of the state, that they tended as well to violate the letter and spirit of the Soviet legal code, that they succumbed to what, from the perspective of their professed ideology, were the worst aspects of selfish, pecuniary capitalism, was less a concern than the maintenance of Soviet power.

This chapter examines one such area where ad hoc, informal practices that tended to produce better outcomes than those of the formal system overcame formal Soviet procedures and acquired something close to the status of an informal regime supported, if only implicitly, by the Soviet leadership. Specifically, this chapter presents an analysis of Soviet official corruption during the 1965–1990 period with a view to explicating the characteristics of the informal regime as it governed the behavior of Soviet officials at a time when the political leadership increasingly recognized the serious problems of its formal rules and institutions. I focus primarily on the various types of illegal activity in evidence among the political and administrative officials of the Soviet state, the differing levels of punishment allotted to these activities, as well as the uneven geographic distribution of the frequency of official misconduct.

This analysis, as will be argued below, highlights an informal criminological regime used by the Soviet leadership to judge the behavior of Soviet officials; certain "functional" crimes committed by Soviet officials during this time were virtually ignored, even encouraged. Dysfunctional crimes, of course, were punished to the full extent of the Soviet legal code. In a sense, administrative and managerial behavior on the part of Soviet officials that served the purposes of system maintenance, although technically in violation of the strict letter of Soviet law (as well as the ethos of the formal ruling ideology), was deemed acceptable because it went a long way in rationalizing the inherent weaknesses of the formal political and economic system. Soviet officials, in a way, operated under an implicit pact with the regime that entailed the creation and maintenance of a great informal system of state administration. This system had in a number of ways actually strengthened the stability of the Soviet regime and, as such, was rendered for the most part immune from the prejudice of technical legal sanctions.

In an effort to discern important aspects of this phenomenon, the circumstances entailed in the convictions of 855 Soviet officials between 1965 and 1990 are examined with respect to the specific violation of Soviet legality, the geographic setting of the crime, and the penalty imposed on the convicted official. As shall become clear below, these data reveal significant and consistent patterns among the enforcement organs with respect to the types of illegal activities that merit moderate or severe punishment, the timing of enforcement "campaigns," as well as the geographic distribution of cases.[3] These findings provide insight into the politics of official crime and punishment in the Soviet Union.

Officialdom, Corruption, and the Soviet Criminal Code

Interest in the "second" or "shadow" economy in the Soviet Union increased in recent decades as its role in the running of Soviet society likewise increased.[4] By the end of the Brezhnev regime in November 1982, in fact, the pervasiveness of "na levo" (literally, "on the left,") or improper transactions in the country had reached almost unimaginable levels. Ed A. Hewett has argued that nearly 20 million Soviet citizens were engaged either full- or part-time in underground production activities.[5] Such high estimates are no longer relegated to Western scholars. Arkady Vaksberg, an investigative reporter at *Literaturnaya gazeta*, has cited the official estimates of the money generated illegally at between 150 and 200 billion rubles, but argues that the true figure is closer to 400 billion rubles.[6] According to T.I. Koryagina, formerly affiliated with the USSR's State Planning Committee's (Gosplan) Economic Research Institute, the largest area of growth in this illegal economy has taken place in the service sector, where the societal needs are greatest.[7] Finally, the scale of the black market in the USSR had grown so large during the 1980s that two Soviet sociologists estimated that 83 percent of the Soviet population employed the shadow economy to obtain necessary food and services.[8]

Corruption on this scale certainly infected all segments of Soviet society, including the political elite. Given the sheer size of the Soviet state and the penetration of its officials into the society during the past quarter-century, Soviet officialdom, like society in general, was unable to separate itself from reliance on illegal activities; if society in general had come to embrace, if only out of necessity, alternative systems to the distribution of goods and services, so had that class of officials who have been charged with the duty of administering Soviet society. In fact, one can argue that Soviet officials were, by virtue of their strategic positions in the running of the Soviet economy, placed in a day-to-day situation marked by the *increased* opportunity for personal and institutional aggrandizement. In this heavily administered economy marked by a sizeable monetary overhang and severe chronic scarcity, the corruption of its officials was almost inevitable.

The criminal code of the Russian Soviet Federated Socialist Republic (RSFSR) served as the model upon which each Soviet republic based its own criminal code. As a result, most of the major studies of Soviet criminal law have used the RSFSR code as the single best source for analysis.[9] Specifically, the code is divided into two parts: the General, which provides conceptual expositions on what the Soviet state considers crime, punishment, and the limits thereof; and the Specific, composed of twelve Chapters, each of which deal with a specific category of crime as well as respective punishments, which are spelled out in the form of specific Articles. The amended Special Part of the RSFSR criminal code contains 269 Articles. For present purposes, however, only a select number of Chapters and their Articles are relevant for the analysis of official crime and punishment.

It is useful at the outset of this discussion to understand how the RSFSR code defines a Soviet "official." Chapter 7 of the Special Part of the code defines a Soviet official as follows:

> By officials . . . are meant persons who are permanently or temporarily effectuating the functions of representatives of authority, and also who are permanently or temporarily occupying offices in state or social or-

ganizations connected with the fulfillment of organizational-executive or administrative-economic duties, or who are fulfilling such duties in the said institutions, organizations, and enterprises in accordance with a special authorization.[10]

It is clear from the above that the Soviet criminal code assumed a very inclusive view of what constitutes officialdom under Soviet law. As such, persons who in Western political settings would not be considered "officials" of the state certainly would be included in the Soviet case. As might be expected, the level of expectations used to judge the behavior of state officials in the Soviet Union was decidedly higher than that used to judge the actions of private citizens. Given the inclusive definition of officialdom in the Soviet setting, then, a higher standard is applied to even those "lower" officials who might not be considered in such a category in another state.

Several Chapters of the Special Part of the Code are especially relevant to the pattern of corrupt behavior among Soviet officials. Indeed, the vast majority of cases involving the 855 Soviet officials dealt with in this present treatment fall legally under but one of a small number of Chapters in the Code. As mentioned above, Chapter 7 deals with "official crimes," and its five Articles spell out a litany of crimes that appear frequently among the specific cases described in the pages that follow: abuse of office (Article 171), neglect of office (172), receiving (173), giving (174), or acting as an intermediary (174.1) in a bribery scheme, and forgery of official documents (175). Virtually every "transaction" in Soviet society involved the acquisition of any number of official state documents. Individuals in Soviet and post-Soviet society have demonstrated perhaps an over-willingness to employ illicit methods to procure these documents. In very many cases, the bribes and other inducements used to lubricate that Soviet administrative machine were bribes that served only to liberate documents, such as housing permits *(propiski)*, licenses, and other essentials, to which the applicant was legally entitled. We therefore witness numerous cases of Soviet citizens being forced to employ illegal means for the acquisition of materials which, by law, they are clearly entitled. Such were the prerogatives of Soviet officials and, interestingly, the cynical expectations of the average Soviet citizen.[11]

Another area of the criminal code frequented by convicted Soviet officials involves Chapter 6: "Economic Crimes." Given the near state monopoly of economic activity, as well as the distribution of the production thereof, Soviet officials were strategically located in positions that carried with them numerous opportunities for personal aggrandizement. As a result, much of the official corruption encountered in the data entails such economic crimes as private entrepreneurial or middleman activity (Article 153), speculation (154), and illicit trade (156.3).

The onerous set of expectations placed on Soviet managerial officials often compelled them to break the letter of Soviet law for essentially unselfish reasons, or for what might be considered reasons of "system maintenance." The actual procurement process in the Soviet industrial sphere, for example, was far removed from what might appear in a ministry's or enterprise's policies and procedures manual. Indeed, it seems clear that the disposition of the Soviet ruling elite toward the proliferation of technically illegal managerial techniques became over the past twenty-five years one of acceptance and, in a significant sense, encouragement. The utilization of aggressive, inventive, and often free-lance procurement agents, or *tolkachi,* became a Soviet growth industry virtually winked at by enforcement agencies. The demands placed on Soviet officials in this regard does, however, produced a large number of convictions for such things as the issuance of poor-quality, non-standard, or unfinished products (Article 152), distortions of plan quotas, and the padding of production reports to superiors, or *pripiski* (152.1).

Of course, Soviet officials were not immune to the array of clearly criminal activities such as those covered in Chapter 2 of the Special Part of the Code. Here, crimes against socialist ownership are defined, and the student of Soviet official corruption encounters many instances of theft of socialist property (Articles 89, 90, 93.1, 96), embezzlement (92), and swindling (93). In what developed to be a largely barter-based domestic economy characterized by chronic shortages of virtually all valued goods and services, a sizeable monetary overhang, and ample opportunities for report padding and other such accounting practices, Soviet officials in many positions were prone to such violations of Soviet state law.

Data and Methodology

Data on the convictions of 855 Soviet officials during the 1965–1990 period were gathered from Soviet press translations as they appeared in the Western publication *The Current Digest of the Soviet Press* (here-inafter *CDSP*), a weekly survey of a wide array of Soviet newspapers, trade journals, and other printed media, and reprints or abstracts articles appearing in the Soviet press. *CDSP* has been widely used by students of the Soviet system and has been the source of data for a number of related studies of Soviet official corruption.[12] A review of the approximately 1,300 issues of *CDSP* that cover the time period under scrutiny produced some 343 articles containing rich information concerning the convictions of the 855 individual Soviet officials referred to above.

It is worth noting that perhaps as many as an additional 100 articles from the Soviet press dealing with official corruption were consulted but excluded from this study due to their lack of relevant information about one or another important detail of the respective case. Often, the criminal act is discussed in rich detail, the reporter explicating the long and complicated network of individuals involved in the crime, with no mention of the exact penalty or penalties distributed. In other cases, vague references may be made to a number of unnamed accomplices who have received "just punishments" for their crimes against Soviet law. Of course, in neither of the above types of cases would these individuals be included in the analysis.

Finally, as is the practice in the Western media, reporters may follow and write several stories about particularly newsworthy trials; as a result, a review of the Soviet media will turn up several articles from different media sources that deal with the same crime, involving the same individuals. The data set constructed for this study involves only those stories that appear as the result of a *conviction* of Soviet officials, not those dealing merely with charges brought against officials. In addition, individual convictions of Soviet officials appear only once in the data set, regardless of how many times the description of the events leading up to the conviction, or the conviction itself, is repeated in the various Soviet media. In this way, the analysis that follows concerns itself solely with the convictions of Soviet officials for specific violations of the Soviet criminal code. It does not entail a content analysis approach to the manner of Soviet media reporting, but seeks only to identify a discrete set of convictions.

Specifically, the details expounded in the Soviet press articles were coded with respect to several important considerations. The data set on convicted Soviet officials contains (1) the name of the official convicted, (2) the official post occupied at the time of the criminal act(s), (3) the geographic location of the criminal activity, (4) the nature of the criminal charges brought against the official, (5) the monetary value of the criminal activity (if applicable), and (6) the penalty assigned the convicted official. This data collection method provided cases from each of the fifteen Soviet republics, from the majority of the USSR's different *oblasti,* and from each of the leadership periods contained in the quarter-century of Soviet history covered in this study. As such, it permits the analysis of these social phenomena from spatial, temporal, and political perspectives.

At this point, however, a word of caution is in order. Research constructed along these lines must be cognizant of variations in the reporting of certain types of crimes in the Soviet press. This concern goes beyond the expected tendency of the media to focus attention on high-profile cases, or cases involving particularly bizarre occurrences. Of special interest, and itself no doubt worthy of separate scrutiny, is the bias of central newspapers to select out stories from prominent places, such as Moscow and Leningrad or Russia and the Ukraine, over equally important stories from less prominant places, such as Sochi and Baku or Georgia and Azerbaidzhan. Might these expected prejudices of the major newspapers skew the distribution of cases reported in the press? No doubt they do. In addition, the media-based data for research into criminal convictions must also pass through the filter of the gatekeepers at the *CDSP*. Everthing that was said above about the selection criteria of Soviet newspapers must be said also of the editors at *Current Digest*. Each of these concerns notwithstanding, however, sufficient faith can be placed in the data. While the number of cases from the Russian Republic is rather high (thus seeming to support a possible bias inflating reports of RSFSR cases), large numbers also appear from the Soviet periphery (Azerbaidzhan, Georgia, Uzbekistan).

When the fact of Russia's population vis-à-vis the other republics is taken into account, any bias in favor of "central places" seems to be quite minimal. Enough cases emerge from outside the major cities, from outside the European sections of the USSR, and from outside the so-called "center" to suggest that the data are generally representative of the true state of affairs in the country. While it must be admitted that the present data, as in many other analyses of Soviet politics and society, are "softer" than the researcher would want, the nature of the distribution of cases does extend confidence in any general statements that emerge from the analysis.

Findings

The specific politics of anti-corruption in the Soviet Union, at least as it applies to officials of state, becomes clear in the analysis of the data. As is detailed below, certain patterns emerge with respect to the geographic distribution of corruption cases, the severity of the penalties handed down by the Soviet courts, and the specific timing of the anti-corruption activities of the enforcement agencies. Evidence of "campaigning" by the enforcement agencies of the Soviet state is visible, as is the prescriptive flavor of such campaigns. The small number of convictions and the relatively modest penalties allotted to officials convicted of "system maintenance" crimes reveals an official state bias in favor of certain "criminal" behavior on the part of Soviet officials. In sum, the analysis of these cases provides an initial look into the informal "rules of the game" governing the individual behavior of Soviet officials. The relatively large number of cases provides an enhanced level of confidence in the validity of the findings.

Incidence and Categories of Official Crime

With respect to the RSFSR criminal code, the convictions of Soviet officials detailed in Soviet press translations during the 1965–1990 period fall predominantly into two categories of violations: crimes against socialist property (Chapter 2 crimes) and official crimes (Chapter 7 crimes). Combined, over 84 percent of all the reported convictions of Soviet officials are captured by these two categories of crime (see Table 3.1).

Specifically, 39 percent of the 855 official convictions coded fell under the rubric of crimes against socialist property. While Chapter 2 of the criminal code is comprised of thirteen separate articles, many with quite pointed subsections, within this crime category two specific articles account for the vast bulk of convictions. Violations of Articles 89 (theft of state or social property) and 92 (embezzlement and misappropriation) combined accounted for 319 of the 336 Chapter 2 crimes (i.e., 95 percent). The remaining seventeen cases of crimes in this category pertaining to crimes against socialist

Table 3.1

Official Convictions and the Soviet Criminal Code, 1965–1990 (by Republic)

	RUS	UKR	BEL	EST	LAT	LIT	MOL	GEO	ARM	AZR	KAZ	UZB	TAD	TUR	KIR	Total
Property Crimes																
Theft	74	16	1	1	0	4	1	10	0	40	3	9	0	0	0	159
Embezzlement	98	13	0	0	0	0	1	15	1	15	5	2	5	5	0	160
Negligent Destruction	1	2	0	0	0	0	0	0	0	0	0	0	0	0	0	3
Lack of Protection	6	0	0	0	0	0	0	5	0	3	0	0	0	0	0	14
Personal Crimes																
Aggravated Homicide	1	0	0	0	0	0	0	0	0	0	0	0	0	0	0	1
Grave Bodily Injury	1	0	0	0	0	0	0	0	0	0	0	0	0	0	0	1
Beatings	2	0	0	0	0	0	0	0	0	0	0	0	0	0	0	2
Ownership Crimes																
Extortion	15	4	0	0	0	0	0	0	0	13	1	5	2	0	4	44
Economic Crimes																
Poor-Quality Output	13	2	0	0	0	0	0	0	2	0	0	0	0	0	0	17
Report Padding	18	6	0	0	0	0	2	6	0	0	0	2	0	0	0	34
Entrepreneurialism	2	0	0	0	0	0	0	0	0	0	0	0	0	0	0	2
Speculation	8	0	0	0	0	1	0	1	0	4	2	0	0	3	0	19
Illegal Trade Alcohol	1	0	0	0	0	0	0	0	0	0	0	0	0	0	0	1
Violating Trade Rules	3	0	0	0	0	0	0	0	0	7	0	0	0	0	0	10
Poaching	1	0	0	0	0	0	0	0	0	0	0	0	0	0	0	1
Precious Metals	1	0	0	0	0	0	0	0	0	0	0	0	0	0	0	1
Official Crimes																
Abuse of Authority	53	15	1	0	0	0	8	10	5	24	5	0	2	1	9	133
Exceeding Authority	2	1	0	0	0	0	0	2	0	0	1	0	0	0	1	7
Neglect of Duties	28	13	0	2	0	0	7	18	10	10	0	8	0	4	1	101
Taking a Bribe	57	10	0	0	0	0	0	11	5	26	2	16	0	0	0	127
Giving a Bribe	5	3	0	0	0	0	0	0	0	0	0	0	0	0	0	8
Middleman in Bribery	1	0	0	0	0	0	0	0	0	0	0	0	0	0	0	1
Forgery	8	0	0	0	0	0	0	0	1	0	0	0	0	0	0	9
TOTALS	399	85	2	3	0	5	19	78	24	142	19	42	9	13	15	855

property involved the related crimes of negligent destruction or damage to state or social property (Article 99) or of displaying an unconscientious attitude toward the protection of state or social property (Article 100).

An even greater percentage of the total convictions noted during the 1965–1990 period entailed violations of various articles of chapter 7 of the code: Official Crimes. Forty-five percent of the 855 cases recorded involved violations of the canons of official conduct. Within this category of crime, three specific articles stand out as especially noteworthy and together comprise the vast bulk (91 percent) of Chapter 7 crime in the USSR: taking a bribe (Article 173), abuse of authority (Article 170), and neglect of official duties (Article 172). Convictions for violations of these three articles combine for 361 of the 386 Chapter 7 crimes. With respect to bribery, a crime taken quite seriously by the higher Soviet authorities, 127 convictions were documented for Soviet officials accepting a bribe. There are three related bribery statutes that bring the total number of bribery-related cases to 136. If these additional cases are added to the mix, then 370 of the 386 Chapter 7 crimes involved one of the following transgressions: abuse of authority, bribery, and neglect. No other "official crime" accounts for more than ten specific convictions.

Roughly 10 percent of the 855 cases chronicled in Soviet press translations involved what the RSFSR code referred to as "economic crimes" (Chapter 6). Thirty-four convictions of officials for report padding (Article 152.1) were cited, along with a lesser number of convictions for speculation (Article 154) and for the issuance of poor-quality goods (Article 152). Of the remaining fifteen Chapter 6 convictions, ten entailed violations of trade rules. Under the broad rubric of economic crime in the Soviet Union, it is interesting to note that, combined, the number of convictions cited entailing the padding of reports of production activities to superiors *(pripiski)* to show plan fulfillment or over-fulfillment, and the employment by Soviet officials of aggressively entrepreneurial procurement agents *(tolkachi),* amount to only thirty-six total convictions over a twenty-five-year period—4 percent of the total number of convictions detailed during this time. Of even more interest, though, is that Soviet press translations during this time cite but two convictions of *tolkachi,* despite their highly questionable status under Soviet law. Further discussion of this finding will be provided below.

Official Crime and Punishment

The patterns that emerge from an examination of the penalties allotted to Soviet officials convicted during the 1965–1990 period reveal the rather serious ramifications involved in undesirable official behavior. Of the 849 cases for which the data reveal levels of punishment, fully 57 percent ($n = 480$) involved a prison sentence, what in Soviet legal jargon is referred to as "deprivation of freedom." Variations in both the likelihood and the severity of the prison sentences is clear when penalties are broken down with respect to the categories of the legal code itself (see Table 3.2). Of those categories for which the available date provide a large number of cases, property crimes committed by Soviet officials are punished the most severely. Those officials convicted of such a category of crime are most likely (in 75 percent of the 335 cases) to be sentenced to prison, and are most likely to spend a considerable period of time there (mean sentence length equals almost eleven years). In fact, the odds of being sent to prison for a Chapter 2 crime are over 6 to 1 when compared to the next less severe penalty, removal from office. Also reflective of the seriousness with which such pecuniary property crimes are viewed is the high number of death penalties handed down for crimes such as theft and embezzlement. Indeed, of the thirty-two death penalties described in Soviet press translations, twenty-three (72 percent) involve these Chapter 2 crimes. In like fashion, officials convicted of extorting bribes are almost certain to be sentenced to jail time, although the mean sentence length (8.3 years) is somewhat less than for the previous category of crime.

The second most likely penalty for officials convicted of violating one or another article of the legal code is removal from office. Approximately 25 percent of the officials in the present sample met up with such a fate. Again, Table 3.2 reveals that this penalty is the "punishment of choice" for convictions for official crimes outlined in Chapter 7 of the legal code. However, Chapter 7 convictions bifurcate into two categories with respect to punishment. If the official is convicted of bribery, he or she is quite likely (over 80 percent of the time) to be sentenced to a penal colony. If one permits the grouping of the three bribery articles in Chapter 7 with the extortion crime in Chapter 5, then the regime's absolute policy with respect to this quite ubiquitous Soviet phenomenon becomes quite clear: 85 percent (151 of the 177 cases) of the convictions related to bribery eventuate in a rather

Table 3.2

Official Crime and Punishment, 1965–1990

	Repri-mand	Probation, Work, Fine	Removal from Post	Prison (Mean Sentence)	Death Penalty	Total
Property Crimes	9	13	39	251 (10.7)	23	335
Theft	0	7	3	134 (9.7)	15	159
Embezzlement	6	0	30	116 (11.9)	8	160
Negligent Destruction	0	2	0	1 (3.0)	0	3
Lack of Protection	3	4	6	0 (—)	0	13
Personal Crimes	0	0	0	3 (4.8)	1	4
Aggravated Homicide	0	0	0	0 (—)	1	1
Grave Bodily Injury	0	0	0	1 (11.0)	0	1
Beatings	0	0	0	2 (1.8)	0	2
Ownership Crimes	0	0	1	42 (8.3)	0	43
Extortion	0	0	1	42 (8.3)	0	43
Economic Crimes	14	8	21	42 (6.7)	0	85
Poor-Quality Output	0	6	5	6 (2.5)	0	17
Report Padding	8	2	14	10 (6.7)	0	34
Entrepreneurialism	0	0	0	2 (6.0)	0	2
Speculation	0	0	0	19 (8.1)	0	19
Illegal Trade Alcohol	0	0	0	1 (2.0)	0	1
Violating Trade Rules	6	0	2	2 (3.5)	0	10
Poaching	0	0	0	1 (15.0)	0	1
Precious Metals	0	0	0	1 (9.0)	0	1
Official Crimes	65	13	154	142 (9.0)	8	382
Abuse of Authority	30	2	83	17 (7.6)	1	133
Exceeding Authority	0	0	6	1 (n.a.)	0	7
Neglect of Duties	35	8	50	6 (2.8)	0	99
Taking a Bribe	0	0	13	105 (9.7)	7	125
Giving a Bribe	0	3	2	3 (8.7)	0	8
Middleman in Bribery	0	0	0	1 (13.0)	0	1
Forgery	0	0	0	9 (7.1)	0	9
Totals	88	34	215	480	32	849*

*Total reflects incomplete data on penalties for six specific crimes.

lengthy term of incarceration. In addition, seven Soviet officials during this time period were executed for bribe taking.

On the other hand, mindful of the often contradictory demands placed on Soviet officials at virtually all levels of the system, Soviet jurists have given people convicted of official crimes other than those associated with bribery much less severe penalties. Convictions in the areas of (1) abuse of authority, (2) exceeding authority, and (3) neglect of duties, produce non-prison penalties at a ratio of greater than 9 to 1 (224 to 24) over prison penalties. In fact, there is even a fair chance (31 percent of the 239 cases) that such a conviction will result merely in a reprimand or fine. One is left with the impression that convictions for Chapter 7 offenses (official crimes) will be rather mildly punished if the particular offense is considered non-pecuniary. On the other hand, the likelihood of severe penalties for Chapter 7 convictions rise as the "selfishness quotient" of the crime rises.

It is worth noting, however, that even being removed from office is not necessarily a sentence from which it is impossible to recover, especially at lower levels. The Soviet press describes a number of cases where a convicted official reappears in a different location in a parallel position of authority, hired by the local authorities after a superficial background check. Of course, such cases appear in the Soviet press only after the official in question has been apprehended for yet another violation. Such Soviet press articles display the appropriate amount of incredulity with respect to the laxity of those who hired the recidivist.

If one considers the first three categories of punishment as reflecting what the regime considered less severe criminal activities, and the categories involving a prison sentence and/or the death penalty as reflecting those crimes seen as most undesirable, then the distribution of punishments can yield interesting patterns. Overall, 60 percent of all punishments cited above fall into the categories of punishment associated with serious crimes. Within individual categories of official convictions, crimes of property, person, and ownership are clearly punished more severely than those involving economic and official crimes. In each of the latter two categories, a convicted official is more likely not to receive a prison sentence; combined, these two areas of convictions produce lesser sentences in 59 percent of the cases.

Table 3.3 takes this analysis a bit further by highlighting the geographic distribution of penalties for official convictions. If the punishments extended for specific crimes are good indicators of the degree to which specific criminal activities are viewed as threatening to the regime, then two republics stand out as noteworthy for higher-than-usual levels of serious crime. Both the RSFSR and Azerbaidzhan produced a disproportionate number of serious penalties. In each republic, the ratio

Table 3.3

Categories of Punishment for Official Crimes, 1965–1990
(by Republic)

	Repri-mand	Probation, Work, Fine	Removal from Post	Prison	Death Penalty	Total
RSFSR	38	17	61	270	9	395*
Ukraine	16	9	18	39	2	84*
Belorussia	0	1	0	1	0	2
Estonia	0	0	0	3	0	3
Latvia	0	0	0	0	0	0
Lithuania	0	0	0	5	0	5
Moldavia	3	0	13	2	0	18*
Georgia	5	1	50	20	2	78
Armenia	7	0	10	7	0	24
Azerbaidzhan	18	3	24	84	13	142
Kazakhstan	1	1	4	10	3	19
Uzbekistan	0	2	14	24	2	42
Tadzhikistan	0	0	2	7	0	9
Turkmenistan	0	0	8	4	1	13
Kirgizia	0	0	11	4	0	15
Totals	88	34	215	480	32	849*

*Totals reflect incomplete data on penalties for six specific crimes: four from the RSFSR, one from the Ukraine, and one from Moldavia.

of serious penalties to less serious penalties surpassed 2 to 1. In no other republic of the former Soviet Union with a large number of convictions can the same be said. On the other hand, the pattern of punishment of convicted officials from several other republics (e.g., Moldavia, Georgia, and Armenia) shows a likelihood of fewer penalties. The issue of the geographic factors of Soviet official crime and punishment is discussed in greater detail below.

The Geography of Official Crime

The data on reported convictions between 1965 and 1990 reveal an uneven geographic distribution of convictions. Approximately 47 percent ($n = 399$) of all the cases cited in Soviet press translations involved convictions of officials attached to Russian Republic units (see Table 3.4, page 87). Such a distribution, it would be expected, would be consistent with population distributions across Soviet republics.

Russia, with some 142 million people in its territory, should show, *ceteris paribus*, the largest raw number of official convictions. If there were anything like a uniform number of officials per capita in the USSR, and if levels of official corruption were likewise uniform throughout Soviet society, it would be expected that the largest republic would have the largest number of official convictions. This expectation, at least with respect to the largest republic, is borne out by the numbers. With this bias in mind, however, it is useful for the sake of comparing the *rates* of corruption with respect to their geographic distribution to attempt to control for differences in population across Soviet republics. When the figures are thus compared, the specific characteristics of the overall distribution of the cases reveals interesting patterns and raises additional questions.

After Russia, the republic with the next highest incidence of official corruption convictions is Azerbaidzhan. Fully 142 convictions of officials of the Azerbaidzhan Republic were described in Soviet press translations. Controlling for population, then, Azerbaidzhan supports the highest corruption saturation rate[13] of any Soviet republic. During the time period under study, Azerbaidzhan evidenced an official corruption rate of almost twenty-two convictions per one million population (see Table 3.5, page 88). This rate is approximately eight times as high as that of the Russian Republic and over 50 percent higher than even the republic with the second highest official corruption saturation rate, Georgia.

That such a large number and percentage (16.6) of total Soviet convictions for official corruption should come from Azerbaidzhan, with some 6.5 million people (only 2.4 percent of the total Soviet population), might seem anomalous. On the other hand, such a finding is not totally unexpected. Certain areas within the Soviet Union have become infamous with respect to the question of corruption. The Caucasus shows an extraordinarily high level of convictions, with a regional rate (16.27) six or seven times that of any other geographically defined group of republics. The three Soviet republics with the highest official conviction saturation rates are Azerbaidzhan, Georgia, and Armenia. With a combined regional population of approximately 15 million people, or 10 percent that of Russia alone, the Caucasus produced a number of official convictions almost half that of Russia. The data from the 1965–1990 period certainly seem to support the findings of more qualitative analyses of the link between corruption and culture in the Caucasus.[14]

Table 3.4

Geographic Distribution of Soviet Official Convictions, 1965–1990 (by year)

	64	65	66	67	68	69	70	71	72	73	74	75	76	77	78	79	80	81	82	83	84	85	86	87	88	89	90	Totals
RSFSR	6	16	3	0	3	4	5	3	10	14	18	15	11	22	18	18	27	43	15	44	32	29	25	12	2	1	3	399
Uk	0	0	0	2	0	0	1	4	0	16	0	0	3	8	2	3	4	1	6	14	0	1	1	13	6	0	0	85
Belo	0	0	0	0	0	0	0	0	0	0	0	0	0	0	0	0	0	0	0	0	2	0	0	0	0	0	0	2
Geo	3	0	0	0	1	2	2	0	0	0	16	0	10	2	0	0	9	4	0	6	10	9	0	0	1	1	0	78
Mold	0	0	0	0	0	0	0	8	0	0	0	0	0	0	1	0	0	0	1	0	6	0	1	3	1	1	0	19
Arm	0	0	0	0	0	0	0	0	0	0	0	2	1	3	0	0	0	1	2	0	0	0	0	0	0	14	0	24
Azer	0	0	0	0	0	0	5	0	21	0	0	9	0	7	26	11	10	16	11	19	2	2	0	1	3	0	0	142
Uzb	0	0	0	0	0	0	0	0	0	0	0	3	0	0	5	0	0	4	1	0	15	7	1	1	0	3	5	42
Kaz	0	0	0	0	0	1	3	0	0	0	0	0	0	1	4	0	1	0	0	0	3	0	0	4	2	3	0	19
Tad	0	0	0	0	0	0	0	0	0	0	0	0	0	2	1	0	4	0	0	0	0	0	0	0	0	0	2	9
Turk	0	0	0	0	0	0	0	0	0	0	0	0	0	0	0	0	0	5	0	0	0	0	8	0	0	0	0	13
Kirg	0	0	0	0	0	0	0	0	0	0	0	0	0	0	0	0	0	4	0	0	0	2	9	0	0	0	0	15
Est	0	0	0	0	0	0	0	0	0	0	0	0	0	2	1	0	0	0	0	0	0	0	0	0	0	0	0	3
Lat	0	0	0	0	0	0	0	0	0	0	0	0	0	0	0	0	0	0	0	0	0	0	0	0	0	0	0	0
Lith	0	0	0	0	0	0	0	0	0	0	0	0	0	0	4	0	1	0	0	0	0	0	0	0	0	0	0	5
Totals	9	16	3	2	4	7	16	15	10	51	34	29	25	47	62	32	56	78	35	91	64	50	46	34	15	20	10	855

Table 3.5

Saturation Rates of Soviet Official Convictions
(by Republics, 1965–1990)

Republic	Population	Officials Convicted	Rate*
RSFSR	142,000,000	399	2.81
Ukraine	50,000,000	85	1.70
Belorussia	10,000,000	2	0.20
Total Slavic	202,000,000	486	2.41
Estonia	1,400,000	3	2.14
Latvia	2,600,000	0	0.00
Lithuania	3,550,000	5	1.41
Total Baltic	7,550,000	8	1.06
Georgia	5,200,000	78	15.00
Armenia	3,300,000	24	7.27
Azerbaidzhan	6,500,000	142	21.85
Total Caucasus	15,000,000	244	16.27
Kazakhstan	15,650,000	19	1.21
Uzbekistan	15,500,000	42	2.71
Turkmenistan	3,200,000	13	4.06
Kirgizia	3,900,000	15	3.85
Tadzhikstan	4 500,000	9	2.00
Total Central Asia	42,750,000	98	2.29
Moldavia	4,100,000	19	4.63
USSR Totals	271,400,000	855	3.15

*Rate is equal to the number of convicted officials per 1,000,000 population; assuming a uniform officials-to-population ratio throughout the USSR, rates comparisons may produce general statements regarding the relative level of official corruption in the various republics.

On the other end of the spectrum, official corruption seems to be decidedly less prevalent in the northwestern sector of the Soviet Union. The three Baltic republics exhibited significantly less corruption than any other region of the USSR, totaling a mere eight reported cases and a population-controlled saturation rate of 1.06 over the twenty-five-year span of this study. Belorussia, bordering on the Baltic region, also exhibited modest numbers of reported official convictions and a saturation rate of 0.20 official convictions per one million population. If one compares, then, the evidence from Soviet press translations with respect to the Caucasus (15 million people, 244 convictions) and the four northwestern republics (17.5 million people, 10 convictions), the geographical variation in official corruption rates is obvious.

Such a marked difference in this social phenomenon certainly merits additional research into the cultural and economic bases of corruption in the former Soviet Union and elsewhere.[15] On the latter score, it is instructive to compare in a cursory way the varying republic corruption saturation rates with some standard economic measures to establish the potential for further research in this area. Table 3.6 represents simple rank orderings of the Soviet republics according to both their levels of official corruption and a number of economic development scales. In general, the data seem to provide general support for the notion that corruption may indeed be symptomatic of certain levels of socio-economic development.

In addition to the particular nature of the geographic and economic distribution of official corruption convictions cited above, the data reveal an interesting geographic anomaly with respect to the level of punishment for these crimes. At the highest level of punishment, the death penalty, the evidence reveals a decidedly skewed record that seems to discriminate on the basis of nationality. The *Current Digest of the Soviet Press* reported details of thirty-two individuals being executed for official corruption in the Soviet Union during the 1965–1990 period. All of the death sentences were handed down in the fifteen years between 1973 and 1987. Consistent with the figures on overall official corruption convictions, 8 of the first 9 officials executed for official crimes were from Azerbaidzhan, and 13 of the 32 total executions involved officials from this republic. Two Georgian officials, a *raiispolkom* chairman and an enterprise manager, were executed for bribery and embezzlement, bringing the number of executions of Caucasus officials to 15, approximately half of the executions evident during the period.

The famous Uzbek cotton scandal and the resultant purge of the Uzbek party and state organs that made prosecutors Telman Gdlyan and Nikolai Ivanov household names in the Soviet Union also produced two executions. In 1986 the Uzbek minister of the Cotton-Processing Industry, V. Usmanov, was executed for falsifying production reports to the central authorities. The following year, A.K. Karimov, first secretary of the Bukhara *oblast* party committee, was executed for

Table 3.6

Official Corruption and Economic Development by Republic, 1965–1990
(Numerical Rankings)

SSR	Official Corruption Saturation Rate (1965–1990)	Vermishev Coefficient of Economic Development (1965)[1]	Per Capita National Income (1970)[2]	% Total Population Employed In Industry (1970)[3]	Horse-power per Agricultural Worker (1970)[4]	Income per Kolkhoz Family Member (1966)[5]
Azer	1	14	13	10	9	14
Geo	2	9	10	11	15	6
Arm	3	10	9	5	10	13
Mold	4	7	7	15	14	10
Turk	5	11	15	12	7	7
Kirg	6	12	11	9	6	12
Russ	7	3	3	2	4	5
Uzb	8	13	12	13	8	11
Est	9	2	1	1	2	1
Tad	10	15	14	14	11	15
Ukr	11	4	5	4	12	8
Lith	12	5	4	6	5	3
Kaz	13	8	8	7	1	4
Belo	14	6	6	8	13	9
Lat	15	1	2	3	3	2

Sources:
[1] K. Vermishev, *"Ob urovne ekonomicheskogo razvitiia soiuznoi respubliki,"* *Voprosy ekonomiki* 1970, No. 4, p. 128.

[2] Gertrude E. Schroeder, "Regional Differences in Income and Levels of Living in the USSR," in V.N. Bandera and Z.L. Melnyk, eds., *The Soviet Economy in Regional Perspective* (New York: Praeger, 1973), p. 169.

[3] *Itogi vsesoiznoi perepisi nasleniia 1970 goda* (Moscow: Statistika, 1972), vol. 2; Table 28.

[4] *Narodnoe khoziastvo SSSR* (Moscow: Tsentral'noe Statisticheskoe Uprav-lenie, 1970), p. 374.

[5] Schroeder, "Regional Differences," p. 178.

accepting bribes in the amount of 6 million rubles. Overall, 6 Central Asian officials were issued death penalties for official corruption. The remaining 11 executed officials worked in the core Slavic republics; 9 from Russia and 2 from the Ukraine.

An Informal Criminology of System Maintenance

Several observers of the behavior of individuals in political office have noted some beneficial aspects of corruption as they pertain to the performance of needed system functions. Corruption, especially in what were called at the time the "new states" of the decolonized Third World, has been said to (1) encourage capital formation, (2) cut bureaucratic red tape, (3) reduce bureaucratic rigidity, (4) promote entrepreneurial behavior, (5) reduce elite cleavages, (6) reduce ethnic discrimination, (7) promote national integration, (8) lessen the potential for political violence, and even (9) attract quality personnel to government service.[16] In sum, these students of the developing world raised the possibility that corruption was not totally dysfunctional, not totally undesirable; in fact, in many ways corruption helped stabilize the political and economic machinery of these fragile states. Of course, this notion of corruption as a "functional dysfunctionality," popular especially in the late 1960s, generated much debate and eventually many of its more extreme claims of functionality were weakened as a result.

Whether or not the Soviet Union during the decline of its economic sector resembled in important ways the underdeveloped "new states" of the post-colonial Third World, over the years many observers of the Soviet system noted both the extreme level of official corruption in the USSR and its limited functionality in the performance of system maintenance. In his important 1952 work on the "informal organization" of Soviet enterprises, Joseph Berliner spoke of the structure of expectations on economic managers that compelled them to engage in legally suspect procurement procedures.[17] John Kramer distinguished between official corruption for *private* gain and official corruption for *bureaucratic* gain, and argued that the Soviet enforcement organs have been encouraged to look the other way regarding illegal activities considered by the higher leadership to be beneficial to the maintenance of economic production and efficiency.[18] In his view, "undeniably, corruption has made important contributions to [the Soviet economy's] efficient functioning."[19] Richard Ericson, analyzing resource allocation under centrally planned economies, concluded that certain illegal activities on the part of Soviet economic managers in particular, and the second economy in general, could "consistently and . . . efficiently allocate productive material inputs" despite serious institutional constraints.[20] As mentioned at the beginning of this chapter, James Millar has explicated what he called Brezhnev's "Little Deal," which allowed for the creation of an entire series of informal "rules of the game" governing both private and official behavior.[21] Finally, Gregory Grossman, one of the most prominent contributors to the literature on Soviet corruption, has argued that for the Soviet elite as well as the masses, corruption has become a "major regular method of solving . . . problems in the social environment."[22]

Each of these students of Soviet politics has raised the question of the role played by certain types of technically illegal official behavior. Each has supported to one degree or another the premise that "corruption" on the part of Soviet officials should not be considered bereft of positive social functions. Perhaps of most theoretical importance, though, in the present context, are a number of related points made by Samuel Huntington in his important work on order and change in developing societies. There, in an extended analysis of corruption, Huntington presents several arguments that seem relevant to the present discussion and that may shed light on the analysis presented in this chapter. To his mind, corruption "may help stimulate economic development . . . [by] surmounting traditional laws or bureaucratic regulations which hamper economic expansion."[23] In this sense, Huntington argued that "in terms of economic growth, the only thing worse than a society with a rigid, overcentralized dishonest bureaucracy is one with a rigid, overcentralized honest bureaucracy."[24]

To be fair to Huntington's argument, however, he is the first to admit that a society marked by a high degree of corruption will not benefit from additional corruption, but he is clear with respect to the following:

> Like machine politics or clientelistic politics in general, corruption provides immediate, specific, and concrete benefits to groups which might otherwise be thoroughly alienated from society. *Corruption may thus be functional to the maintenance of a political system in the same way that reform is. Corruption itself may be a substitute for reform and both corruption and reform may be substitutes for revolution.*[25]

It can be argued in this regard that for Brezhnev corruption was indeed a "substitute" for reform. The flowering during the Brezhnev years of a series of "coloured markets" at differing variances from Soviet law, while at the same time the formal mechanisms of the Soviet state were deteriorating, together seems to argue in support of the notion put forth by Millar, in particular, and Huntington, more generally, that in the Soviet case corruption of a certain type was explicitly accepted and implicitly encouraged as a partial substitute for serious reform of for-

mal institutions. That is, the Brezhnev leadership seemed to have countenanced the development of a series of informal social patterns, many
of which were quite clearly illegal, in recognition of the system-
maintenance functions they performed.

Returning to the specific aspect of the phenomenon analyzed in this
chapter, evidence of further partial support for this claim can be found.
It is certainly no surprise that the Soviet leadership's application of its
own criminal code can be said to aim at the performance system-
maintenance functions, nor should it be surprising if evidence is found
that this effort was indeed successful. Legal codes in all states seek to
perform these functions.

What is interesting in the Soviet case during the 1965–1990 period
is not that the formal operation of the Soviet criminal code with respect
to official behavior should aim at encouraging legal behavior and dis-
couraging illegal behavior, or that the net product of these incentives
and disincentives should be enhanced system stability. Rather, evidence seems to support the claim that to a significant degree during
this period of Soviet history an *informal* operation of the Soviet criminal system encouraged certain behaviors and discouraged others. Like
the formal operation of the criminal code, the informal regime used to
judge official behavior during this time sought to enhance system
maintenance. However, unlike the formal operation of the criminal
code, the informal application of the code *cannot* be said to have
encouraged "legal" behavior and discouraged "illegal" behavior. On
the contrary, the informal operation of the criminal code encouraged
those behaviors, *legal or illegal,* that were considered by the Soviet
leadership to increase the stability of the regime. In a word, the formal
operation of the Soviet criminal code during the 1965–1990 period, in
the face of increasing economic and political stress, gave way to the
operation of an informal mechanism which, in the eyes of the Soviet
leadership, more effectively met the requirements of system maintenance. To use "Huntingtonian" language, faced by the development of
events with the options of engaging in significant reform of formal
institutions or the encouragement of certain types of what were perceived to be "positive" corruption, the Soviet leadership, especially
under Brezhnev, opted for the latter.

The demonstration of the existence of such an informal regime is,
however, somewhat problematic. By its very nature, estimating the
true level of official crime in any society is made all the more difficult

by the fact that such behavior is, by definition, behavior that is hidden. Most quantitative studies of official corruption are forced, from a certain perspective, to rely not on direct measures of the extant level of corruption, but instead on those of state measures of anti-corruption. In studying the convictions of state officials, one is studying anti-corruption just as much, if not more, than one is studying corruption. A greater number of convictions of state officials in the Caucasus, for example, can be validly seen both as evidence of greater corruption there, as well as evidence of a greater sensitivity to corruption (producing a more vigilant anti-corruption stance defined in terms of increased prosecutions and convictions). As a result, more convictions can signal both greater levels of corruption and lesser levels of corruption. Given these constraints, one is forced to agree with F.J.M. Feldbrugge, who, in his important related work, argued the following:

> Any political and socio-economic system which practices and tolerates wide-spread corruption develops a set of informal rules regulating corruption. Vicious penalties for corrupt high officials then do not indicate official intolerance of corruption, but rather serve as a signal that the informal rules have not been observed (too high bribes extracted, too much ostentation). The informality of the rule system easily accommodates local divergencies, such as the specific economic climates of Transcaucasia and Central Asia.[26]

In the Soviet case, then, measures of official crime must be viewed with a healthy level of suspicion. If, as argued above, it is useful to view the convictions of Soviet officials as evidence of the anti-corruption stance of the law enforcement agencies of the state and, by extension, of the higher Soviet leadership, the scholar interested in gaining some insight into the informal organization of Soviet crime and punishment patterns must also speculate about areas of illegal activity that are rarely punished. That is, by the nature of the phenomenon, students of official corruption must study, in a sense, both the event (prosecution, conviction, and sentencing patterns of the ubiquitous crime) and the non-event (those of the rarely prosecuted illegal act). It is in this latter area as well that evidence for the existence of an informal Soviet criminological regime appears.

Despite repeated references in both anecdotal and serious analytical accounts of Soviet official behavior that point to the extremely high level of informal and illegal entrepreneurial activity—for example, bartering for mutual support *(krugovaia poruka)*, hoarding of supplies, exaggerated procurement requests *(zaiavki)* to compensate for future unexpected shortfalls, withheld production to fall into the next planning period, the use of accounting "plugs" to balance short-term expectations against future production, the employment of aggressive free-lance procurement agents *(tolkachi)*, and the padding of production reports to guarantee worker bonuses *(premiia)*—analysis of the official convictions during the 1965–1990 period reveals very few instances of officials being punished for such behavior. For instance, it was reported in a leading Soviet legal journal that for the year 1971, 87.7 percent of all those officials convicted of report padding did not lose their jobs, let alone spend time in jail.[27] The data presented in this chapter reveal only three dozens convictions ($n = 36$) of Soviet officials for such crimes as report padding and *tolkach* activities over a twenty-five year period.

Additionally, the temporal and geographic distribution of criminal convictions of Soviet officials during this time points to irregularities in the degree of enforcement of the Soviet legal code. The data displayed in Table 3.4 suggest uneven enforcement of the legal code, the use of anti-corruption "campaigns" with political overtones (political careers in the Soviet Union were built in many cases on an official's anti-corruption *bona fides* [28]), the operative presence of clientelism, and other criteria outside the domain of law enforcement. In sum, a number of informal forces impacted on the nature of Soviet official crime and punishment during this period.

The evidence provided by the examination of 855 reported cases of official convictions during the 1965–1990 period lends further support to the contention that the Brezhnev regime witnessed the development of a number of informal institutional arrangements that were perceived by the Soviet leadership to perform positive functions for the Soviet state. Specifically, in addition to those scholars who have examined the Soviet black market or second economy from this perspective, the analysis provided in this chapter points to the operation of informal yet well-understood, "rules of the game" for the behavior of Soviet officialdom. Illegal activities based on the pecuniary self-interest of the Soviet official were punished more often and more severely than those illegal activities of Soviet officials aimed at rationalizing the irregularities of the formal Soviet institutions. Returning to the quotation that begins this chapter, the formal requisites of Soviet law are often weak sisters to the informal arrangements of Soviet officialdom.

Conclusion

In this chapter I have sought to demonstrate that during the period of decline in the society's economic growth the Soviet leadership allowed the development of a number of informal governing arrangements that took the place of significant reform of the formal government and state institutions. That many of these informal arrangements violated the spirit and letter of Soviet law was a secondary consideration to their impact on the maintenance of the stability of the regime and the society it governed.

James Millar referred in 1985 to "Brezhnev's Little Deal," which tolerated "the expansion of a wide range of petty private economic activities, some legal, some in the penumbra of the legal, and some clearly illegal, the primary aim of which was the reallocation by private means of a significant fraction of Soviet national income according to private preferences."[29] In this chapter, that general argument is extended to the class of officialdom, which operated under an increasingly informal and explicit "little deal" of its own.

A large number of informal and technically illegal measures appropriate for the maintenance of economic growth and, by extension, the stability of the regime, would be permitted and in some cases encouraged by the Soviet leadership. Specifically, evidence has been shown to support the proposition that the Soviet leadership allowed the development of an informal criminological regime that applied selective criteria to the behavior of state and government officials. These selective criteria, it is argued, were *not* necessarily those spelled out in detail in the Soviet criminal code, but rather were modified in practice to allow for certain illegalities, on the condition that these technically illegal acts furthered economic growth, the stability of the regime, and the continued rule of the Soviet powers that be. When official illegalities were considered non-pecuniary and regime-supportive, legal statutes were less stringently applied. When official illegalities were seen as motivated by strictly selfish desires, with no system-support component, they were punished as severely as the law allowed.

Brezhnev's period of stagnation *(period zastoya),* then, was not one bereft of attempts to address the structural flaws of a declining economic system. What *is* true of the period, though, is Brezhnev's general proclivity to eschew formal structural reform in favor of the more passive policy of permitting the development of a wide series of informal arrangements that in many instances supplanted the formal institutions of the state. The black market was allowed to flourish precisely *because* much of the time it distributed goods and services more efficiently than the formal distribution organs of the state. Soviet officials were allowed to engage in extravagant barter deals with suppliers, to hire devious procurement agents, and to create a number of informal bureaucratic and economic mechanisms because in many cases these were *necessary* for even the meager levels of growth enjoyed by the state economy. In this specific way, then, the Brezhnev leadership did witness the corruption of the formal institutions of the Soviet state.

Notes

1. Charles A. Schwartz (1979), "Corruption and Political Development in the USSR," *Comparative Politics,* Vol. 11 (No. 4): 429.

2. James R. Millar (1984), "The Little Deal: Brezhnev's Contribution to Acquisitive Socialism," *Slavic Review,* Vol. 44 (No. 4): 694–706.

3. Related efforts to utilize data from Soviet press translations in the analysis of convictions appear in F.J.M. Feldbrugge (1984), "Government and Shadow Economy in the Soviet Union," *Soviet Studies,* Vol. 36 (No. 4): 528–543; Nicholas Lampert (1984), "Law and Order in the USSR: The Case of Economic and Official Crime," *Soviet Studies,* Vol. 36 (No. 3): 366–385; and Charles A. Schwartz (1979), "Corruption and Political Development in the USSR," *Comparative Politics,* Vol. 11 (No. 4): 425–442.

4. Gregory Grossman (1977), "The 'Second' Economy of the USSR," *Problems of Communism,* Vol. 25 (No. 5): 25–40; Aron Katsenelinboigen (1977), "Coloured Markets in the Soviet Union," *Soviet Studies,* Vol. 29 (No. 1): 62–85; Gerald Mars and Yochanan Altman (1983), "How a Soviet Economy Really Works: Cases and Implications," pp. 259–267 in Michael Clarke, ed., *Corruption: Causes, Consequences, and Control* (London: Francis Pinter); Dmitrii K. Simes (1975), "The Soviet Parallel Market," *Survey,* Vol. 21 (No. 3): 42–52; Konstantin Simis (1977), "The Machinery of Corruption in the Soviet Union," *Survey,* Vol. 23 (No. 4): 35–55; F.J.M. Feldbrugge (1984), "Government and Shadow Economy in the Soviet Union," *Soviet Studies,* Vol. 36 (No. 4): 528–543.

5. Ed A. Hewett (1988), *Reforming the Soviet Economy: Equality versus Efficiency* (Washington, D.C.: The Brookings Institution), p. 180.

6. Arkady Vaksberg (1991), *The Soviet Mafia* (New York: St. Martin's Press: 133.

7. *Trud,* August 12, 1988, p. 4.

8. Galina Belikova and Aleksandr Shokhin (1989), "The Black Market: People, Things, and Facts," *Soviet Sociology,* Vol. 28 (Nos. 3/4): 51.

9. George L. Kline (1965), "Economic Crime and Punishment," *Survey*, Vol. 57 (No. 3): 67–72; Nick Lampert (1984), "Law and Order in the USSR: The Case of Economic and Official Crime," *Soviet Studies*, Vol. 36 (No. 3): 366–385; Maria Los (1982), "Crime and Economy in the Communist Countries," pp. 121–137 in P. Wickman and T. Dailey, eds., *White Collar and Economic Crime* (Lexington, MA: Lexington Books); Yuri I. Luryi (1986), "The Use of Criminal Law by the CPSU in the Struggle for Reinforcement of its Power and in the Inner-Party Struggle," pp. 91–114 in Dietrich Andre Loeber, ed.. *Ruling Communist Parties and their Status Under Law* (The Hague: Martinus Nijhoff); Freidrich Neznansky (1985), *The Prosecution of Economic Crimes in the USSR* (Falls Church, VA: Delphic Associates); Stanislav Pomorski (1978), "Crimes against the Central Planner: *Ochkovtiratel'stvo'*," pp. 291–311 in Donald D. Barry, et al., eds., *Soviet Law after Stalin*, vol. II (Alphen aan den Rijn: Sijthoff & Noordhoff).

10. *Vedmosti RSFSR* (1982), No. 49, item 1821.

11. For more on the expectations of Soviet citizens with respect to questions of crime and punishment, refer to the results of a public opinion survey conducted by the USSR Academy of Sciences' Sociological Research Institute published in *Sotsiologicheskie issledovania*, No. 2 (April–June 1983): 121–126, reprinted in *Current Digest of the Soviet Press*, Vol. 35 (No. 26): 3.

12. F.J.M. Feldbrugge (1984), "Government and Shadow Economy in the Soviet Union," *Soviet Studies*, Vol. 36 (No. 4): 528–543.

13. For additional information on the concept of a "saturation rate," a term coined by T.H. Rigby, refer to Rigby's *Communist Party Membership in the USSR, 1917–1967* (Princeton: Princeton University Press, 1968). See also Jerry F. Hough (1977), *The Soviet Union and Social Science Theory* (Cambridge, MA: Harvard University Press), pp. 125–139.

14. Gerald Mars and Yochanan Altman (1983), "How a Soviet Economy Really Works: Cases and Implications," pp. 259–267 in Michael Clarke, ed., *Corruption: Causes, Consequences, and Control* (London: Francis Pinter).

15. Louise I. Shelley (1980), "The Geography of Soviet Criminality," *The American Sociological Review*, Vol. 45 (No. 1): 111–122.

16. Joseph S. Nye (1967), "Corruption and Political Development: A Cost–Benefit Analysis," *American Political Science Review*, Vol. 51 (No. 2): 417–429; Nathaniel H. Leff (1964), "Economic Development through Bureaucratic Corruption," *American Behavioral Scientist*, Vol. 8 (No. 3): 8–15; see also on this topic Gabriel Ben-Dor (1974), "Corruption, Institutionalization, and Political Development: The Revisionist Theses Revisited," *Comparative Political Studies*, Vol. 7 (No. 1): 63–83; David H. Bayley (1966), "The Effects of Corruption in a Developing Nation," *Western Political Quarterly*, Vol. 19 (No. 4): 719–732; Colin Leys (1965), "What Is the Problem about Corruption?" *Journal of Modern African Studies*, Vol. 3 (No. 2): 215–230.

17. Joseph S. Berliner (1952), "The Informal Organization of the Soviet Firm," *Quarterly Journal of Economics*, 66, 3, pp. 342–365.

18 John M. Kramer (1977), "Political Corruption in the USSR," *Western Political Quarterly*, Vol. 30 (No. 2): 213–24.

19. Ibid., p. 223.

20. Richard E. Ericson (1984), "The 'Second' Economy and Resource Allocation under Central Planning," *Journal of Comparative Economics*, Vol. 8 (No. 1): 2–3.

21. James R. Millar, "The Little Deal: Brezhnev's Contribution to Acquisitive Socialism," p: 697.

22. Gregory Grossman (1979), "Notes on the Illegal Private Economy and Corruption," in *Soviet Economy in a Time of Change*, Joint Economic Committee of the Congress of the United States (Washington, D.C.: U.S. Government Printing Office): 840.

23. Samuel P. Huntington (1968), *Political Order in Changing Societies*, New Haven: Yale University Press), p. 68.

24. Ibid.

25. Ibid., p. 64 (emphasis added).

26: F.J.M. Feldbrugge (1984), "Government and Shadow Economy in the Soviet Union," *Soviet Studies*, Vol. 36 (No. 4): 542.

27. *Sotsialisticheskaya zakonnost'*, No. 5 (May 1973): 8–13, reprinted in *CDSP*, Vol. 25 (No. 39): 14.

28. Indeed, the connection between changes in the leading party cadres in specific geographic locations just prior to dramatic increases in convictions of Soviet officials merits additional study. A cursory look at this relationship shows that much can be learned from such an examination. For example, in Azerbaidzhan an important leadership change preceded the noticeable crackdown in that republic in the 1977–1982 period. In April 1977, a new ethnic Russian party second secretary (Yuri Pugachev) was appointed to Baku. In like fashion, a new Georgian MVD chief, Guram I. Gvetadze, was appointed in May 1979 with a resultant increase in official corruption convictions. Similar patterns exist for the Ukraine (Aleksei A. Titarenko was named second secretary in Kiev in October 1983), Uzbekistan (both first and second secretaries were replaced in 1983), and Armenia (a new first secretary was appointed in May 1988).

29. James R. Millar (1985), "The Little Deal: Brezhnev's Contribution to Acquisitive Socialism," p. 697.

4

COMBATING CORRUPTION IN SOVIET SOCIETY

Peter the Great could not deal with the great number of administrative crimes, . . . his control ultimately proved ineffective, and . . . his punishments did not constitute a deterrent.

—Hans J. Torke[1]

The above quotation serves to remind the reader that much relevant to official misconduct in the Soviet Union had its antecedents deep in Russian history. Professor Torke's words describe the problems of crime and punishment in the pre-Petrine Russian civil service, yet in many ways seem applicable to the late Soviet period. As the preceding chapter has attempted to demonstrate, the final decades of Soviet rule, like Russia under the tsars, were marked by a high degree of ambiguity with respect to the question of official crime and punishment. Just as certain types of technically illegal activity by regional Russian prefects alleviated the treasury demands of the central imperial court (and were thus permitted in practice), official misconduct during the period of Soviet power also frequently served the purposes of the central authorities. In like fashion, all the technology and advanced control mechanisms of the Soviet state often accomplished little in making the geographical vastness of Soviet territory a useful ally in the development of even staggering cases of localized corruption.

These similarities notwithstanding, however, the specific nature of Soviet ideology, the organization of government, and the structure of economic activity combined to produce a political system within which the control function became both critical and, to put it kindly, ubiquitous. In a word, the overly ambitious goals of the Soviet state necessarily produced overly ambitious mechanisms of control. The differences between the tsarist Russian state and the Bolshevik Soviet state in this respect revolve around the differences between the undemocratic authoritarian designs of the former and, for much of its existence, the anti-democratic totalitarian designs of the latter. Like the tsarist state, the Soviet state in the final analysis was incapable of exercising its control functions with the level of success necessary to ensure the regime's survival. In this sense, then, the examination of the Soviet state's failed efforts to compel the desired behavior even among its officialdom presents a microcosm of its overall failure with respect to its ability to remold society in general. That official and societal corruption were most prevalent in the final decades of the Soviet Union, after several generations of the Soviet population were educated and socialized according to the dictates of Soviet ideology, speaks directly to Lenin's error in stating: "Give us the children and we shall change the world." This failure of the Soviet regime to create the so-called "new soviet man," even among its leading officials, necessitated the creation of a wide array of institutional mechanisms aimed at official control.

The Control Organs

The issue of administrative control has been a constant problem for Russian governments, both prior to and after the 1917 revolution. In general terms, and despite varying degrees of harshness connected with the enforcement of prescribed official behavior, both tsarist and Soviet systems were patently unable to exercise a sufficient degree of control over their respective public officials. Describing the state of affairs in pre-Petrine Russia, Hans Torke has argued that "because organs of effective control were thus wanting, it was necessary in Muscovy to proceed in a preventative fashion and to rely upon the impact of prohibitions (or the fear of exposure for abuses, through complaints and denunciations) and punishments."[2] Likewise, Marc Raeff has concluded that "to a much greater degree than was the case in the West, [the bureaucracy] had no overall control and direction, for there were no constituted bodies to limit its capricious tyranny or to make abuses known to higher institutions."[3] With respect to Russian officialdom, then, there did not exist anything close to a "well-ordered police state."

Of course, the Bolsheviks assumed power with a radical ideology that saw the state itself in extremely negative terms. The state for Marxists served to perpetuate the exploitation of the proletariat and was the manifestation of the class conflict. As such, the state was the enemy of the proletariat, but would gradually "wither away" under socialism and communism as class antagonisms likewise faded. Considerable debate raged within early Bolshevik circles about just when the state would wither away and what should be done in the meantime. Lenin's answer to the latter question involved seizing state power to control the state itself. Lenin's goal of transforming the inherited Russian state into a popularly administered "commune state" entailed placing strict limits on the bureaucratic apparatus of power. However, Lenin was not successful in diminishing state power in Soviet Russia. On the contrary, state power expanded greatly. As Robert C. Tucker has aptly put it, "history has its ironies, and one of them is that Lenin did go down in it as, among other things, a state builder."[4] The administrative state became a necessity in building communism, in reshaping society and its public officials, and in dealing with both external and internal "enemies."

With respect to official conduct and corruption, several institutions were created to police the state and its officials. That these institutions ultimately failed, for a number of reasons, to control Soviet officialdom does not belie the fact that a prevailing modus operandi of party rule in the USSR was based on the axiom of organization distrust. That is, despite the extremes that the growth of the Soviet state approached, a significant amount of ambivalence toward the state maintained itself in the USSR. Perhaps due to the rather ambitious goals of the regime and the great amount of coercive power that was seemingly necessary to achieve them, the control organs of the state were indeed based on the organizational *ethos* of distrust, even of its high officials.

The Party Control Committee

The history of party control institutions can be traced back to the origins of the All-Russian Extraordinary Commission for Combating Counter-Revolution, Speculation, and Sabotage (Vecheka or Cheka), which soon after its inception in December 1917 extended its domain to include the actions of Soviet officeholders (at which point the post-script "and Misuse of Authority" were added to the name). Like many other Soviet institutions, the one responsible for supervision and control of party members has undergone various formulations and reorganizations. For present purposes, it is instructive to review Khrushchev's experimentation in the area of party control because his attempts to improve this function reveal many of its inherent problems.

In 1963 Khrushchev created the Party–State Control Committee (KPGK) and appointed Aleksandr Shelepin, a party secretary, power-ful member of the CPSU Presidium,[5] and the erstwhile head of the KGB, to be its chairman. As its official name, "The Committee of Party–State Control of the Central Committee of the Communist Party of the Soviet Union and of the Council of Ministers of the CPSU," indicates, the power of this institution extended to both party and state officials, giving it a wide area of control. Its chairman was entitled to ex officio membership in the USSR Council of Ministers. On paper, at least, this control organ was given very extensive powers over all aspects of life, and could investigate, reprimand, and dismiss officials at all levels of the social system.[6] With only a few exceptions, lower party organs throughout the Soviet Union operated subsidiary units, headed in most cases by party secretaries.

The problem for Khrushchev's institutional marriage of party and state control organs was that the KPGK was not performing any real control function over party members. The Communist Party would not permit even a partially non-party organ to supervise, discipline, and potentially expel party members. Past institutional history had established the precedent; notwithstanding certain periods when, for somewhat diabolical purposes, Stalin had merged the two inspectorates, that party and state officials would be supervised separately. Khrushchev's reform posed a threat to party officials in that it opened up the possibility of higher levels of scrutiny from outside the party apparatus. Like so many of the other major changes instituted by Khrushchev, the Party–State Control Committee was abandoned soon after the first secretary was ousted. In December 1965, fourteen months after the palace coup that replaced Khrushchev, the hybrid Party–State Control Committee was abolished.

The Brezhnev–Kosygin leadership returned this aspect of control to the *status quo ante bellum*: separate control organs for the party apparatus and for the state machinery. The Party Control Committee was recreated, and, to scrutinize the state bureaucracy, a new People's Control Committee was formed. The Communist Party itself would adjudicate internal party affairs, including the maintenance of party discipline and morality. Of some importance to the issue of official corruption, especially with respect to party members, is the fact that no criminal indictment could be served to a member of the CPSU without the permission of the party itself. As the party's investigative, adjudicative, and punitive organ, the Party Control Committee stood at a critical point in the supervision and control of party cadres.

The Party Control Committee was directly responsible to the Central Committee of the Communist Party of the Soviet Union (CPSU). It was charged with the duty of maintaining party discipline and the proper personal behavior of party members. According to Hough and Fainsod, this control organ tended in practice to concentrate on the investigation of complaints of "incorrect conduct" on the part of Communists[7] and to evaluate appeals from members of the party who had been disciplined for perceived wrongdoing.[8] In a sense, then, the Party Control Committee served as an informal party "supreme court" that handled internal party disputes, questions of party discipline for improper conduct or violation of party rules, and the like. It seems as though the Party Control Committee served as the final arbiter of appeals from Communists expelled from the Party for disciplinary reasons. The decisions of the Party Control Committee were frequently published, either in the popular press, such as *Pravda,* or in more specialized party journals.

The CPSU was a federal organization, having parallel party institutions at all levels of Soviet society: all-union, republic, region, city, and district. In like fashion, the Party Control Committee had subsidiary offices at lower levels, called Party Commissions at the local level. This hierarchical structure provided a quite extensive apparatus of scrutiny of the behavior of members of the Communist Party. During the period of the joint Party–State Control Committee, this network entailed over 3,000 coordinated committees from the all-union level down to individual collective farms.[9] Even with the bifurcation of the party and state sides of this inspectorate, a sizable structure of party control remained. The head of the Party Control Committee, technically elected by the members of the party Central Committee formed at each of the CPSU party congresses, was in most cases a Soviet party official of very high standing, often a full voting member of the party's highest decision-making organ, the CPSU Central Committee Polit-buro. Heads were: Aleksandr N. Shelepin (1963–1966), Arvid Pel'she (1966–1983), Mikhail S. Solomentsev (1983–1988), Boris K. Pugo (1988–1991). Like Shelepin, Boris Pugo, Gorbachev's Latvian chair-man of the Party Control Committee, assumed the post with several years experience in the KGB apparatus (from 1980 to 1984 Pugo was chairman of the Latvian KGB). It is an interesting irony that Pugo, the ringleader of the August 1991 putsch against Gorbachev, had just three years earlier been named by Gorbachev to the post of guardian of party discipline.

While during the Khrushchev period of the unified Party–State Con-trol Committee the party units were not enthusiastic about the idea of state interference in party affairs, there has been a consistent tendency of supervisory party organs to interfere in the domain of state officials. In the Soviet literature, this problem is referred to as *podmena*, or the tendency of party officials to usurp the functions and authority of state functionaries. In these cases, the zealousness with which the party's "right of verification" (*pravo kontrolya*) was exercised serve to dimin-ish the effectiveness of the state organs. State officials, wary of criti-cism from party "checkers," soon assumed a much more passive attitude toward their duties, waiting instead for the inevitable instruc-tions from the party offices. In such a way, the party control mechanism acted as a fetter on the efficient functioning of the state institutions.

The People's Control Committee

A key aspect of Bolshevik ideology related to the general prohibition against private control over the means of production was the notion that the average citizen could take an active role not only in the labor force, but also as guardian of managerial decision making. For this reason, from the very beginning of the Soviet state a sizable number of individuals has been involved either full- or part-time in various as-pects of popular control over government and economic managers. While the modern version of the People's Control Committee was created with the December 6, 1965 decision by Khrushchev's succes-sors to discontinue his hybrid Party–State Control Committee, the no-tion of popular control had a long history in the USSR.

While Lenin envisioned popular control to include a wide array of concerns, ranging from the old tsarist notion of "state control" (*gosudarstvennyi kontrol*) as the independent auditing of government accounts, all the way to the forwarding of recommendations for the more efficient functioning of the administrative routines of state government, his relatively short time in power did not allow for the establishment of such a popularly based structure of people's control. Stalin's notion in this realm was much more narrow than Lenin's; after Lenin's death in January 1924 Stalin basically advocated the old approach of inspectors *qua* auditors. His approach, interestingly, was the more generally accepted within the new state bureaucracy, staffed as it was in the 1920s by a large number of former tsarist officials.

In February 1920, Lenin established a new and expanded organization of popular control, the People's Commissariat of Workers' and Peasants' Inspection, usually referred to as RABKRIN, the acronym for "workers and peasants." The statute establishing RABKRIN empowered the organization to monitor "all the organs of state administration, the economy, and social organizations."[10] In addition, RABKRIN was to supervise the Bureau of Complaints and was encouraged to make administrative reform recommendations. The intent of the new Soviet leaders with respect to this organ of popular state control seems to have been sincere, with overtones of what one scholar of the organization has called "democratic idealism."[11] However, as happened much later under Khrushchev, at the March 1922 Eleventh Party Congress this independent state people's inspectorate was incorporated into the Central Control Commission (TsKK), the control commission of the party. These two inspectorates would remain unified until the first year of the great purge, 1934.

During the remainder of Stalin's life the precursor of the People's Control Committee went through various organization arrangements, from the Commission of Soviet Control (KCK), to the People's Commissariat of State Control (NKGK), to the USSR Ministry of State Control (MGK). In many ways, though, these reorganizations under Stalin produced the same result: a sharply reduced role for popular state control. During the initial post-Stalin years the organization was involved in the rehabilitation of many victims of Stalin's "cleansings," serving as a sort of appellate court for those purged from the party ranks. It took a full decade for Stalin's politically motivated state and party control machinery to be depoliticized and dismantled. Only in the late Khrushchev period, after several temporary and unsatisfactory institutional arrangements, did some stability in the area of people's control reemerge.

The People's Control Committee *(Komitet narodnogo kontrolya,* or KNK), which relied quite heavily on citizen volunteers, was responsible for checking on the work of governmental and economic administrators. In the mid-1970s, almost 10 million Soviet citizens were actively engaged in volunteer work in some regular capacity for the People's Control Committee. These volunteers were elected to some 659,000 posts and 649,000 groups located in virtually every type of Soviet state enterprise, including the military and central state ministries. In addition, some 20 million citizens were utilized in ad hoc inspections, bringing the army of citizen inspectors to a staggering total.[12] According to reports, it was not at all irregular for upwards of 10 percent of an enterprise's employees to be involved in volunteer work connected to the People's Control Committee. Potentially, then, the People's Control Committee held out the promise of a powerful system of checks on the activities of responsible cadres attached to state managerial and production units.

This potential popular check against the officials, however, was never fully realized in practice. Much of the problem with the People's Control Committee during the final decades of Soviet rule revolved around its relationship with the Communist Party of the Soviet Union. As has been mentioned above, Khrushchev's melding of the party and state control functions into the single Party–State Control Committee was seen by many in the party as an undesirable check on party activities by individuals connected to the state apparatus. When Brezhnev announced the new separate organization of these control units in December 1965, a great deal of behind-the-scenes debate had still to be worked out. It took three full years from the announcement of the formation of the People's Control Committee before the actual statute describing its details appeared. Like its predecessor under Khrushchev, the People's Control Committee was to work under the guidance of both the USSR Council of Ministers (state) and the CPSU Central Committee (party). However, there was to be no formal attachment to the latter. According to Jan S. Adams, who has written the definitive work on the history of popular control in the USSR, the People's Control Committee was declared in the statute to be subordinated to the state alone: its members were to be confirmed by the USSR Council of Ministers, and its chairman was to be appointed by the USSR

Supreme Soviet.[13] This arrangement followed the argument that the soviets at each level of the Soviet state apparatus were the most appropriate places to anchor popular participation in state management.

This statutory separation of organization ties between the People's Control Committee and the Communist Party of the Soviet Union, however, did not stand up to practice. While the party leadership was quite uncomfortable with the notion of those outside the party apparatus engaging in party control, they quickly arrogated for themselves the right to monitor state managers and enterprises. For example, despite the strict wording of the statute creating the People's Control Committee, the party controlled the selection and appointment of committee members at various levels in the Soviet administrative hierarchy. As Adams has put it:

> the party's responsibilities with regard to appointments were no less real for being unstated in the statute, and the party's guidance of People's Control activities was not diminished when the "CPSU" was removed from the corporation letterhead.[14]

Despite this strong "guiding" presence of the Communist Party in the activities of the People's Control Committee, the KNK's impact on Soviet society seems to have been quite beneficial. The registering of complaints by ordinary citizen volunteers provided a positive function on at least three grounds. First, by providing a genuine outlet for individuals who were sincerely interested in bettering the management of the state, the KNK mobilized an important clientele and thereby provided these individuals with feelings of increased efficacy vis-à-vis their government. Second, the processes instituted by the People's Control Committee actually did provide increased efficiency in the management of state agencies, especially at the enterprise and shop levels. Finally, while it is clear from the record that the overtly volunteer and part-time elements of the People's Control Committees had severely constrained punishment powers, the scrutiny of these people's inspectors could not be totally ignored. Complaints against their actions, both work-related and personal, were not to be taken lightly by state officials. This having been said, however, the press of the late Soviet period was full of bizarre stories of forged accounting books, stolen materials, barter deals, and outright theft of socialist property. Perhaps the best summary of the success or failure of the People's

Control Committees lies in accepting the fact that even if a net positive result obtained from its activities, the level of graft, corruption, and mismanagement in the Soviet system was so extreme as to make the KNK's best efforts appear marginal in the final analysis.

The Ministry of Internal Affairs' OBKhSS

Many observers have chronicled the long tradition of disrespect for state property among Russians of the old regime. This disrespect became a much more pronounced problem under the Soviet system of government in that practically everything was the property of the state. What made the problem even more serious for the Soviets is the fact that socialist property, as distinguished from personal property, included virtually all the income-producing property of the Soviet state. Such a state of affairs made the protection of socialist property in its three forms (state property, cooperative property, and the property of social organizations) that much more important.[15] The practice of Soviet law enforcement, reflecting this status, consistently meted out higher penalties for crimes against socialist property than for those against personal property,[16] even though all property crimes are grouped together under the same chapter in the Soviet criminal code.

Valerii Chalidze has argued that "the theft of private property is regarded by all except actual thieves as criminal and shameful, whereas the average citizen regards the theft of public property, unless it is on a large scale, as innocent and normal behavior."[17] This perception is supported by a number of public opinion surveys conducted in the USSR by Soviet academicians. For example, the USSR Academy of Science's Sociological Research Institute conducted survey research during 1983 on the question of citizens' attitudes toward legal norms. The results published in the journal *Sotsiologicheskiye issledovania* (Sociological Research) revealed that while 92.6 percent of the respondents were in favor of the strict criminal penalties against "an attempted theft of valuables from an apartment" (with the remaining 7.4 percent giving "no response"), a mere 16.6 percent of the respondents favored the strict penalties associated with the existing laws against "petty theft at an enterprise." The author of the article, analyzing the results of the survey, cited "flaws in citizens' legal upbringing" and concluded that "a large portion of the respondents attach no particular significance to petty thefts of socialist property or to mismanagement."[18] It is little wonder, given this widespread attitude toward socialist property, that such crimes constituted the second largest category of crime in the USSR, after general hooliganism.[19]

Popular attitudes toward the theft of socialist property in the Soviet Union were so lax that the Soviet regime created a special investigatory structure within the apparatus of the Ministry of Internal Affairs (MVD) specifically to combat crimes against socialist property. Regular police departments at each level of the administration of justice were organized into the following sections: the regular uniformed service *(naruzhnaia sluzhba),* criminal investigation (ORUD), internal passports, visas, and registration (OVIR), motor vehicles, prosecution and preliminary investigation, training and administration, and, of special concern presently, the Department for the Struggle against the Theft of Socialist Property (OBKhSS). The OBKhSS was created in the 1970s in order to combat such white-collar crimes as embezzlement, falsification of plan records, and other related economic crimes. It played an important role in the investigation of embezzlement and theft in the Soviet system. The OBKhSS maintained a system of informants in Soviet organizations and enterprises to detect bribery, embezzlement, and other forms of misconduct involving socialist property.[20] The creation of such a specifically focused entity within the police force reveals both the scale of crimes against socialist property and the seriousness that marked the Soviet authorities' attempt to confront the problem. As in all states, it is difficult to separate out general popular attitudes from those held by Soviet officials. The evidence that has emerged in other chapters (i.e., almost four in ten convictions of Soviet *officials* chronicled in Soviet press translation involved crimes against socialist property) seems to support the notion that Soviet officials shared with the general population the heightened proclivity to view socialist property as "no one's" property, thereby making it all the more likely to be violated.

The Procuracy

The prerevolutionary Procuracy and the tsarist judicial system, the origins of which can be traced back to the early eighteenth century, were formally abolished by a decree of the Council of People's Commissars of the Russian Soviet Federated Socialist Republic (RSFSR) on November 24, 1917, scarcely a month after the Bolshevik seizure of power. A significant amount of idealist experimentation followed, with a utopian emphasis on more informal and popular methods of resolving questions of public order and morality. Like so much else in Soviet Russia of the time, however, the idealist notions soon surrendered to more realistic discussions of crime and punishment.

These discussions on the topic of establishing a more formal set of legal institutions eventuated in early 1922 in the creation of the Soviet Procuracy *(Prokuratura)* within the People's Commissariat of Justice. The draft decree stated that the Procuracy was to engage in "supervision over the legality of the activity of central agencies of Soviet power and also supervision and direction of the activities of the people's procurators."[21] This charge given to the Procuracy reflects again the ambivalent feelings of the early Bolshevik rulers toward the state. As one student of the Procuracy has put it, "the *prokuratura* was founded upon the bureaucratic trend in Soviet jurisprudence which was concerned that state administrative organs and officials not have unrestricted power and that those restrictions should be based on law."[22] As one might suspect, however, significant changes occurred in this orientation of the Procuracy during the Stalin period.

Stalin utilized the judicial system as a political tool during the well-chronicled purge trials of the 1930s. Andrei Vyshinskii, the chief theoretician of the Stalinist, dictatorial trend in Soviet law, was also the chief state prosecutor at the purge trials. During the 1930s, the Leninist notion of popular participation in the system of justice was discounted severely. Speaking to an assembled group of Ukrainian prosecutors in 1936, Vyshinskii stated that "the old twaddle about the mobilization of social active workers . . . all that must be put aside, something new is needed at the present time." His approach to the question of law was made clear in his 1938 speech to the First Congress of the Sciences of Soviet State and Law in which he defined law as a system of rules reflecting the will of the state and guaranteed by the state's monopoly of coercive power.[23]

On June 20, 1933, the Procuracy of the USSR was established as a separate entity, no longer subordinate to the People's Commissariat of Justice. The new constitution of 1936 detailed that the newly centralized Procuracy would be headed by the procurator general of the USSR, with functional independence of its subordinate organs from all horizontal authorities. Procurators at all levels were to be named by the procurator general of the USSR.[24] Thus began the modern version of the Soviet Procuracy.

Changes in the administration of Soviet justice came swiftly after the death of Stalin. This new mood briefly entailed a new wave of more idealistic notions about the role of the general population in the judicial system; the so-called Comrades' Courts *(tovarishcheskie sudy)* reappeared in October 1959. By the time Khrushchev was ousted in 1964, there were roughly 200,000 Comrades' Courts in existence dealing with over 4 million cases a year. By the mid-1970s, the number of the popularly based bodies had risen to over 300,000.

Article 164 of the 1977 Soviet Constitution states that the Procuracy is vested with "supreme power of supervision over the strict and uniform observance of laws by all ministers, state committees and departments, enterprises, institutions and organizations, executive-administrative bodies of local Soviets of People's Deputies, collective farms, cooperatives and other public organizations, [and] officials and citizens" of the USSR. This centralized structure was to exercise these powers "independently of any local bodies whatsoever" (Article 168). The procurator general of the USSR was appointed by the USSR Supreme Soviet and would serve, along with all subordinate procurators, a five-year term of office. In such a way, the Procuracy would ensure the uniform compliance of the Soviet legal code. All public prosecutors, from the municipal or village level up to the all-union level, were subordinated to the procurator general of the USSR in a strictly unified and hierarchical structure.

The importance of the Procuracy in the realm of official crime is clear from the wording of Article 164, which empowered the prosecutors to scrutinize virtually all aspects of the application of justice in the USSR. No suspect could be arrested, no search for evidence could take place, no prosecution of cases could be pursued, and no appeals could be entertained without the authorization of the Procuracy. It also supervised prisons, prisoners' complaints, and the actions of the police. During the late Soviet period, some 15,000 lawyers (or 12 percent of the legal profession) were directly employed by the Procuracy. If one adds the additional 18,000 investigators, the Procuracy directly employed or supervised over one-quarter of the legal professionals in the USSR.[25]

As is obvious from the above description of the Procuracy's authority in the administration of Soviet justice, the potential for abuse was quite high. Among the cases reviewed as part of the research for this book, many instances of abuse of prosecutory power were evident. Local prosecutors frequently engaged in overt intimidation of political enemies, or attempted after the fact to reopen cases where political enemies were exonerated. For example, *Izvestiia* reported in 1972 a typical case that occurred in Archangel City in the northwestern portion of the Russian Republic.[26] A private citizen, in this instance a female pensioner, was wrongly prosecuted for slander by the local procurator's office after she voiced criticism of a local official, who, she claimed, was using his position for personal gain. As the story describes, the official exercised influence over the local prosecutor's office to silence his critic; she was charged, prosecuted, and convicted of slander. Eventually, the Archangel municipal party committee *(gorkom)* reprimanded the judge who convicted the critic, as well as three officials of the district prosecutor's office. The offending official in question, the director of a municipal repair and construction administration, was dismissed from his post. Such cases were not rare occurrences in the Soviet Union.

Soviet Whistleblowers and the Control Function

Ideological Foundations of Popular Control

As has been shown, perhaps to the extent of no other country, the Soviet Union encouraged the development of a large number of institutions devoted either partially or entirely on the control of state administration and the behavior of its officials. Moreover, traditionally there has been state-sponsored encouragement of popular participation in these formal institutions, as shown in the large number of citizen volunteers in the work of the People's Control Committees, the Comrades' Courts, and so on. Such a formal predisposition to popular control, moreover, is quite consistent with a Marxist-Leninist view of the state as a negative social entity destined to whither away gradually as socialism develops into communism. Friedrich Engels, in *The Origins of the Family, Private Property, and the State,* wrote that

> as the state arose from the need to keep class antagonisms in check, but also arose in the thick of the fight between the classes, it is normally the state of the most powerful, economically ruling class, which by its means becomes also the politically ruling class, and so acquires new means of holding down and exploiting the oppressed class.[27]

This danger, inherent in the nature of the state, even under socialism, required vigilance with respect to control. As one scholar has put it,

Almost the entire experience of the Russian Communists as a conspiratorial group within the autocratic czarist state served to confirm in their eyes Engels' characterization of the repressive and administrative apparatuses of the state as class-dominated structures whose raison d'être was the strangling of social change. Following the revolution, the Bolsheviks found themselves attempting to remold and direct a vast, hostile, and sluggish administrative apparatus which they could neither wholly abolish nor completely control. The "withering away of the state" as postulated by Engels and the role of the state apparatus in a revolutionary society continued to vex Soviet administrators and theorists.[28]

One way out of this dilemma, of course, was the mobilization of the population for the aim of governing the activities of the state.

The idea of popular participation in the running of the state strikes at the most idealistic or utopian aspects of the Soviet ideology. While Lenin may have been more sanguine with respect to the role to be played by the common man in governing (and thereby controlling) the state, Marx's often quoted passage from *The German Ideology* provides a strong ideological basis for the popular element in the running of the state:

in a communist society, *where nobody has one exclusive sphere of activity* but each can become accomplished in any branch he wishes, society regulates the general production and thus makes it possible for me to do one thing today and another tomorrow, to hunt in the morning, fish in the afternoon, rear cattle in the evening, criticize after dinner, just as I have a mind, without ever becoming hunter, fisherman, shepherd or critic. . . . And out of this very contradiction between the interest of the individual and that of the community the latter takes an independent form as the State, divorced from the real interests of individual and community, and at the same time as an illusory communal life, always based, however, on the real ties existing in every family and tribal conglomeration . . . and especially . . . on the classes, already determined by the division of labor, which in every such mass of men separate out, and of which one dominates all the others.[29]

For Marx, then, under socialism, as the state is withering away, this artificial division of labor, which categorizes individuals into, *inter alia,* the governors and the governed, and which perpetuates class antagonisms and the domination of the ruling class over all others, must be checked. In practical terms, erasing the line between those categories is critical in controlling the state and is manifested in an active and positive "checking" role for the citizenry.

In the work of Lenin one finds further support for the idea of active involvement by the ordinary citizen in controlling the activities of the state bureaucracy. Upon returning to Russia in April 1917, Lenin supported the power of the soviets in their struggle against the Provisional Government in part because of the former's ability to control the latter. One of the functions of the soviets during this revolutionary period, he wrote, was to ensure that the state bureaucracy would be "replaced by the direct rule of the people, or at least placed under special control."[30] Lenin's support for the soviets as against the Provisional Government was not based solely on his firm negative conviction that Aleksandr Kerensky and the Provisional Government had to go and that the soviets were the only logical alternative to it. His support for the soviets had a more positive element in that they offered popular control of government through the mobilization of the citizenry.

Soviet ideology, then, encouraged popular participation in controlling the state, even if this activity took place outside formally constituted institutions of the state. To be sure, the soviets at times purposely blurred the lines between officials of the state and the public—for example, in seeking the mobilization of the general population for many state tasks. One such area of popular mobilization involves the encouragement of what has come in the literature to be called whistleblowing. As a form of criticism from below, citizen complaints simultaneously provide a channel of grievances for ordinary citizens as well as useful information about official abuse. In the latter capacity, whistleblowing provides yet another potentially powerful check on abuses and corruption within the class of officials charged with the running of the state.

Whistleblowing in Comparative Perspective

Most of the research into the phenomenon of whistleblowing has focused on its characteristics in American settings. Little research into what might be called "comparative whistleblowing" has taken place, thus rendering the bulk of this research relevant to the West. Whistleblowing has been defined in a number of ways. Miceli and Near call it the disclosure by organization members of illegal, immoral, or illegitimate practices to persons or organizations who may be able to effect action.[31] Jill Graham views whistleblowing as a form of "principled organizational dissent" constituting "a protest and/or effort to change the organizational status quo because of a conscientious objection to current policy or practice."[32] Common to virtually all definitions of whistleblowing is the notion that the person blowing the whistle is an agent of change who has a disagreement with his or her organization and discloses information to others as a means to effect change.

Scholars have focused attention on three main variables to explain who engages in whistleblowing and why.[33] First, research has attempted to determine the degree to which individual personality characteristics are predictive of who might engage in whistleblowing. Second, some have looked to organizational attributes, such as organization size, the nature of the internal organizational structure, whether the organization is public or private, and the individual whistleblower's position in the hierarchy. Finally, others have examined what might be called situational pressures or incentives: the initial response of the whistleblower's immediate superior, the seriousness of the charge in question, and so on. In general terms, the extant research on whistleblowing in Western organizations has sought to determine whether there exists a set of distinctive personality characteristics shared by whistleblowers, or whether whistleblowers are more or less typical kinds of decision makers. If the former were to hold true, organizational and situational variables would be less important in analyzing whistleblowing since, in this case, whistleblowers would be seen as "born, not made." If whistleblowers are not in any important sense "different" from non-whistleblowers, then the most fruitful avenue of investigation would be to look at the critical organizational and situational variables. Some of the findings emerging from this literature may be helpful in shedding light on whistleblowing in the Soviet Union.

Considerable debate exists within the literature as to the importance of these three general areas of explanation. From the perspective of organizational attributes and the likelihood that different types of organizations will exhibit different likelihoods of whistleblowing, some encouragement has been provided by those working in the area of organizational theory. There has been a long-standing concern that organizations discourage non-conformity and independent judgment. Max Weber's fear that the rationalization of the workplace encourages a habitual deference to authority and rule rigidity has been echoed by many contemporary writers. Organizations are likely to insist on conformity as a condition of advancement, promoting only those who can be trusted. But the question of how one's position and responsibilities in the organization might affect one's exposure to wrongdoing, sensitivity to such issues, and willingness to challenge superiors on an issue of principle are clearly complex and the logic is sometimes contradictory.

One might expect higher-ranking officials to be more prone to whistleblowing due to the fact that they are closer to the actual locus of policymaking and have more invested in the success of the organization. On the other hand, low-level support personnel are often privy to the most sensitive information in an organization by virtue of their role in the production and distribution of critical documents. Similarly, a bureaucratic account of the organization might lead one to expect that whistleblowers would tend to be younger employees with relatively few years of service who have not yet been rendered "mindless cogs" or whose unwillingness to demonstrate fealty to particular superiors has left them stranded at the bottom of the hierarchy.

With respect to situational variables, scholars have taken note of such factors as the initial response of one's superior, the seriousness of the issue, and whether or not others in the workplace were also aware of the behavior in question. Others attempt to simulate the decision-making process of whistleblowers in an effort to discern the degree of rationality in the choices made by organizational critics. Jill Graham, for example, provides an account of the whistleblower that sees the awareness of an issue, the perceived seriousness of the issue, the attribution of personal responsibility, and the perceived feasibility of response as the key determinants of the decision by a whistleblower to respond to a perceived instance of wrongdoing.[34] In like fashion, Miceli and Near find "some evidence of a 'subjectively rational' decision process . . . whereby observers of wrongdoing weigh costs and benefits [which] suggests that, to the extent organizations and individuals can influence these costs and benefits, the level and nature of whistleblowing will change."[35] Unfortunately, however, much of the research into the individual personality characteristics of whistleblowers has pointed to the conclusion that such a rational calculus is hardly present in most cases.

Jos, Tompkins, and Hays found that "committed" whistleblowers "do not appear to be concentrated in any particular position in the organizational hierarchy nor do they share common organizational histories."[36] What these whistleblowers have in common is a number of interesting personality traits that combine to distinguish them from non-whistleblowers. First, they are often described as those being most closely committed to the organization's goals.[37] Second, they exhibit little of the cynicism or disillusionment that might be suspected in such organizational dissent, being described rather as patriotic and traditional. Third, whistleblowers are more likely than non-whistleblowers to reject relativistic claims about morals. That is, in their view universal moral rules are supported and should be applied without exception. Fourth, whistleblowers score higher on a "social responsibility scale" than do non-whistleblowers; these individuals take their responsibilities seriously and seek to see them through to completion. Fifth, whistleblowers are very often distinguished from their work colleagues because, unlike the latter, who also recognize the improper behavior, whistleblowers are capable of acting on this knowledge. This has led scholars to the conclusion, backed up by a variety of measurement techniques, that whistleblowers respond differently to social cues of conformity.[38] Jos, Tompkins, and Hays argue that

> the overwhelming majority of whistleblowers contacted are apparently uninterested in regulating their behavior to conform to particular situations. . . . They are unlikely to look to others or to aspects of the situation for cues to appropriate behavior. Instead, their behavior is consistent across situations because they rely on their own attitudes and beliefs, which include a strong endorsement of universal moral standards as a guide.[39]

From an organizational point of view, then, the personality of whistleblowers as described above indeed makes them "difficult people." In some sense, much of the literature supports the view that whistleblowers really are peculiar people who seem especially resistant to broader organizational influences and pressures and who do not seem to calculate in the way most theories of organizational behavior assume people calculate. If this personality-based explanation of whistleblowers in Western organizational settings is at all generalizable to whistleblowing in the Soviet Union, it may help explain why organizational dissent still occurs in a society that is characterized by administrative corruption on such a large scale, a long history and a general acceptance of legally proscribed activities, a marked degree of cynicism with respect to the formal rules of the society, and a much greater potential for incurring rather severe reprisals for dissent.

Whistleblowing in the Soviet Union

Comparatively little analytical work has been done on the phenomenon of whistleblowing and its role in citizen control in the Soviet Union, although this modest body of literature that does exist has produced some quite interesting findings. Nicholas Lampert has provided the best analysis of citizen complaints and their impact on Soviet society. He examined seventy cases of Soviet whistleblowing as reported in the Soviet national press in the 1979–1983 period with the aim of shedding some light on this neglected area of research. Focusing on the characteristics of the whistleblowers, their occupations, the types of organizations within which the complaints arose, the specific type of charge leveled, and the motives of the whistleblower, Lampert went a long way in providing a snapshot of the organizational dissenter in the Soviet Union.[40]

Based on a close reading of the seventy Soviet press cases, Lampert found that 38 percent of the whistleblowers came from managerial or technical posts within the organization in question, 23 percent fell into the category of "activists," such as active party members or rank-and-file volunteers of the delegated People's Control units. Roughly 38 percent of the cases emerged almost equally from either individual or group complaints from manual workers connected to the organization.[41] He found only a single case of a complaint from a consumer.

On the one hand, the almost total lack of consumer complaints in the sample is quite odd, especially given the notoriously low quality of most Soviet consumer goods. Indeed, the work of Theodore Friedgut has shown that the number of non-organizational citizen complaints and requests for services reaches astronomical numbers.[42] On the other hand, though, this particular finding is more understandable, as Lampert himself explains: the sample is skewed away from the voluminous amount of consumer-generated complaints by the fact that such stories are rarely if ever reported in the Soviet press. This claim is certainly corroborated by the present author who, in reviewing over 200 Soviet press articles on corruption between 1965 and 1990, found only the odd story about what is most mundane in Soviet society. In a word, the press in the Soviet Union, as elsewhere, self-selects the more interesting stories for investigative reporting.

These Soviet whistleblowers and the cases of abuse that they report emerge from a wide variety of organizations. Lampert found that 41 percent of the cases involved service organizations such as transportation, education, housing, and trade. An additional 27 percent of the complaints referred to abuses in industrial enterprises, 17 percent in construction, and 13 percent in the area of agriculture. In a word, from the reported cases he examined, Lampert found all areas of the Soviet structure being affected.[43]

With respect to the nature of the complaints raised by these whistleblowers, the findings may be somewhat unreliable by virtue of the fact that almost all the consumer complaints dropped out of the sample. That being said, however, the intra-organizational complaints likewise revolved around a wide array of abuse. Roughly one in five complaints entailed charges of report padding, and an equal number alleged improprieties in the calculation or distribution of wages and bonuses. An additional one-fifth of the cases involved allegations of improper managerial practice that either aimed at self-aggrandizement or the favoring of one employee over others.[44] Interestingly, cases of bribery, one of the most ubiquitous types of abuse in the Soviet Union, are virtually non-existent in press reports of whistleblowing; only four of Lampert's eighty examples of offenses involved bribery. As he explains, "if complaints about bribery are relatively few, this is not surprising. It is a transaction in which both the bribe-giver and bribe-taker are breaking the law, and it is relatively easy to conceal from outsiders."[45] All sorts of other complaints appear in these press reports: forgery, bartering, plagiarism, drunkenness, safety violations, quality violations, and so on.

Based on the admittedly impressionistic picture presented by Lampert, a decidedly different view of the motives of whistleblowers appears in the Soviet Union. Recalling the general conclusion reached about organizational dissenters in the West as presented in the preceding section of this chapter, in which it was alleged that whistleblowers' personalities, their perceptions of right and wrong, their appreciation of rules and their universal application, and their insensitivity to social cues about appropriate behavior all combined to distinguish them from non-whistleblowers, the conclusion was that "whistleblowers are born, not made." Lampert's general findings contest this image of the whistleblower. After reviewing possible motives for whistleblowing in the Soviet case, Lambert cites a Soviet source who contends that in the USSR only "about 10 percent of complaints to the press were motivated by a general 'search for justice.' " Ninety percent were allegedly of a decidedly personal or selfish nature.[46] We are left to agree with Lampert's ultimate position that such distinctions may often be false ones, obfuscating an already complex psychological motive.

Of equal importance in cases of alleged official wrongdoing, of course, is the response to the complaints and the future prospects of the complainant. Whistleblowing research is full of instances of rather severe reprisals against critics, and this is no different in the case of the Soviet Union. As Lampert puts it,

> it is clear from almost every story that there is little love lost between the management and their critics. By raising a fuss, and above all by trying to take the complaint outside the organisation, they will quickly be seen as troublemakers, as "scribblers" *(pisaki)* and "nit-picking critics" *(kritikany)* who are out to slander the management, to tarnish the name of the whole collective, and in general to make life harder for everyone.[47]

Given the general level of law-breaking that took place in the everyday activities of most Soviet citizens, to say nothing of the routinized-but-illegal activities of Soviet managers, and given the role this law-breaking had in maintaining both the individual and collective standard of living in that country, it is clear why there should have been extreme pressure against whistleblowing in the USSR. What, then, were the prospects of success or failure for organizational dissenters and critics in Soviet society?

Before the recent demise of Soviet power in Russia, the likelihood of success for a critic depended on a number of factors. According to Lampert, management had a number of weapons it could use against any whistleblower: (a) support from the remainder of the work force, (b) support from the all-important party secretary, (c) the possibility of penalizing organizational dissenters through sanctions of the Soviet labor law, and, finally, (d) the pressing of counter-charges of malpractice against the whistleblower himself. Critical in all these deliberations on the part of the accused manager or management was anticipating the reaction of the relevant party officials. Now that the party itself is no longer the "leading and guiding force of Soviet society"—and, in fact, has been rendered illegal in many parts of the former Soviet Union—this calculus has changed drastically.

Under the old system, a whistleblower depending on collective support from the organization work force was often left disappointed. The Soviet system of remuneration left a sizable portion of the average worker's salary in the hands of management because of the bonus *(premiia)* system. Some portion of enterprise profits were often redistributed as salary bonuses to the rank-and-file worker, representing in not a few cases upwards of 40 percent of the worker's take-home pay. Such a system made workers loathe to support a whistleblower who might in fact be seen as a naive do-gooder who could upset the delicate balance in the organization.

This reluctance to buck management on the grounds of salary concerns, of course, is not unique to the Soviet case. What did make this reluctance a bit more compelling was the assumption that the party secretary would in most cases stand behind the local enterprise management. The reasons for this were quite clear: party secretaries themselves were evaluated on the economic results of the enterprises under their supervision; the situation compelled close ties and mutual support between party and state officials at most levels of the system. As a result, unless a whistleblower's charges involved grievous wrongdoing, the momentum of the situation conditioned the party secretary to support management. In most cases, the tendency of the party officials was to respond to complaints with merely some sort of token gesture. Soviet workers were well aware of the obstacles confronting them in this regard and often reasoned that supporting a whistleblower carried too many risks, with too few potential benefits.

Such risks, of course, were only compounded by the possibility that higher-ups would institute reprisals against the whistleblower (and his or her supporters). Such cases were all too frequent in the latter decades of the Soviet Union, as shown in the press articles describing the suppression of criticism by higher authorities. Despite rather specific legal safeguards against such things, it was not difficult for a Soviet manager to transfer or fire troublesome employees. While there are numerous cases of such chastised employees successfully exposing the improper actions of managerial superiors, the successes were hardly the rule. In Lambert's sample, 26 of the 66 individual whistleblowers under study were fired from their jobs at some time during their confrontation with management, and 13 others received a lesser penalty. From his estimate, only about one-third of the whistleblowers examined came through the process relatively unscathed by their superiors.[48]

Very often, as a result of a perceived lack of positive response from management or party officials, committed whistleblowers will petition the press for help. In many instances, the press plays a crucial role in compelling real action. Such was the case in the Soviet Union; even though the press under Soviet rule was an arm of the state, and worked under some frustrating constraints, it did not relinquish totally its role as the government's "fourth estate."[49] Every Soviet newspaper had a complaints department and actively encouraged citizens to write on matters of concern. In not a few instances, the public exposure given to extreme cases of mistreatment of organizational critics was instrumental in restoring the whistleblower to his or her job and in having penalties applied to the guilty parties. Again, however, such cases seem to have been the exceptions and not the rule. Even with press reports of the whistleblower's case, Lampert's sample revealed serious penalties falling on guilty managers only 11 percent of the time.[50]

Lambert's extended scrutiny of the phenomenon of whistleblowing in the Soviet Union led him to the following conclusion, which meshes well with one of the central themes of this book:

> [T]ypically the whistleblower gets much rougher treatment than the offenders complained about. From the standpoint of hardened Soviet executives this is only natural. Organisations, and ambitious individuals, cannot survive in the Soviet environment without day-to-day breaches of law, and even if this allows one to gain a little extra personal reward as well, that too is part of the rules of the game. The critics appeal to law and to official values in pursuit of their claims, but this quickly marks them out as misfits in real life.[51]

One of the themes defended in this book has been the notion that violations of socialist legality in the Soviet Union during the last quarter-century of its existence were almost inevitable. The demands on Soviet managers (and private citizens for that matter) were such that the regime itself was compelling its servants to break the law. In addition, it has been argued that the party and state leadership, as well as the control and enforcement organs of the state, were quite cognizant of the politically and ethically ambiguous nature of crime and punishment in a declining Soviet state. Given this state of affairs, one must agree with Lambert's conclusions about the "social misfit" role of whistleblowers in such a social environment.

The Cadres Weapon and the Control of Officialdom

While the above institutions represent the Soviet regime's more active control mechanisms, another method of control makes explicit the notion of an embedded "institutional mistrust" referred to earlier. Like its tsarist predecessor, the Soviet state was a colonial power and, as such, ruled over a vast geographic empire composed of a multitude of peoples representing sometimes strikingly different ethnicities, religions, cultures, languages, customs, traditions, and histories. Colonial empires, whether Roman, Hungarian, Ottoman, British, Russian, or Soviet, present a similar challenge to the dominant group: the challenge of control. In large part, as exemplified by the constant concern of those in power in Moscow with the related issues of nationalism, separatism, regionalism *(oblastnichestvo),* localism *(mestnichestvo),* and the development of local satrapy headed by "little tsars," guaranteeing the proper behavior of officials outside the center has been at the root of the problem of centralized colonial control. The recent events of the late 1980s and early 1990s reveal that such a constellation of forces is not to be taken lightly in any state, even one like the Soviet Union with a sizable and determined apparatus aimed at ensuring predictability in these matters. As John H. Miller has put it,

> Multi-ethnic polities have opted usually for one of two strategies to maintain their cohesion. One has been the promotion of loyalty to the multi-ethnic system by encouraging the autonomy of local communities, or elites, or their specific contribution to the "commonwealth," or both. The other has been the control or suppression of centrifugal tendencies often accompanied by a policy of assimilation to the 'central' culture. . . . A predictable feature of such control would be strict supervision from the centre over the selection of administrative personnel in ethnic minority or ethnically mixed areas. The USSR must certainly be classified among the polities inclining towards the latter strategy.[52]

In maintaining centralized control of the non-Russian Soviet "colonies," Moscow employed the "cadres weapon" to place faithful officials at all levels of the administrative hierarchy. Such a "weapon" entailed much more than the regular employment of the *nomenklatura* system.

The Nomenklatura *System*

Briefly, the *nomenklatura* system entailed the arrogated right of the Communist Party to recruit and place responsible cadres in all positions of importance within the Soviet system. In such a way the central authorities ensured the political loyalty of those individuals in key positions throughout the political-administrative hierarchy. Several million positions in the state and party structures, public organizations, trade unions, scientific institutions, and other institutions were staffed through the *nomenklatura* system. It represented in essence a system of official co-optation, rather than one marked by competition based on qualifications, experience, or training, although these factors entered the *nomenklatura* process in somewhat devalued forms.[53]

The system operated in a relatively straightforward manner. Every party committee, from the Central Committee of the CPSU at the top of the party pyramid to the roughly 3,500 *raion* (district) party committees *(raikomy)* at the bottom, compiled and maintained two lists. The first list, called the basic *(osnovnaya)* list, was composed of the array of specific posts that the party committee at that level was responsible for filling. A second list, referred to as the registered *(uchetnaya)* list, was made up of the names of persons seen as appropriate to fill those important posts. In most cases, the second secretary of the party committee at each level was charged with the responsibility of maintaining this cadres system. Such authority made the second party secretary a powerful person at each level of the political and administrative system in the Soviet Union. While it cannot be said that only members of the Communist Party were given these important posts, the fact that the Communist Party apparatus was able to screen all suitable applicants for key posts in Soviet society points to a high level of potential control by the party.

With respect to the system requisite of control, especially salient in the Soviet case, this cadres power provided the central authorities with a more consistent, if less direct, method of addressing the question of official control. Critical to the deployment of the cadres weapon is the party committee second secretary and, in many cases, his relationship with the party committee first secretary. Scholars have commented that such a cadres system "can easily be used . . . to protect the incompetent."[54]

Brezhnev's "Trust in Cadres" and the Decline of Control

The cadres policy of Brezhnev's successors can certainly be seen as a response to the policies pursued in the area of personnel during the 1965–1982 period. Likewise, in reviewing Brezhnev's disposition on personnel questions, a policy position variously labeled "Stability of Cadres," "Trust in Cadres," "Respect for Cadres," or "Faith in Cadres," one must assuredly view it as a calculated response to the erratic cadres policy of his immediate predecessor Nikita Khrushchev. Indeed, Khrushchev's mismanagement of the regional party and state cadres was prominent among the causes of the coup of October 1964.[55]

The origins of the Brezhnev cadres policy lie in the "hare-brained" organizational schemes of Khrushchev. Khrushchev's erratic policy with respect to leading cadres was at the root of his internal opposition and certainly contributed to the drive to remove him from his leadership past. The immediacy of the problem is revealed by the fact that within two weeks of the ouster of Khrushchev, the erstwhile leader's approach to personnel selection had been reversed. In the first edition of the CPSU's theoretical journal, *Partiinaia Zhizn,* to appear after the coup, the first part of a two-pronged attack on the reversed policy was articulated:

> Without according assistance to lower-level officials, without knowledge of [their] circumstances, a demanding attitude can easily boil down to leadership "in general," which often leads to the unjustified reshuffling of cadres.... Indisputedly, bad officials must be replaced. The renewal of cadres is a natural phenomenon. Not infrequently, however, there are still efforts to represent frequent changes of them as a virtue.[56]

The second overt criticism of Khrushchev's policy of limited tenures, constant reshuffling, and "systematic renewal" of cadres was voiced in the first post-coup edition of the important journal *Kommunist:*

> Recently, however, work with cadres and the rational employment of them has been subjected to artificial complications. The frequent restructurings and reorganizations have entailed repeated mass reallocation of officials. This switching around of cadres has not allowed them

to concentrate on the decision of long-term questions of economic development of the oblast, krai, or raion, and has imbued officials with a feeling of lack of self-confidence which hinders them from working calmly and fruitfully.[57]

Brezhnev's first act as general secretary of the Communist Party of the Soviet Union, then, was to reassure the party *apparatchiki* that jobs, their influence, and their perquisites would not be touched.[58] In his first major public speech to the party members, at the Twenty-third Party Congress in March 1966, Brezhnev was quick to state his policy in explicit terms:

> The frequent restructurings and reorganizations of Party, Soviet and economic bodies that were carried out in recent years had a negative effect on the selection, promotion and training of cadres. As a rule, they were attended by an unwarranted shuffling and replacement of cadres, which engendered a lack of self-assurance in officials, prevented them from demonstrating their abilities to the full and created the soil in which irresponsibility could sprout. . . . We are pleased to be able to remind the Congress that the November, 1964, plenary session of the C.P.S.U. reunited the province industrial and rural Party organizations into single entities, thereby restoring the Leninist principle of Party structure and eliminating the serious errors that have been committed in this matter. *(Applause.)* Also reinstated were the rural district Party committees, which in a short time have firmly reasserted their status as militant and authoritative propagators of Party policy in the countryside. *(Applause.)* . . . The development of the principle of democratic centralism has found expression in the further strengthening of the principle of collective leadership at the center and in the localities, in the enhancement of the role of the plenary sessions of the C.P.S.U. Central Committee and also of plenary sessions of local Party organs, in the manifestation of complete trust in cadres and in the improvement of inner-Party channels of information.[59]

Thus, by early 1966 Brezhnev had reinforced the earlier comments of Aleksei Kosygin, who some six months earlier spoke at the September 1965 Plenary Session of the CPSU Central Committee. Kosygin had assured the audience that "stability of cadres" would govern his attitude toward government personnel as well:

> Many thousands of able and competent organizers of socialist produc-
> tion have grown up in the country during the years of Soviet rule. At
> present more than 2,000,000 specialists with a higher or specialized
> secondary education are employed in industrial enterprises. More then
> 4,000,000 Communists are working in them. This is an immense force,
> by relying on which we can resolve the most complex tasks. The Party
> and the people hold the cadres of specialists and production organizers
> in high esteem, place great confidence in them and give them all pos-
> sible support in their complex and socially useful work.[60]

Within months of the mid-October 1964 removal of the first secretary, the Brezhnev–Kosygin leadership had stated in no uncertain
terms its policy toward cadres. For almost twenty years after the fall of
Khrushchev the resultant leadership, even after the decline of its initial
collective nature, maintained a rather consistent personnel policy
marked by the extremely slow turnover of elites at all levels of the
Soviet system. Both the genesis of the "stability of cadres" policy and
its subsequent effects on the Soviet system, however, merit specific
consideration as they directly impinge upon both the issue of elite
control and the prerogatives and the necessities faced by the post-
Brezhnev political leadership.

Western analysts' characterizations of the roots of Brezhnev's "stability of cadres" policy revolve around two basic and related themes. The
first, and perhaps the more standard of the two explanations, stresses
Nikita Khrushchev's treatment of the party and state cadres, especially
those in the CPSU Central Committee, and points to Brezhnev's reversal
of that cadres policy as evidence of his attempt to appease the powerful
national and regional officialdom. The adopted "stability of cadres" policy
was, seen in this light, a necessary policy, almost dictated from below, for
Brezhnev to adopt if he wished to build personal authority.[61]

Robert A.D. Ford's depiction of the events surrounding the adoption
of this policy can be seen as a classic example of this first type of
explanation:

> Khrushchev's reforms were tolerated until he began to tinker with the
> structure of the Party and introduced changes that would have reduced
> the power of the thousands of small Party bosses all over the country.[62]

Throughout 1960–1961 a "bloodless purge" of the majority of regional
party bosses revealed that even that group of officials who, in effect,
had salvaged Khrushchev's career during the 1957 Anti-Party Group

coup attempt, could not count on Khrushchev for personal job security.[63] Indeed, by the early 1960s, approximately two-thirds of the RSFSR *obkom* first secretaries installed by Khrushchev in the mid-1950s had been replaced.[64] According to this first school of thought, the rapid pace of regional elite turnover created a sense of frustration and insecurity that would eventually contribute greatly to Khrushchev's removal from power in 1964.

These frustrations and the sense of career instability were only intensified by further actions taken by Khrushchev in the first three years of the new decade. In October 1961, the Party Rules were changed and Khrushchev, for the first time, instituted minimum turnover quotas as well as limited office tenures for party committee members at virtually all levels of the system. Following on the heels of these cadres policy changes was perhaps the most self-damaging of all Khrushchev's schemes. In November 1962, the CPSU first secretary initiated a sweeping administrative reorganization that

> split a large proportion of the regional party organizations into two, one for industry and one for agriculture, each with its own regional committee [obkom], executive bureau, and secretariat. This not only created further administrative confusion, but struck directly at the incumbent *obkom* first secretaries by duplicating the offices and thus sharply reducing their individual power and status.[65]

This series of attacks on the powerful regional party elite, according to this explanation of the fall of Khrushchev and the genesis of "stability of cadres," had gone too far. The new leadership quickly reunified the party apparatus, restoring, in 75 percent of the cases, the erstwhile *obkom* first secretary to his former leadership post. Scholars stressing these events in their analyses argue that Brezhnev "apparently concluded that his own political fortunes [were] best served by identifying his administration with cadres stability,"[66] which without doubt would "foster support for [the] regime within this crucial elite group."[67]

A second slant on the origins of Brezhnev's "stability of cadres" policy views it less as a policy dictated from below and more as the result of a Politburo-level compact entered into by the main actors of the October 1964 coup. Seen from this perspective, the conservative cadres policy instituted by Khrushchev's successors was primarily an instrument aimed at facilitating the reintroduction and preservation of oligarchic, or collective, leadership patterns at the apex of the Soviet system. Khrushchev was ousted by his lieutenants in the Politburo "because the strains between the lesser oligarchs and the predominant leader had finally become intolerable. The coup was designed to restore rule by 'pure' oligarchy."[68]

Several scholars have pointed to the existence among the so-called Brezhnev–Kosygin team of a conscious compact about the proper nature of decision making.[69] Rigby himself was the first to proffer the theory of the leadership compact and articulates most explicitly the probable contents of the agreement:

> Whatever private reservations individual leaders may have entertained, it seems likely that, at the least, an implicit compact of this kind [i.e., one aimed at collective leadership and "mutual control"] was at the basis of the agreement and conspiracy to remove Khrushchev, and that this compact probably envisaged the following practical devices to this end:
> 1) Keeping the two top posts in different hands.
> 2) Reducing opportunities for patronage.
> 3) Distributing among leaders seats in the Party Presidium, Presidium of the Council of Ministers and Central Committee Secretariat in such a way as to avoid dangerous patterns of overlap.
> 4) Maintaining countervailing power between topmost leaders.[70]

The "stability of cadres" policy, from this perspective, was adopted as a means of ensuring the integrity of this collective compact. It improved the Soviet leadership style through much of the Brezhnev era because it effectively depoliticized the personnel selection process, thereby limiting much of the intra-elite power struggle. As Gail Lapidus argues, the curtailing of the high elite turnover rates associated with Khrushchev's leadership had "the immediate virtues of preserving stability at the apex and of limiting a potentially destabilizing competition over power and patronage among the elite."[71] Robert Blackwell describes in perhaps the clearest terms just how the Brezhnev cadres policy fit into the overall attitude of the post-Khrushchev Soviet leadership:

> Following N.S. Khrushchev's overthrow, his heirs replaced their patron's freewheeling cadres policy with a far less politicized approach in making personnel decisions. These changes—perhaps one should call

them reforms—have considerably narrowed the tactical options in the leadership struggle and thereby strengthened the institutional restraints against abuses of power by the more ambitious members of the Politburo.[72]

These two foci on the genesis of "stability of cadres," of course, are not at all antithetical. Indeed, they serve to highlight the significant degree of support that the policy must have engendered at the time. Whatever the exact impetus for its adoption, the "stability of cadres," implemented rather evenly for almost twenty years, had a profound impact on the nature of Soviet politics and society; its effects have been extremely far-reaching.

Brezhnev's cadres policy, in a word, entailed the extremely slow turnover of elites at virtually all levels of the Soviet system. This aspect of Brezhnev's "trust" in the party and government cadres revealed itself in a multitude of ways. At the highest political level, change in the composition of the Politburo slowed considerably. Over the first six-and-a-half years after the removal of Khrushchev, only two individuals (Kirill Mazurov and Arvid Pelshe) were promoted to full Politburo membership.[73] Changes at this level remained relatively low throughout the Brezhnev period and by the early 1980s the inner core of the Politburo averaged almost 75 years of age. The average age of the full voting members of the Politburo continued to rise throughout the period, going from 58 in 1966, to 62 in 1972, and to over 70 in 1980.[74] When Brezhnev died in November 1982, twelve full Politburo members remained (at least temporarily); seven were over 70 years of age.[75]

Similarly low turnover rates, as well as parallel aging patterns, emerged at lower levels as a result of "stability of cadres." In the CPSU Central Committee, membership in which defined the true power elite in the Soviet Union, low replacement rates provided further evidence of the "faith" Brezhnev placed in these individuals. The rates of reelection for the living full members of the Central Committee at each of the CPSU congresses during the Brezhnev era attest to the nature of the policy. As Table 4.1 reveals, Brezhnev's Central Committees retained a degree of continuity much higher than either Khrushchev's or Gorbachev's. The 1971 Central Committee membership reflected an 81 percent reelection rate from that of the 1966 Central Committee. Indeed, a full 61 percent of the voting members

Table 4.1

Reelection Rates in the CPSU Central Committee, 1956–1990

Year	Congress	Living Full Members Reelected (%)
1956	20th	63
1961	22nd	54
1966	23rd	76
1971	24th	81
1976	25th	89
1981	26th	89
1986	27th	60
1990	28th	8

elected into Khrushchev's final Central Committee in 1961 still alive in 1971 were reelected into Brezhnev's second "reconstructed" Central Committee.[76] This trend continued: the 1976 Central Committee reelected 89 percent of the living full members of the 1971 Central Committee, and 89 percent of these members, if still alive five years later, were reelected in 1981. Indeed, if one controls for the "automatic" turnover of the worker and peasant representatives, these figures would be even higher.

As a result of these extremely high reelection rates, the age structure of the Central Committee followed that of the Politburo. The average Central Committee member elected at Khrushchev's last Party Congress in 1961 was 52 years of age. Those identical elite elected at Brezhnev's final Congress (Twenty-Sixth) in 1981 averaged 62 years of age. These phenomena have led Jerry F. Hough to remark, "one could say that Central Committee membership in the Brezhnev era almost became a near-life peerage—something that one would normally retain until one died or was forced to retire for reasons of health."[77]

The continuance of such a personnel policy for almost two decades has had dramatic implications for the governance of the Soviet Union. In reviewing briefly the impact that "stability of cadres" has had on Soviet political life, it becomes clear that the cadres policy of Brezhnev's successors must be viewed, first and foremost, as a series of responses to the problems it created. That is, just as Brezhnev's policy with respect to personnel was a conservative reaction to the radical policy of his predecessor Khrushchev, so those of Andropov and Gorbachev must be seen as a more bold response to *their* predecessor, Brezhnev.

The "stability of cadres" policy engendered both positive and negative effects for the Soviet system. In fact, much of the negative aspect of the policy can be seen as the long-term consequences of its short-term benefits.

"Stability of cadres" enhanced the stability of the Soviet national leadership in a variety of ways. First, it limited the "potentially destabilizing competition over power and patronage within the elite."[78] In effect, it depoliticized cadres policy to such an extent that, according to Robert Blackwell, "cadres policy has not been a major weapon of political combat since Khrushchev. . . . "[79]

This depoliticization of Soviet personnel policy, moreover, spilled over into other areas as well. "Stability of cadres" can be seen as an instrumental aspect of a more general and consistent leadership approach:

> [The Brezhnev leadership's] deliberate use of depoliticization as a strategy for the management of economic and social change, . . . the effort to play down, if not remove from public view altogether, the ideological and conflict-provoking aspects of policy-formation and intra-elite relations contrasts sharply with what was a quintessential feature of Soviet political life until recently.[80]

Because of the extended tenures of most responsible positions during "stability of cadres," the Brezhnev period witnessed an increase in the functional specialization of its party and state cadres. Since movement among a variety of functional posts was, by design, curtailed by the cadres policy, the development of more "generalist" skills was discouraged. Cadres' functional skills, as a result, became more compartmentalized and, to a degree, more stable and rational in the process.[81]

A third positive effect of the cadres policy adopted by Brezhnev concerns the regularization of local mobility patterns. While Khrushchev was implementing a policy of increased geographic "circulation" of elites, Brezhnev very early in his tenure advocated the regularized, if more lethargic, mobility patterns. More officials were promoted locally, from within the same organization or geographic region.[82] As Brezhnev himself stated at the 1971 Twenty-fourth Party

Congress, "the Central Committee has pursued a consistent policy of promoting local personnel; people have been promoted to these posts [Republic party secretaries, *obkom* and *kraikom* first secretaries] from the centre only in exceptional circumstances."[83] Again, Brezhnev's goal here was to establish continuity in leadership, sensitivity to local conditions, and increased regularization of the patterns of cadre mobility—all relatively lacking under Khrushchev, where various elites were "parachuted" into posts from without.

Despite these significant benefits of "stability of cadres," the Brezhnev cadres policy, after eighteen years of rather consistent application, seriously jeopardized the long-term interests of the Soviet system. Many of its negative aspects combined to emasculate the Soviet leadership at all levels and engendered the general economic and social malaise that was inherited by Brezhnev's successors.

The most obvious problem caused by Brezhnev's conservative cadres policy, and one chronicled above, was the consistent aging of the elite. By the early 1980s and especially at the higher echelons of the party and government apparatuses, the Soviet leadership resembled a "gerontocracy" that lacked not only the will but the physical wherewithal to implement the needed reforms in the system. Soviet society became moribund as the inner core of the Soviet leadership became feeble, hospitalized, and died one by one. While these key officials experienced their extended illnesses, the apparatuses they governed became even more immobilized and demoralized. The society came to reflect its leaders—during the last half-decade of the Brezhnev era the entire Soviet system lost whatever dynamic element it had theretofore possessed.

The elite aging phenomenon infected other aspects of the political system. The inhibition upon cadre advancement not only divided the elite into distinct and competing age cohorts—the so-called "generation gap" in the elite [84]—but engendered the significant resentment of lower-level cadres who, despite extended experience and advancing age, could not move up the political- administrative ladder.[85] The regional party bosses, once considered to be in "stepping stone" positions ready for promotion to the center, found themselves instead in dead-end jobs. Some 30 percent of the regional party first secretaries of the Brezhnev generation either died in that post, or retired from it out of active political life. Life in the Soviet Republics as a result became increasingly isolated from national politics as the influx of personnel (especially non-Russians) into central leadership posts became increasingly restricted.[86]

At the systemic level, the Brezhnev leadership, at least implicitly, accepted and paid the price of system immobility for the achievement and advancement of depoliticization.[87] As Thomas H. Rigby has put it,

> A "normal" Soviet rate of turnover in senior posts would place extreme strains on an oligarchy concerned to ensure that such appointments do not allow one of their number to acquire too much patronage strength. The solution adopted by the oligarchy has been to cut back turnover well below the "normal" Soviet level, indeed to a level that appears exceptionally modest by any standard. . . . For [this] attempt to stabilize the oligarchy by a system of "mutual control," and certain of the particular devices employed to this end, produce—perhaps inevitably—some serious side-effects, which of their nature seem bound to become more acute as time goes on.[88]

At this level of analysis, the "serious side effects" predicted by Rigby took the form of the ossification of the policies governing the Soviet system. The institutionally entrenched and aging elite of the late Brezhnev period were unable to alter policy to confront the contemporary problems of state. While the trade-off agreed to back in the mid-1960s produced the leadership consensus that marked the Brezhnev period, the dictates of the actuarial tables ensured that as the long-time leaders died off, the carefully built consensus would break down. Thus, while, for its part, the "stability of cadres" policy was successful as a strategy of consensus building through the enlistment and maintenance of key political support systems, it must be regarded as a failure as a strategy for long-term policy innovations and creative and flexible governance. Indeed, this lack of policy innovation and general systemic immobility must be considered the main legacy of the Brezhnev era. It is against this inheritance that Brezhnev's heirs have been inveighing.

No less important were the consequences of Brezhnev's conservative cadres policy for the oversight and control of officials. The "social compact" made by the regime and the elite entailed the "depoliticization" of cadres policy—in effect, the withdrawal of the cadres weapon for the control of elites. Elite turnover was meager, and only the most blatant disregard to state laws and/or socialist etiquette would land an *apparatchik* in trouble. With one of the most effective controlling mechanisms of the state withdrawn, a powerful check on the personal prerogatives of responsible cadres was also withdrawn.

In such an environment, the corruption of Soviet officialdom associated with the Brezhnev regime was inevitable. Allowing state and party officials to engage in "positive" illegalities for the good of the state could not but spill over into their embracing "negative" illegalities as well. It was virtually impossible for the Brezhnev leadership to encourage illegalities of one type without experiencing a parallel increase of the other. The result was a rather large increase in the number of prosecutions and convictions for the latter categories of crime, while the "functional" crimes went uncommented upon. A society governed by such rules in bound to produce high levels of cynicism, both within the general population and among its officialdom.

In Brezhnev's defense, however, he was in a rather difficult position. The engineers of Khrushchev's ouster had entered office as a result of the extreme displeasure on the part of the party and state officials with the former leader's tendency to wield the personnel weapon with what was viewed as excessive zeal. In good part, the Brezhnev–Kosygin "electoral mandate" was the depoliticization of this check. In addition, as has been argued throughout these pages, increasingly prevalent within the upper leadership during the Brezhnev period was the realization that for the Soviet system to muddle through economically and politically without thoroughgoing reform, which was itself deemed unacceptable, Soviet officials had to be extended far greater latitude with respect to their personal behavior. In the absence of major reforms, then, Brezhnev's effective use of the cadres weapon entailed at least two major threats to the general secretary: the evaporation of his personal authority, and the even further decline of administrative efficiency and morale (and, hence, short-term societal living standards). Such was the nature of both Brezhnev and the times in which he ruled the Soviet Union that dangers like these were to be avoided at all costs.

The Cadres Weapon after Brezhnev

After the many years of rather conservative personnel turnover at all levels of the Soviet system that marked the Brezhnev period, Brezhnev's successors engaged in a rigorous cadres replenishment program. The new leaders, with the exception of Konstantin

Chernenko, who was wedded to the practices of his mentor, grasped the opportunity to replace elites of the Brezhnev mold with a cohort more consistent with their ideas and ideals for the Soviet future. Within six years of Brezhnev's death 90 percent of the roughly 150 regional party bosses had been replaced. At a rate approaching the hectic years of the Khrushchev era, the Soviet Union under both Yuri Andropov and Mikhail Gorbachev witnessed a thoroughgoing replacement of cadres, within both the Communist Party and state apparatuses.[89]

In the highest party circles, elite turnover increased dramatically. For example, Brezhnev's "trust in cadres" policy manifested itself in the high level of stability in the CPSU Central Committee. As Table 4.1 shows, during Brezhnev's period atop the party, reelection rates in the Central Committee were quite high, causing a general aging of the elite. While neither Andropov nor Chernenko lived long enough to witness the first post-Brezhnev Party Congress elect a new Central Committee, Gorbachev presided over two such congresses. The reelection rates of members of the Central Committee, the true "power elite" of Soviet politics, declined precipitously as new elites entered the national scene. The 1986 Twenty-seventh Party Congress elected a Central Committee that left out 40 percent of the sitting members. As the crisis of perestroika deepened in the late 1980s, Gorbachev's cadres policy began exacting a greater toll on the political elite. His final Central Committee, elected in 1990, saw over nine out of ten of its incumbents replaced as new, untraditional segments of the party were brought into greater representation.[90]

In general, Gorbachev's cadres policy entailed a rate of elite turnover twice that of Brezhnev's. Moreover, a large percentage of those party and state *apparatchiki* that were removed by Andropov and Gorbachev were not gracefully shifted to other posts with impressive titles and alternative opportunities for the perquisites of office. For example, among the powerful regional party first secretaries, referred to by Stalin as the "generals" of the Communist Party, sixty-five of the first 146 replaced after Brezhnev, a full 45 percent, were ushered into forced retirement from active politics. Recalling the nature of the intra-elite "compact" that undergirded Brezhnev's eighteen-year rule, it is hardly surprising that Gorbachev's rule was consistently in trouble from within or that the putsch of August 1991 should have been attempted. The failed coup of 1991 was no less an "institutional coup" than the one that successfully toppled Khrushchev twenty-seven years earlier.

Assessing the prerequisites for reform in the Soviet Union at the beginning of the Gorbachev era, George W. Breslauer argued that the general secretary

> must bring in people who are not only beholden to him for their new jobs but also share his general orientation, who agree with his view that what is needed now is to get the country moving again. He needs people who agree that the country cannot afford to continue a relaxed style of political administration. In many instances these will be individuals with whom Gorbachev has worked in the past and with whom he therefore shares experiences and old-boy ties, and, partly for that reason, shares a common orientation as well. In other instances, through reports of trusted associates, he may bring in people whom he knows, share his general outlook.[91]

Clearly at the root of Breslauer's conception of reform necessities is Gorbachev's cadres policy. His reference to "a relaxed style of political administration" may seem a bit euphemistic, but in effect Breslauer is calling for a rigorous cadres policy that entails a reinvigoration of the personnel weapon as a means of controlling the behavior of the elites.

In like mind, at the end of the Chernenko interregnum Robert A.D. Ford identified two major obstacles to serious reform in the Soviet Union. The first was "the immense power of the middle-level and provincial Party officials to resist change." The second obstacle that faced Gorbachev was comprised of the "strong doubts on the part of the Party leaders about the ideological and political consequences of effective reform."[92] Both of these obstacles to reform required a rigorous cadres policy which sought to reconstitute Soviet officialdom. Gorbachev did indeed embrace such a personnel policy. His cadres policy went beyond the normal "authority-building" strategies implied by the related notions of patronage and clientelism so prevalent in the literature on Soviet elite politics. In retrospect, Gorbachev was engaged in much more than building his own personal power by replacing Brezhnev loyalists with Gorbachev loyalists. He frequently replaced officials he himself had named a few years earlier because of their inability or unwillingness to implement policies to his liking. In a word, Gorbachev attempted to wield the cadres weapon so long in disuse in Soviet politics; in the main, he did so successfully.

It is important to keep in mind, however, that Gorbachev's prospects for restructuring Soviet politics and society did not in the final analysis depend on his cadres success. While it is indeed true that Gorbachev used an aggressive cadres policy to replace hundreds of party and state officials at all levels of the Soviet system, such an instrumental success did not in any way guarantee his programmatic or policy success. Gorbachev's cadres policy aimed at controlling the Soviet elite, in terms of their personal behavior, their official actions, and their adopted orientation to the future Soviet Union. It is somewhat ironic that despite tremendous changes in personnel, shortened tenures in office, the elevation of a new generation of leadership, and increased openness about what ailed the system, the cadres weapon from a policy perspective was far from lethal. In the new political atmosphere that Gorbachev himself had helped create, the old tools of the Soviet upper leadership became extremely blunt instruments.

Conclusion

As the above treatment has shown, the mechanisms of party, state, and popular control of officials in the Soviet Union were quite numerous. What is more, given the size, pervasiveness, and legal mandates enjoyed by these anti-corruption instruments, they possessed both the ideological and physical means to engage in potentially sweeping control activities. That official corruption, black marketeering, organized crime, and other assorted *regularized* and *institutionalized* violations of Soviet law developed to a level unparalleled certainly in European history raises serious doubts about the overall willingness of the Soviet state and its leadership to employ these vast controlling mechanisms in any objective, uniform, and consistent manner.

Such doubts are further reinforced by the existence within Soviet history of periods of time marked by the extremely efficient operation of such control mechanisms, in some cases over vast portions of the society. One need not cite the extreme case of the terroristic collectivization of agriculture in the 1929–1932 period when the coercive powers of the state manifested themselves quite remarkably. Nor is it necessary to describe the details of the Stalinist purge of the political elite starting in December 1934 and extending through 1938. While both cases show the darker side of the state's coercive ability when it was firmly committed to such goals, these instances represent but the extremes of a more generic argument.

Given the potential of the Soviet Union's controlling capabilities and the extremely uneven application of these capabilities in practice, it is necessary to investigate the social and political functions of anti-corruption efforts within the Soviet system of governance. That is, the high measure of arbitrariness in the application of state power with respect to corruption within society in general, but especially as it was applied to Soviet officialdom, suggests the politicization of this critical state function. As the following chapter will attempt to show, the "politics" of corruption and anti-corruption revealed this element of politicization and arbitrariness, serving a number of purposes in regulating both "high" and "low" politics in the Soviet Union.

Notes

1. Hans J. Torke (1988), "Crime and Punishment in the Pre-Petrine Civil Service," pp. 5–21 in Ezra Mendelsohn and Marshall S. Shatz, eds., *Imperial Russia, 1700–1917: State, Society, Opposition* (Dekalb, IL: Northern Illinois University Press), p. 17.

2. Ibid., p. 13.

3. Marc Raeff (1983), *The Well-Ordered Police State: Social and Institutional Change through Law in the Germanies and Russia, 1600–1800* (New Haven: Yale University Press), p. 217.

4. Robert C. Tucker (1990), *Stalin in Power: The Revolution from Above, 1928–1941* (New York: W.W. Norton), p. 25.

5. Immediately after Khrushchev's ouster in October 1964, the name of the leading party organ of the CPSU Central Committee was changed from "Presidium" back to "Politburo," its original name before being changed in 1952.

6. Leonard Schapiro (1971), *The Communist Party of the Soviet Union* (New York: Vintage Books), p. 600.

7. In Soviet parlance, only actual members of the Communist Party of the Soviet Union can properly be referred to as "Communists." At its peak in the late 1980s, the CPSU had approximately 19 million members.

8. Jerry F. Hough and Merle Fainsod (1979), *How the Soviet Union Is Governed* (Cambridge: Harvard University Press), p. 218.

9. Jan S. Adams has cited data indicating that in September 1963 there were 3,166 party–state control committees at various levels (127 at the *oblast* level and above, 1,057 city and district committees, 348 committees attached to industrial zones, and 1,634 control committees for state and collective farm production associations). See Jan S. Adams (1977), *Citizen Inspectors in the Soviet Union: The People's Control Committee* (New York: Praeger Publishers), p. 79.

10. Jan S. Adams, *Citizen Inspectors in the Soviet Union: The People's Control Committee*, p. 25.

11. Ibid., p. 26.

12. This set of figures comes from Hough and Fainsod (1979), *How the Soviet Union Is Governed,* p. 302.

13. Jan S. Adams, *Citizen Inspectors in the Soviet Union: The People's Control Committee,* p. 97.

14. Ibid., p. 100.

15. For more on recent developments in the area of Soviet property law, see Randy Bregman and Dorothy C. Lawrence (1990), "New Developments in Soviet Property Law," *Columbia Journal of Transnational Law,* Vol. 28 (No. 1): 189–206.

16. Stanislaw Pomorski (1977), "Criminal Law Protection of Socialist Property in the USSR," pp. 223–245 in *Soviet Law after Stalin,* Vol. 1 (Leyden: A.W. Sijthoff), p. 230–231.

17. Valerii Chalidze (1977), *Criminal Russia: Essays on Crime in the Soviet Union* (New York: Random House), p. 190.

18. A.S. Grechin (1983), "Experiment in the Sociological Study of People's Feelings on Law and Order," *Sotsiologicheskiye issledovania,* No. 2 (April–June): 121–126. Cited in *Current Digest of the Soviet Press,* Vol. 35 (No. 26): 3.

19. Stanislaw Pomorski, "Criminal Law Protection," p. 239.

20. Louise I. Shelley (1990), "The Second Economy in the Soviet Union," pp. 11–26 in Maria Los, ed., *The Second Economy in Marxist States* (New York: St. Martin's Press), p. 21.

21. Cited in Gordon B. Smith (1978), *The Soviet Procuracy and the Supervision of Administration* (Alphen aan den Rijn: Sijthoff & Noordhoff), p. 6.

22. Ibid.

23. Ibid.

24. F.J.M. Feldbrugge, G.P. Van Den Berg, and William B. Simmons, eds. (1985), *Encyclopedia of Soviet Law,* 2d rev. ed. (Dordrecht: Martinus Nijhoff), p. 623.

25. Gordon B. Smith (1988), *Soviet Politics: Continuity and Contradiction* (New York: St. Martin's Press), p. 144.

26. "The House on Liternaya Street," *Izvestiia,* January 19, 1972, p. 3. Appears also in *Current Digest of the Soviet Press,* Vol. 24 (No. 3): 27.

27. Cited in Neil J. Smelser, ed. (1973), *Karl Marx on Society and Social Change* (Chicago: University of Chicago Press), p. 19.

28. Theodore H. Friedgut (1979), *Political Participation in the USSR* (Princeton, NJ: Princeton University Press), p. 33.

29. Cited in Robert C. Tucker, ed. (1972), *The Marx–Engels Reader* (New York: W.W. Norton), p. 124.

30. Cited in Theodore H. Friedgut, *Political Participation in the USSR,* p. 38.

31. Marcia P. Miceli and Janet P. Near (1985), "Characteristics of Organizational Climate and Perceived Wrongdoing Associated with Whistleblowing Decisions," *Personnel Psychology,* Vol. 38, pp. 525–544.

32. Jill W. Graham (1986), "Principled Organizational Dissent: A Theoretical Essay," *Research in Organizational Behavior,* Vol. 8 (No. 1): 1.

33. Philip H. Jos, Mark E. Tompkins, and Steven W. Hays (1989), "In Praise of Difficult People: A Portrait of the Committed Whistleblower," *Public Administration Review,* Vol. 49 (No. 6): 552–561.

34. Jill W. Graham, "Principled Organizational Dissent," pp. 20–22.

35. Marcia P. Miceli and Janet P. Near, "Characteristics of Organizational Climate," p. 542.

36. Philip H. Jos, Mark E. Tompkins, and Steven W. Hays, "In Praise of Difficult People," p. 556.

37. Myron Glazer (1983), "Ten Whistleblowers and How They Fared," *The Hastings Center Report*, Vol. 13 (December): 33–41.

38. See Mark Snyder (1974), "The Self-Monitoring of Expressive Behavior," *Journal of Personality and Social Psychology*, Vol. 30 (No. 4): 526–537.

39. Philip H. Jos, Mark E. Tompkins, and Steven W. Hays, "In Praise of Difficult People," p. 557.

40. See Nick Lampert (1983), "The Whistleblowers: Corruption and Citizens' Complaints in the USSR," pp. 268–287 in Michael Clarke. ed., *Corruption: Causes, Consequences and Control* (New York: St. Martin's Press); and Nicholas Lampert (1985), *Whistleblowing in the Soviet Union: Complaints and Abuses under State Socialism* (New York: Shocken Books).

41. Nicholas Lampert, *Whistleblowing in the Soviet Union*, p. 109.

42. Theodore H. Friedgut, *Political Participation in the USSR*, pp. 224–234.

43. Nicholas Lampert, *Whistleblowing in the Soviet Union*, pp. 109–110.

44. Ibid., p. 110.

45. Ibid.

46. Ibid., pp. 111–112.

47. Ibid., p. 117.

48. Ibid., p. 121.

49. For a fine overview of party–media relations, see Thomas F. Remington (1988), *The Truth of Authority: Ideology and Communications in the Soviet Union* (Pittsburgh, PA: University of Pittsburgh Press), especially pp. 133–155.

50. Nicholas Lampert, *Whistleblowing in the Soviet Union*, p. 141.

51. Ibid., p. 145.

52. John H. Miller (1977), "Cadres Policy in Nationality Areas: Recruitment of CPSU First and Second Secretaries in Non-Russian Republics of the USSR," *Soviet Studies*, Vol. 29 (No. 1): 3.

53. See Bohdan Harasymiw (1984), *Political Elite Recruitment in the Soviet Union* (London: Macmillan), especially pp. 160–173.

54. Ronald J. Hill and Peter Frank (1986). *The Soviet Communist Party*, 3d ed. (Boston: Allen and Unwin), p. 89.

55. T.H. Rigby (1970), "The Soviet Leadership: Towards a Self-Stabilizing Oligarchy?" *Soviet Studies*, Vol. 22 (No. 2): 173.

56. *Partiinaia zhizn*, 1964 (No. 20): 6.

57. *Kommunist*, 1964 (No. 16): 7–8.

58. Robert A.D. Ford (1984), "The Soviet Union: The Next Decade," *Foreign Affairs* 62 (No. 5): 1133.

59. *Pravda* and *Izvestiia*, March 30, 1966.

60. *Pravda* and *Izvestiia*, September 28, 1965.

61. For more on this "authority-building" strategy, see George Breslauer (1982), *Khrushchev and Brezhnev as Leaders: Building Authority in Soviet Politics* (London: George Allen & Unwin).

62. Robert A.D. Ford, "The Soviet Union," p. 1133.

63. Jerry F. Hough (1979), "The Generation Gap and the Soviet Succession," *Problems of Communism*, Vol. 28 (No. 4): 2.

64. T.H. Rigby (1978), "The Soviet Regional Leadership: The Brezhnev Generation," *Slavic Review*, Vol. 37 (No. 1): 5.

65. Ibid., p. 6.

66. Robert E. Blackwell, Jr. (1979), "Cadres Policy in the Brezhnev Era," *Problems of Communism*, Vol. 28 (No. 2): 29.

67. T.H. Rigby (1978), "The Soviet Regional Leadership," p. 8; Jerry F. Hough (1979), "The Generation Gap," p. 3; R. Judson Mitchell (1982), "Immobilism, Depoliticization, and the Emerging Soviet Elite," *Orbis*, Vol. 26 (No. 3): 592.

68. T.H. Rigby (1970), "The Soviet Leadership," p. 173.

69. Ibid.; Grey Hodnett (1975), "Succession Contingencies in the Soviet Union," *Problems of Communism* (March–April): 1–21.; Gail Lapidus (1977), "The Brezhnev Regime and Directed Social Change: Depoliticization as Political Strategy," pp. 26–38 in Alexander Dallin, ed., *The Twenty-Fifth Congress of the CPSU: Assessment and Context* (Stanford: Hoover Institution Press); and Robert E. Blackwell, Jr., "Cadres Policy in the Brezhnev Era."

70. T.H. Rigby (1970), "The Soviet Leadership, p. 175.

71. Gail Lapidus, "The Brezhnev Regime," p. 35.

72. Robert E. Blackwell, Jr., "Cadres Policy in the Brezhnev Era," p. 29.

73. Grey Hodnett, "Succession Contingencies," p. 8.

74. Jerry F. Hough (1980), *Soviet Leadership in Transition* (Washington, D.C.: The Brookings Institution), p. 61.

75. Archie Brown (1983), "Andropov: Discipline *and* Reform?" *Problems of Communism*, Vol. 32 (No. 1): 26.

76. Jerry F. Hough (1976), "The Brezhnev Era: The Man and the System," *Problems of Communism*, Vol. 25 (No. 2): 3. Compare this fact to the following: the 1961 Twenty-second Party Congress, convened eight years after the death of Stalin, elected a Central Committee with only two "leftovers" from Stalin's final Central Committee of 1952.

77. Jerry F. Hough (1982), "Changes in Soviet Elite Composition," pp. 39–64 in Seweryn Bialer and Thane Gustafson, eds., *Russia at the Crossroads: The 26th Congress of the CPSU* (London: George Allen & Unwin), p. 47.

78. Gail Lapidus, "The Brezhnev Regime," p. 35.

79. Robert E. Blackwell, Jr., "Cadres Policy in the Brezhnev Era," p. 38.

80. Gail Lapidus, "The Brezhnev Regime," p. 26.

81. R. Judson Mitchell, "Immobilism, Depoliticization, and the Emerging Soviet Elite," pp. 592–594; T.H. Rigby (1978), "The Soviet Regional Leadership," p. 22.

82. T.H. Rigby, ibid., p. 13.

83. *XXIV S''ezd, stenograficheskii otchet*, Vol. 1, p. 124.

84. Jerry F. Hough (1980), "Soviet Leadership in Transition."

85. T. H. Rigby (1978), "The Soviet Regional Leadership," p. 5.

86. R. Judson Mitchell, "Immobilism"; John H. Miller, "Cadres Policy in Nationality Areas."

87. R. Judson Mitchell, ibid., p. 491.

88. T.H. Rigby (1970), "The Soviet Leadership," pp. 179, 190–191.

89. See, for example, Gordon B. Smith (1987), "Gorbachev's Council of Ministers," *Soviet Union,* Vol. 14 (No. 3): 343–363.

90. For more on the increase in non-traditional representation in the Gorbachev period, refer to William A. Clark (1991), "Token Representation in the CPSU Central Committee," *Soviet Studies,* Vol. 43, No. 5 (October): 913–929.

91. George W. Breslauer (1986), "The Nature of Soviet Politics and the Gorbachev Leadership," pp. 11–30 in Alexander Dallin and Candoleeza Rice, eds., *The Gorbachev Era* (Stanford, CA: Stanford Alumni Association), p. 18.

92. Robert A.D. Ford (1984), "The Soviet Union: The Next Decade," pp. 1138–39.

5

THE POLITICS OF CORRUPTION AND ANTI-CORRUPTION IN THE SOVIET SYSTEM

> The underlying dilemma of Soviet law has been defined as one be-
> tween legality and arbitrariness. . . . [But] if one recognizes the exis-
> tence of an hierarchically organized elite, which strives towards the
> acquisition of all political and economic power, . . . then the dilemma
> can be defined as one between legality and political expediency, and
> much of the irrationality of official behavior disappears.
> —F.J.M. Feldbrugge[1]

One of the arguments presented in the preceding pages has been that in viewing the impact of corruption and those state-sponsored efforts to combat corruption in the post-Khrushchev period of Soviet history a significant degree of arbitrariness or, as Feldbrugge puts it, political expediency can be discerned. This arbitrariness has been attributed to a number of causes, not the least of which are (a) the ambiguous feelings on the part of the political leadership with respect to the net effect of corruption on society, and the stability certain types of corruption afforded to their political position; (b) the dubious capability of the state to root out such a widespread and culturally accepted form of private activity; (c) the appreciation by the leadership of the fact that economic managers in the Soviet command economy faced a number of competing demands from above, many of which compelled them for essentially unselfish reasons to engage in technical violations of the law; and (d) given the pervasiveness of corruption among the political elite, the role of corruption and anti-corruption in the making and breaking of individual political careers, as well as in personal authority-building efforts. The present chapter focuses on this final source of arbitrariness in the regime's response to corruption among its public officials: the politicization of official corruption and anti-corruption in the high politics of the Soviet system.

As has been well chronicled in the literature on Soviet criminal policy, one of the hallmarks of state action against crime has been the enforcement "campaign." As Gordon B. Smith has described them, campaigns are

> the coordinated efforts of several law enforcement related agencies and institutions to reduce the incidence of certain types of crime. . . . Ideally, campaigns represent an integrated, total approach to combating crime, incorporating investigations, prosecution, follow-up supervision, and preventive measures. . . . Campaigns against crime assume a central position in the Soviet system of criminal justice. In actuality, campaigns serve four separate functions; (1) to uncover, punish and, by example, prevent violations; (2) to communicate new policies or laws to officials and the public; (3) to inform Party and state officials of the state of legality in a region; and (4) to provide an outlet for ritualistic participation in government.[2]

In centrally ordered or directed campaigns, there is some evidence that the local organs of law enforcement treat their orders from above as an enterprise manager might view his: as quotas to be filled. Smith studied the pattern of activity of the Soviet Procuracy between 1955 and 1976; he came to the conclusion that the accelerated pace of procuratorial activity toward the end of the plan period suggests that the Procuracy "is engaged in some 'storming' of its own in order to fulfill its quota of investigations."[3] Given the Soviet penchant for quantitative quotes, the idea of prosecutors being assigned central numerical targets is not at all out of the question.

Of course, not all anti-crime campaigns occurred on orders from the center. As is well known by students of Soviet politics, the ability of the central authorities to control regional and local officials was somewhat limited. As shall be discussed below, it was not at all rare for local elites to enact anti-crime campaigns for their own reasons. While antiseptic, anti-crime programs were generally neutral in a political sense, such was not the case in anti-corruption campaigns directed at Soviet officials. Here, the stakes were much higher. Instances of factional infighting through the use of anti-corruption campaigns were, therefore, much more delicate operations and were usually enacted only after some amount of care had been taken in planning the course of the campaign.

Campaigns are sometimes associated with extensive press coverage; often, the Soviet authorities would use reports of arrests, convictions, and the like to signal individuals throughout the system with respect to alterations in the "rules of the game." However, the amount of press coverage is incidental to the nature of the campaigns themselves. That is, anti-crime campaigns often occurred without a corresponding media component. In fact, for our present purpose of shedding light on the politics of campaigns against Soviet officials, there is in all likelihood a reduced role for the media in the campaign.

This chapter seeks to highlight the politicized character of anti-corruption campaigns during the last twenty-five years of the Soviet Union. While the sections that follow describe the "high" politics of the national elites as a critical factor in making sense of the patterns of official crime and punishment in the Soviet Union, it must be remembered that because the ability of central authorities to control events in the republics, territories, regions, cities, and precincts of the country was quite circumscribed, similar politicized and faction-based anti-crime and anti-corruption campaigns were evident at lower levels of the system as well.[4] If the localized variants are at all similar to the national anti-corruption campaigns, this chapter will have succeeded in demonstrating the politicized and arbitrary elements of the Soviet practice of combating official corruption.

Andropov's Rise to Power

Personal Career Background

Yuri Vladimirovich Andropov was born on June 15, 1914, in a small town between the Black and Caspian seas in southwestern Russia, in what later came to be under Soviet organization Stavropol' territory *(krai)*. His father, Vladimir Andropov, worked for the local administration of the Russian railroad. In his middle-to-late teens, Yuri Andropov worked at a number of odd jobs: telegraph operator, trainee projectionist, and boat hand on the Volga River. The last job may have seemed somewhat promising to the young Andropov, for in 1932 he entered the Rybinsk Water Transportation Technicum, located in Yaroslavl *oblast,* and graduated in 1936. His first job after graduation entailed organizing the local youth at a Rybinsk shipyard for Komsomol activities. He simultaneously worked as a Komsomol secretary at the Water Transportation Technicum. A year later, Andropov was promoted within the Yaroslavl Komsomol organization to the post of *oblast* Komsomol Secretary. Between 1938 and 1940, he served as the Yaroslavl region's Komsomol first secretary, and became a member of the Communist Party at this time.

By the time the war broke out with Germany's invasion in the summer of 1941, Andropov was still in the Komsomol, now as first secretary of the Karelo-Finnish Republic Komsomol organization. Finally, in 1944, at the age of thirty, Andropov was promoted out of the youth organization and into active party work. He served as second secretary of the Petrozavodsk city party committee *(gorkom)* within the Karelo-Finnish Republic until 1947, when he was elevated to the post of republic second secretary. Andropov's next major move came in 1953 when he was moved to ambassadorial work in Budapest. By 1954 Andropov was Soviet ambassador to Hungary and, as has been well chronicled in numerous works, played a relatively duplicitous role in the Soviet crushing of the short-lived Hungarian revolution of 1956. After the reestablishment of pro-Soviet sentiment in the Hungarian government, Andropov was assigned the role of chief of the CPSU Central Committee Department for Liaison with Communist and Workers' Parties of Socialist Countries, a post he would hold for ten years. While in this position, Andropov was elevated in 1962 to the CPSU Central Committee Secretariat. In 1967, he was made chairman of the KGB, giving up his status of party secretary at this time. This loss, however, was made up for by his being named a candidate member of the Central Committee Politburo. As KGB chairman, Andropov pursued a hard line against the growing dissident movement, and emphasized the creation and maintenance of discipline in society at large.

During the April 1973 plenum of the Party Central Committee, four new members were added to the ruling Politburo, the final three up to full voting status: Grigorii Romanov (the 53-year-old first secretary of the Leningrad City party committee), Andrei Gromyko (the 64-year-old USSR minister of foreign affairs), Marshal Andrei Grechko (the 70-year-old USSR minister of defense), and Yuri Andropov (the 59-year-old chairman of the KGB). The advancement of Andropov, while not unexpected, seemed at the time to be the most dramatic. The KGB chief had been a non-voting member of the Politburo since 1967, but his promotion broke a two-decade KGB absence from the Politburo's voting ranks.

In retrospect, the promotion seems less significant in this regard since Andropov in all likelihood was advanced as much due to his personal abilities and ties with Brezhnev as to his institutional connections. In 1967, Brezhnev had selected Andropov to replace then–KGB chief Vladimir Semichastny, and he owed his candidate membership in the Politburo to the general secretary. By 1973, Andropov had had significant experience in bloc relations through his ambassadorship as well as in foreign affairs generally. Given what at the time seemed to be his unquestioned loyalty to Brezhnev, his considerable foreign policy experience at a time of détente's greater East–West contacts, his six-year tenure as a candidate member, as well as the obvious need to readmit the intelligence bureaucracy into the key party decision-making apparatus, Andropov's promotion to full membership in the Politburo seems logical. Moreover, given the traditional competition between the Soviet military and the KGB, it came as no surprise when the KGB chief and the defense minister were promoted to equal rank at the same time.

Kremlinologist Michel Tatu argued at the time that the events of the April 1973 plenum represented a necessary but, from the party's perspective, undesirable dissemination of political power. In his view, the ruling triumvirate of Leonid Brezhnev, Aleksei Kosygin, and Nikolai Podgorny was only able to win approval for Brezhnev's far-reaching policy of détente in Europe and cooperation with Washington on the condition that the nominees of the traditional hard-line elements—the KGB and the army chiefs—were brought into the Politburo as counterweights.[5] A second, less provocative thesis seems to possess some degree of explanatory power. Based on the fact that the policy of rapprochement with the West did not meet with unanimous approval in the Politburo, and in fact probably was contributory to the ouster of Ukrainian party boss Petr Shelest in 1972, this second theory postulates that Brezhnev and his colleagues, in an effort to ensure accountability, co-opted the KGB and the Armed Forces into the leadership.

While on the one hand presenting a united front to the world during the initial implementation of a controversial policy, the Politburo elites, by giving the KGB and the Armed Forces full representation, also made these centers of political power co-responsible for unquestioned obedience to Politburo decisions in the future.

Whatever the reasons behind Andropov's promotion to full voting status in April 1973, his power within the leading party organ gradually built throughout the remainder of 1970s. Within two years, he was given the title of Soviet Army General, and the awarding of medals and orders so prevalent during the second half of the Brezhnev period also blessed Andropov. By the time the Brezhnev leadership was in its final year, Andropov had become as decorated as almost any figure on the political scene; four Orders of Lenin, three Orders of the Red Banner of Labor, a Hero of Socialist Labor medal, a Gold Medal Sickle and Hammer, an Order of October Revolution, as well as an Order of Sukhe-Bator (from Mongolia) and the Grand Cross for Military Services (from Peru), and other medals adorned his chest.

It has been argued elsewhere that Andropov had by the late 1970s benefited from a conscious strategy of utilizing the major achilles heel of the political elite—corruption—as a vehicle by which both the reputation of the KGB and its leader, as well as its ability to make or break political rivals, would be enhanced to the point that Andropov himself could become a serious contender for political power upon Brezhnev's eventual death. As KGB chief, Andropov knew better than any other living soul in the Soviet Union just what scale of elite corruption existed in the system; under the Brezhnev leadership virtually every official, from the lowliest enterprise manager to the all-union Politburo, was potentially vulnerable to charges of abuse of office, bribery, black marketeering, and other related illegalities. Using anti-corruption campaigns at various levels of the Soviet system, then, the KGB chief was able to manipulate events in such a manner as to slowly but inexorably weaken both Brezhnev and any potential check to his own career. Solovyev and Klepikova have described the major pillars of Andropov's politicized anti-corruption system as his "Caucasian Rehearsal."[6] In this instance, Andropov played out a series of orchestrated events in Georgia and Azerbaidzhan through the use of local proxies (in this case, Eduard Shevardnadze and Geidar Aliev) that served his purposes of personal and institutional advancement through calculated political infighting. That such a strategy, if indeed it existed, was successful can be inferred, of course, from subsequent events that culminated in Yuri Andropov's elevation to the position of general secretary of the Communist Party of the Soviet Union four days after the death of Leonid Brezhnev in November 1982. The details of Andropov's use of corruption and anti-corruption speaks volumes to the notions of arbitrariness and political expediency raised throughout this work.

Shevardnadze, Aliev, and the Caucasian Strategy

While the term "coattails" is a common concept used to describe electoral "halo effects" in Western democracies, administered societies such as that in operation in the Soviet Union are much more prone to patron–client relationships, or, as it has been called, clientelism.[7] One of the best metaphors to describe this phenomenon is that of *seilschaften*. Jozsa describes the concept in generic terms as follows:

> in mountaineering jargon the term *seilschaften* stands for a "roped-party" of climbers whose mutual aid, protection and support enable them to scale heights that would be beyond their individual powers.[8]

With respect to the operation of patron–client relations as they existed in the Soviet Union, Grey Hodnett has argued that such a relationship is extant and operating when both the patron and the client are simultaneously engaged in

> (a) promotion of one's interest as a continuing member of the leadership; (b) promotion of one's factional interests; (c) promotion of functional sympathies; (d) promotion of interests associated with one's general policy sympathies; (e) promotion of sectoral ("party," "governmental," etc.), organizational (departmental, ministerial, etc.), or geographic (province, region, republic) interests; (f) promotion of interests associated with one's past career experiences; [and] (g) promotion of interests arising from one's membership in various age, social background, ethnic, and educational categories.[9]

The basis of the Solovyov and Klepikova thesis concerning Andropov's personal political strategy is the existence of such patron–client relationships with key individuals at lower levels of the Soviet socio-political administrative hierarchy. Three individuals above all others seem to have been critical in the development during the 1970s of anti-corruption forces sympathetic to Andropov's professional and personal political strategy: Eduard Shevardnadze, Mikhail Gorbachev, and Geidar Aliev. To varying degrees, each can be considered to have been part of the same *seilschaft* chain of ambitious party and state officials that was headed by Yuri Andropov. The political career of each was tied to some extent to that of Andropov and at the root of this relationship was the *seilschaft* dynamic of anti-corruption.

The career of Eduard Shevardnadze, one of the most important Soviet and post-Soviet national figures of the past ten years, provides ample evidence of the impact anti-corruption can have on an individual's rise to political prominence. Whatever the real mix of motives for engaging in anti-corruption efforts, the fact of the matter is that in the final years of the Soviet period, significant reputations were built through rigorous and successful campaigns against corruption, abuse of office, speculation, and the like. In many ways, the path of Shevardnadze's rise from obscure Komsomol positions in his native Georgia to national prominence as Gorbachev's minister of Foreign Affairs and, later, the president of an independent Georgia, was paved by his successes as an anti-corruption policeman.

Eduard Amvrosievich Shevardnadze was born on January 25, 1928, in the small town of Mamati, Georgia. His father Amvrosi was a teacher. The young Shevardnadze was heavily involved in local Komsomol organizations, and by his eighteenth birthday was serving as an instructor in one of the departments of the *raion* Komsomol organization. Eduard's older brother Ippokrat had already embarked on what in itself would be a successful political career (he eventually rose to the position of chairman of the Georgian Republic's State Committee for Vocational and Technical Education before his death in 1978), and Eduard seemed early on to be destined for the same type of promising career.

While studying at the Georgian Central Committee's Higher Party School in Tbilisi, from which he graduated in 1951, he continued his rise through the Georgian Komsomol organization. Like his future patron Mikhail Gorbachev, Shevardnadze spent the whole first phase of his career in the Komsomol, eventually heading the entire Georgian youth league (1957–1961). Simultaneously, Gorbachev was the head of the Stavropol' Krai Komsomol organization, and the two became acquainted with each other at this time. Finally, at the age of thirty-three Shevardnadze made the logical and predictable switch out of the Komsomol to the party organization, becoming a Georgian *raion* party committee first secretary.

For our present purposes, though, his transfer out of the party apparatus after only three years is the most telling and significant change in his career. In 1964, Shevardnadze was named to the post of first deputy minister for the Maintenance of Public Order for the Georgian Republic. In the next year, he was promoted again, to become the Georgian Republic Minister for the Maintenance of Public Order. In 1968, the name of this ministry was changed throughout the Soviet Union to the Ministry of Internal Affairs. Shevardnadze remained the highest ranking police official in Georgia, a republic notorious throughout the USSR for its level of graft, corruption, and bribery, until the fateful year of 1972. In that year, the man whose political career he had had a hand in destroying, the corrupt Georgian Communist Party first secretary Vasilii Mzhavanadze, was forced to resign from his position of Georgian party boss. Shevardnadze was named as his replacement.

The details of the attack on Mzhavanadze are somewhat confusing and entail some rather bizarre plot twists. At the time of his forced retirement from political life in September 1972, Vasilii Pavlovich Mzhavanadze had been first secretary of the Georgian Communist Party for almost twenty years. That Mzhavanadze was a skillful politician is surely evidenced by the fact that having been named to his post in 1953 (the year of Stalin's death), he had survived the harebrained personnel whirlwind of Nikita Khrushchev and had lasted well into Brezhnev period—all this in a republic that was notorious for crime, corruption, and graft. One of Mzhavanadze's major political liabilities, it turns out, was his wife Viktoria. A very strong-willed woman, her proclivity for living a grandiose life-style compelled her to develop solid working relationships with some of Georgia's most notorious mafiosi. She dabbled in the black market, wore opulent jewelry, and entertained the rich and famous of Tbilisi society in lavish soirees. Her presence cast such a wake through Georgian society that the period of Mzhavanadze's rule was referred to as "the Victorian Era." For Shevardnadze, the ambitious fighter of high-level corruption with a well-positioned protector as the head of the all-union KGB, Viktoria represented what was worst about the Soviet "new class."

The story has been told that at a dinner party held by the first secretary, Shevardnadze spied on the hand of Viktoria Mzhavanadze an eight-carat diamond ring being sought by Interpol, the ring having been stolen some years earlier in Western Europe. Shevardnadze found out that the ring had been given to the "first lady" of Georgia by one of her admirers, the black marketeer Otari Lazishvili. This damning evidence was sent by Shevardnadze, along with other details of corruption by the Mzhavanadzes, to Andropov in Moscow. When the Georgian newspaper *Zarya Vostoka* (Dawn of the East) published in 1972 an exposé revealing the presence in the Georgian Black Sea resort city of Sukhumi of an underground firearms factory, Andropov and Shevardnadze had all the evidence they needed. Andropov allegedly convinced Brezhnev that Mzhavanadze had to go and suggested his own protégé, Eduard Shevardnadze, as his replacement as Georgian party boss. At forty-four Shevardnadze became the youngest sitting republic party first secretary in the Soviet Union.

Notice of Mzhavanadze's dismissal appeared in *Zarya Vostoka* on September 30, 1972. Citing a plenary session of the Georgian Communist Party Central Committee held the day before, the announcement read:

> The plenary session of the Georgian Communist Party Central Committee complied with the request of Comrade V. P. Mzhavanadze that he be retired on pension in view of his age and in this connection relieved him of his duties as first secretary and member of the Bureau of the Georgian Communist Party Central Committee.

Despite this innocuous wording, the nature of the dismissal was clear. Mzhavanadze was at the time a candidate member of the CC CPSU Politburo; he also was removed from this key post.

While this point may seem to be the end of the story, such was not the case. Andropov was seemingly not satisfied with the camouflaged firing of Mzhavanadze. He wished to pursue the matter and arrest Viktoria, and he compelled Shevardnadze to continue with the case. Some rather bizarre developments then took place. Shevardnadze, supported by Andropov, brought Viktoria Mzhavanadze in for questioning by the police authorities. So frightened by the tone of the questions about the diamond ring, the former first lady immediately flew off to the Ukraine to commiserate with her sister, who just so happened to be the wife of Petr Shelest, the recently deposed party boss of the Ukraine who had lost his post in May 1972 over disagreements with Brezhnev. Both women were close friends of Leonid Brezhnev's wife, also named Viktoria. Shevardnadze pressed for the right to extradite Viktoria Mzhavanadze from Kiev, where she was now living permanently with her sister and famous brother-in-law, back to Tbilisi for criminal proceedings. Brezhnev himself adamantly refused to allow it. As Solovyov and Klepikova describe this odd set of occurrences: "In these events one can hear the echoes of a Shakespearian drama: two sisters, the wives of overthrown rulers of republics, pursued by an implacable fate in the person of the man heading up the union-wide secret police."[10] Otari Lazishvili, well protected under the rule of Mzhavanadze, was spooked by the turn of events under Shevardnadze. He ran for protection to the Moscow office of Roman Rudenko, the USSR procurator general and former Soviet chief prosecutor at the Nuremberg war trials. Andropov allegedly had Lazishvili arrested right in Rudenko's outer office.

As has been chronicled above, some observers have placed Shevardnadze at the center of a plan inspired by Yuri Andropov to use the anti-corruption successes associated with the police and KGB role to bolster the latter's position within the central political leadership structure. As Solovyov and Klepikova interpret Shevardnadze's anti-corruption strategy in Georgia, it was part of Andropov's overall "Caucasian strategy," which also involved Shevardnadze's corollary in Azerbaidzhan, Geidar Aliev, in a growing challenge to Brezhnev and his supporters. It is rather difficult to assess the validity of such claims one way or the other, but it is rather interesting in this connection to note that despite the fact that Shevardnadze was named in 1972 to be the head of the entire Georgian party apparatus, thus making him one of a small group of fourteen republic party bosses, and despite the fact that he replaced Mzhavanadze, a man who at that time was a candidate member of the ruling Soviet Politburo, Shevardnadze was not even promoted to membership in the CPSU Central Committee until 1976, four years later. On first glance, this incongruity certainly seems to fit into the Solovyov and Klepikova version of events if one sees this snub of Shevardnadze with respect to the Central Committee as a sign of Brezhnev's displeasure over role of the former in the fate of his close friend Mzhavanadze. By way of comparison, Mikhail Gorbachev was elevated to the Central Committee in April 1971, at the first plenary session of the Central Committee following his promotion to first secretary of the Stavropol' *kraikom.*

On the other hand, however, things are not so clear. The historical record indicates that not a single person was added to the ranks of the Central Committee at any time between the Twenty-fourth Party Congress that convened in March–April 1971 and the Twenty-fifth Party Congress of February–March 1976, when Shevardnadze was voted into the Central Committee; the "snub" may not have been a snub at all. In any event, Shevardnadze was elevated further in 1978 to a non-voting candidate's seat on the ruling Politburo. At this same time, Gorbachev was promoted from his post in Stavropol' to the Secretariat in Moscow. The following year, Gorbachev would join Shevardnadze as a candidate member of the Politburo.

A second individual allegedly involved in Andropov's "Caucasian strategy" was Geidar Aliev, during the last dozen years of the Brezhnev regime the first secretary of the Azerbaidzhan republic party organization. Aliev was born into a relatively poor blue-collar family on May 10, 1923, in Nakhichevan, a decidedly rural region in Azerbaidzhan. His early youth period was not outstanding, and he trained for a career in teaching. After graduating from a pedagogical technicum in his hometown in 1939, Aliev continued his studies at the M. Azizbekov Industrial Institute of Azerbaidzhan in Baku, the republic capital some 536 kilometers from Nakhichevan. Upon his graduation in 1941, Aliev was immediately recruited into the local NKVD apparatus (NKVD was the Soviet acronym for People's Commissariat of Internal Affairs, later changed to the Ministry of Internal Affairs, or MVD). He would spend the next twenty-six years in the Azerbaidzhan police and state security (KGB) organizations, making a name for himself in combating corruption and graft in another notorious section of the country. One of Andropov's first appointments upon his elevation to the chairmanship of the USSR Committee for State Security (KGB) in 1967 was to name Aliev his chief lieutenant in Azerbaidzhan. Aliev replaced Semen Tsvigun, who headed the organization between 1963 and 1967, and stayed in this post until 1969 when, like Shevardnadze a few years later, the successful anti-corruption efforts in the republic would jettison him to the top party post of republic party first secretary. Interestingly, Tsvigun, Aliev's boss at the Azerbaidzhan KGB until 1967, was Leonid Brezhnev's brother-in-law, being married to Vera Petrovna, the younger sister of Brezhnev's wife Viktoria Petrovna. In

1967, Tsvigun was promoted by Brezhnev to the second-in-command position at the all-union KGB, all the better to keep a close eye on his new KGB chairman Andropov. His role as Brezhnev's "eyes and ears" in the KGB was, as might be expected, a rather delicate assignment; as shall be discussed later in this chapter, Tsvigun met a rather unfortunate fate once his brother-in-law and benefactor left the scene.

Unlike Shevardnadze, in whose case the patronage lines are not so definitively drawn, Aliev was clearly an Andropov man. In addition to Aliev being one of Andropov's first appointments upon the latter's taking control of the all-union KGB leadership, a similarly close parallel occurred in late 1982. Immediately upon being selected to the top Soviet leadership position in November 1982, Andropov brought his protégé Geidar Aliev to Moscow, to the post of first deputy chairman of the USSR Council of Ministers. Concomitant with this promotion, Andropov moved Aliev into a full voting seat on the Politburo as well. The timing of the promotions and the men's past close relationship suggested at the time that Andropov had chosen Aliev as his man to succeed the sitting Soviet premier, the seventy-seven-year-old Nikolai Tikhonov. Aliev never achieved this critical post in the Soviet leadership hierarchy, but it seems a fair bet to assume that if Andropov's poor health had not cut short his life so soon after he became party general secretary, Geidar Aliev would indeed have become the Soviet head of government.

Aliev served as party boss of Azerbaidzhan between 1969 and 1982, or for slightly over half of the total time period examined in the present study. During his reign as republic first secretary, 135 out of the total 142 convictions (95 percent) of Azerbaidzhani officials chronicled in the Soviet press took place. In his final six years in office in Baku, during a time when Andropov was waging an anti-corruption campaign that aimed to elevate that status of the KGB and the Andropov patronage network, and during a time when Brezhnev's health and political position were both in decline, Aliev too turned up the heat at home. Between 1977 and 1982, the year Andropov rewarded Aliev with promotion to Moscow, the former head of the Azerbaidzhan KGB initiated anti-corruption charges that resulted in 93 of the 135 cases (69 percent) of the publicized convictions referred to above. Aliev's effort in the Caucasus was well-coordinated with Andropov's higher-profile effort at the national level. The two worked in tandem, promoting their factional and personal interests. One Soviet observer remarks that "it was a real battle against real corruption. . . . Targets of Aliev's attack on corruption were without doubt members of a mafia—the mafia which had operated under the sphere of influence of the previous regime."[11] The useful side benefit of such a campaign, of course, was personal: Aliev's reputation as a fighter of official corruption garnered him the nickname "Hammer of the Mafia."

Arkady Vaksberg, in his exposé of the "Soviet mafia," focused a considerable amount of attention on Aliev's role in both Azerbaidzhani and national political developments. He argues that Aliev, not unlike a number of new political bosses, used the cadres weapon to consolidate his own personal position of power in Azerbaidzhan. In his words, "having seized and consolidated his power as top dog in the republic, Aliev began weeding the ranks in an effort to get rid of those who had been put in positions of power by his predecessors and to replace them throughout with his own men."[12] Aliev's own republic machine required that several powerful people be disposed of politically. Primary among these displaced persons was Gamboi Mamedov, the Azerbaidzhan chief prosecutor who had been on unfriendly terms with Aliev for a number of years. In the usual—if not institutionalized— pattern, false charges of corruption (in this case, accepting bribes and stealing socialist property) were leveled against a political opponent for decidedly political purposes. Such a motive for the charges is clear by the chain of events that followed:

> Mamedov was expelled from the party and a criminal charge was brought against him. It was the usual pattern: a campaigner against the mafia is revealed himself to be a mafioso—a bribe-taker and a thief. "Witnesses" against him were being got ready. Unlike Averbukh [another unfortunate undesirable], he didn't shelter in hideaway flats but took up residence with his sister in Leningrad. Probably they could have located him if they had really wanted to. But Aliev did not institute a search. There was an unspoken agreement which suited him better. "If you keep quiet, you'll be left in peace. If you don't, do not blame me for the consequences." By this time Aliev feared no one and nothing. And Mamedov knew this and kept quiet. Moreover, he came himself from a nomenklatura background and was perfectly aware of the rules of the game.[13]

In a system characterized by elite life-styles that very often entail petty and not-so-petty violations of the law, the usefulness of anti-corruption as a mechanism to control political opponents or, as in the case described above, to run them off the local scene, accrues only to those who can bring the necessary power to bear on a situation. Aliev's local machine and his Moscow benefactor Andropov provided him with just such power.

Chapter 3 chronicled the fact that over the 1965–1990 period Azerbaidzhan had the highest number of convictions of Soviet officials outside of the much larger Russian Republic. Controlling for population, Azerbaidzhan's official corruption "saturation rate" was by far the highest in the entire Soviet Union, roughly eight times that of Russia, thirteen times that of the Ukraine, and even 50 percent greater than the level of official corruption in Georgia, which itself is notorious for graft and corruption. Aliev was at the center of this anti-corruption effort, and in so doing he was involved in promoting his personal, institutional, and *seilschaft* interests. As has been described above, the major actors of this patronage chain were Andropov, Shevardnadze, Aliev, and Gorbachev, the individual prospects of the latter three men inexorably linked to those of Andropov. The prospects of the KGB seemed to brighten in the late 1970s and early 1980s, along, of course, with those tied to its success.

Law and Order and the Rise of the KGB

One of the major elements of patronage politics in the Soviet Union, as in any society, was the promotion of one's own institutional bases. If the descriptions of the Soviet Union as a "bureaucracy writ large" are at all accurate, then it should not be surprising that the interest politics of the Soviet Union revolved around a competition between and among institutions of "the state" (i.e., party, state, and government organs in the USSR). It is quite obvious from a "systems" theory perspective that politics in Soviet-type societies was dominated not by "inputs" from the social environment (the development of such private interests was discouraged, oftentimes through the use of physical coercion), but by what Gabriel Almond and G. Bingham Powell called "withinputs": competing and often times mutually exclusive "demands" and "supports" from within the state apparatus itself.[14] Almond and Powell were quite vague about the nature of any such interest articulation by the state itself; in fact, they and other input-oriented systems theorists "black boxed" the state, seeing it as a passive cash register or scale that accounted for the balance of group power located outside the state.

Others, though, have focused explicit attention on the autonomy of the state (defined as the individuals who make up the key offices of public life) as an independent actor in the process of influencing public policy. In studying Western democratic systems, scholars such as Eric Nordlinger and Theda Skocpol have in recent years sought to "bring the state back in," as it were, feeling that its autonomous influence in politics has been neglected.[15] Of course, no such neglect of the state and its various institutions as the main organized actors in politics has been in evidence among those who study the communist or post-communist world. In fact, quite the opposite has, in all likelihood, been the case. The "bureaucratic politics model" introduced by, among others, Graham T. Allison in his study of United States foreign policy decision-making during the Cuban missile crisis,[16] was hardly a shocking revelation to Kremlinologists very used to viewing high politics in the Soviet Union from such a perspective. The ideas of the promotion of institutional interests and political infighting through the use of institutional weapons have been at the root of mainstream conceptions of Soviet politics for many decades.

For Yuri Andropov and his protégés in the Soviet republics, participating in patronage or clientelistic politics in the mid-to-late 1970s entailed, inter alia, the use of anti-corruption campaigns that served a number of purposes:

1. solving short-term and small-scale political problems in the locales (e.g., getting rid of local enemies or challengers for power);
2. building personal patronage networks at the local levels (for each middle-level protégé served as some other group's patron) by freeing up important posts to be filled by one's supporters;
3. building up the authority and power of one's institutional base through a series of political successes (e.g., expanding the KGB's reputation as a political force to be reckoned after the years of relative disgrace associated with the purges and de-Stalinization);
4. weakening the perceived power of one's chief rivals at the top of the political pyramid by successfully destroying any number of the "chains" in a rival *seilschaften*.

Each of these elements of patronage politics was in evidence as part of the modus operandi of the Andropov–KGB network during the final half-decade of the Brezhnev leadership.

Institutionally, Andropov was successful in bettering his own personal prospects for succeeding Leonid Brezhnev by making law and order (and therefore the KGB and police organs) a critical component of domestic politics during the late 1970s and early 1980s. There are several signs that point to this strategy and its relative success.

First, in July 1978 the KGB itself was elevated in stature to a full-fledged state committee. On July 5, 1978, Leonid Brezhnev in his capacity as chairman of the Presidium of the USSR Supreme Soviet signed into force the "Law of the Union of Soviet Socialist Republics on the USSR Council of Ministers."[17] Article 26 of the law listed the USSR State Security Committee as among the USSR Union–Republic State Committees.

For Peter Reddaway, though, the year 1979 is critical in the upgrading of the political power of the KGB.[18] In August of that year, Andropov succeeded in raising the political stakes connected with a renewed push for law and order. On August 11, *Pravda* announced on its front page a CPSU Central Committee resolution with the title "On Improving Work to Safeguard Law and Order and Intensifying the Struggle against Law Violation."[19] The resolution highlighted five main areas of renewed emphasis in the law and order campaign: (1) public order, (2) drunkenness and alcoholism, (3) juvenile delinquency, (4) "mismanagement, wastefulness, report padding, and hoodwinking," and (5) parasitism and speculation. The fourth concern, of course, had an ominous ring to it in that it pointed clearly to Andropov's intention to scrutinize official behavior much more seriously than had previously been the case. The law and order drive was kicked off at the end of the same month by the awarding to Andropov of a medal, this time the Order of the October Revolution.[20]

That this focus on official behavior was at the root of Andropov's law and order drive was pounded home soon thereafter when *Izvestiia* published an interesting article by Vladimir I. Terebilov, the USSR minister of justice. In the article, Terebilov mentioned the Central Committee resolution and inserted the following ominous warning at the close of his remarks:

> In this connection, I would also like to say that the courts cannot and should not ignore the improper behavior of officials who in one way or

another fail to prevent criminal offenses. *No matter what posts these officials hold*, they should bear strict responsibility.[21]

The number of publicized convictions of Soviet officials initiated during the remaining years of Andropov's life went up dramatically. In the four years after the 1979 Central Committee resolution, our survey of the Soviet press captured 249 such official convictions; the previous four-year period reveals only 165. The Russian Republic was especially hard hit; the comparable numbers are 62 in the four years prior to the 1979 resolution, 129 in the four years after.

Such a law and order program, with its emphasis on official behavior, surely was threatening to Brezhnev and his followers. As Brezhnev became more feeble, Andropov's efforts took on a decidedly upperclass accent. The question remains, though: why would Brezhnev countenance such a program from Andropov? Reddaway again provides some interesting insights into the dynamic that energized Soviet high politics at that time:

> An important, perhaps central part of the picture is the fact that, at least from 1978 onwards, Brezhnev's health showed clear signs of decline. The logic of Kremlin politics demanded at this point that his colleagues should lessen their loyalty to him and start discreetly maneuvering for new alignments, each building up his strength through informal alliances and the tentative pushing of new policies, so as to be in a good position to strike, should Brezhnev either stumble politically or fail seriously in health. . . . Thus to maneuver for policies aimed at ending dissent and emigration, attacking corruption, and restoring law and order through tough leadership—this, too, was both to pursue policies acceptable to most colleagues, and also to undermine Brezhnev (even, again, if he tried to "take over" the policies himself and thus head off consequences dangerous to himself). These general points may help us to understand why a politically weakened Brezhnev went along with the law-and-order and anti-corruption campaigns, the drive against dissent and emigration, the steady raising of the prestige of the KGB, and the invasion of Afghanistan, all of which policies (except one) date from the second half of the pivotal year of 1979.[22]

As Reddaway mentions above, Brezhnev attempted to head off Andropov's anti-corruption drive, to co-opt it, so as to avoid being caught up in it himself. In his report to the Twenty-sixth Party Congress in February 1981, for example, Brezhnev attempted to show that he was indeed supportive of a campaign that he must have in reality viewed with a good deal of ambivalence. He praised the KGB as follows:

> The acuteness of the class struggle in the international arena is making high demands on the activity of the state security agencies and on the Party tempering, knowledge and work style of our Chekists. The USSR State Security Committee works efficiently, on a high professional level, and adheres strictly to the provisions of the Constitution and the norms of Soviet legislation. The Chekists keep a sharp and vigilant eye on the intrigues of the imperialist intelligence services. They resolutely curb the activities of those who take the path of antistate, hostile actions, who encroach on the rights of Soviet people and on the interests of Soviet society. Their work merits the deep gratitude of the Party and our entire people.[23]

This Congress also saw an increase in the number of KGB officials among the full members of the Central Committee. Whereas the Twenty-fifth Party Congress of 1976 had elected but a single "Chekist" (Yuri Andropov) to full membership in the Central Committee, in 1981 this number grew to four full members: KGB Chairman Andropov (elected to full membership in 1961), Deputy Chairman Viktor Chebrikov (up from his candidate membership achieved in 1971), Deputy Chairman Georgii Tsinev (up from candidate status achieved in 1976), and First Deputy Chairman Semen Tsvigun (up from candidate membership achieved in 1971).[24] While Brezhnev's comments at the Party Congress provoked "prolonged applause," later developments would show that as he weakened further—both physically and politically—he was unable to protect even his closest friends and family members from the politicized anti-corruption campaign of Andropov and his followers.

The Decline of Brezhnev and the Politics of Succession

Attacks on Brezhnevites

As the anti-corruption campaign initiated in 1979 developed momentum, the leading figures of the Brezhnev leadership grew politically and physically more frail. The combination of these two trends produced a number of thinly disguised challenges to Brezhnev, his immediate family, and his political allies. One such veiled threat to Brezhnev appeared even in the official organ of the CPSU Central Committee, *Pravda*. In a November 1981 article titled "Our Criteria of Morality," the author Feliks Kuznetsov sent what one could call a direct message to Brezhnev and those close to him that enjoyed the pleasures of the high *nomenklatura:*

> When we sometimes encounter aggressive, shameless challenges from latter-day nouveaux riches—for example, when we contemplate stone dachas, zhigulis, volgas, diamonds and furs in the possession of people whose earnings could never provide for the acquisition of such luxury items—why shouldn't we, Soviet socialist society and its law-enforcement and oversight agencies, ask these citizens just what their sources of income are? . . . The problem has to do with moral as well as material losses, and, as is known, these moral losses are inestimable. The consumerist, parasitic psychology that manifests itself in various forms of money-grubbing that are contrary to the norms and laws of socialist development is precisely what continues even today to form a philistine, petit bourgeois ideology and morality. It asserts its own trivial life-style, which has its own cynically materialistic slant and its own system of views, beliefs and human goals and objectives.[25]

The innuendo of this article was made much more clear the following month in *Aurora,* a Leningrad literary magazine. The December 1981 issue was dedicated to Brezhnev's seventy-fifth birthday, but the tribute ended there. The magazine printed a satirical story about a very old writer who was, the story said, "living and does not plan to die." In the Soviet Union, the connection was clear. What is more, the very fact that such a thing could be written in the controlled press spoke volumes to Brezhnev's declining ability to inspire respect and fear among those close to the top of the Soviet *nomenklatura.*[26]

The death of Brezhnev's patron and protector Mikhail Suslov, nine weeks later on December 25, 1982, opened the door for more intrigue. Suslov, a major beneficiary of Khrushchev's ouster (which he helped engineer) in October 1964, had always preferred to be a king-maker rather than a king. As Michel Tatu tells it, Suslov turned down the top slot and put forward Brezhnev as the general secretary.[27] With Suslov out of the Kremlin, the level of anti-Brezhnev activity picked up. It is no coincidence that one of the first major arrests that tied Brezhnev and his family directly to high-level corruption occurred on the very day of Suslov's funeral.

Trade Union Leader Shibaev Is Ousted

One Brezhnevite who was to suffer in Andropov's anti-corruption campaign was Aleksei Ivanovich Shibaev. Shibaev was born into a peasant household on February 21, 1915, in the Russian town of Maslovka, located in what later became Gorkii *oblast*. By the age of fifteen, Shibaev was working as a draftsman and attending factory apprenticeship school, preparing for a career as a red engineer. Ten years later, in 1940, he graduated with a degree in design engineering from Gorkii University's Faculty of Physics and Mathematics. As was common in those days, his graduation from university with a scientific degree made Shibaev a good candidate for recruitment into the Communist Party. Upon graduation, he was admitted to membership. For the next decade-and-a-half, Shibaev worked as a design engineer and director at an aviation plant in Rostov and Saratov. His career took a sudden turn in 1955.

At the age of forty, Shibaev was selected for a position in the Saratov regional party organization. Surprisingly, his first posting was to the delicate job of *obkom* second secretary, in most cases responsible for personnel selection within the *nomenklatura* of the region. He was soon elevated to the post of *obkom* first secretary in Saratov, in which capacity he served between 1959 and 1963. In the latter year, Khrushchev instituted one of his so-called "harebrained" organizational schemes: bifurcating the regional party organs into separate industrial and agricultural organs. Given his background, Shibaev was named head of the industrial side of party affairs in Saratov. This split regional party structure was soon reversed, however; one of the first measures taken by the new Brezhnev–Kosygin team in 1964 was the reunification of the regional party apparatus under a single party first secretary. Shibaev was back in charge of all party affairs in the region, a post he was to hold for twelve more years.

At the first post-Khrushchev Party Congress held in Moscow during March–April 1966, Shibaev headed the delegation from Saratov *oblast* and extended strong support to the Brezhnev leadership. After a delay of almost eighteen months, during which time the post vacated by Aleksander Shelepin remained vacant, Brezhnev appointed Shibaev in

1976 to the post of chairman of the All-Union Central Council of Trade Unions (AUCCTU). Shibaev had absolutely no trade union experience and some have speculated that he represented a compromise candidate between competing interests in the Politburo; in all likelihood, he was not Brezhnev's first choice for the job. Solovyev and Klepikova, two Soviet journalists closely in tune with the high-level political events of that time, have identified Shibaev as a protégé of Suslov.[28] In any event, in his capacity at AUCCTU chairman, Shibaev supported the Brezhnev policy and was by all accounts a loyal bureaucrat who followed orders from his superiors. That he was in favor with Brezhnev, Suslov, and the others in the general secretary's camp is shown by the fact that Shibaev, as was the case with many top national figures of the late Brezhnev period, was adorned with various state medals and orders, among them four Orders of Lenin, the Hero of Socialist Labor, and a Gold Medal Sickle and Hammer.

With the intimidating figure of Mikhail Suslov gone from the leadership in early 1982, and with Brezhnev's health failing, Shibaev was targeted in Andropov's political campaign of anti-corruption. In the immediate week after the death of Suslov, Shibaev was arrested. According to Dusko Doder, the *Washington Post* Moscow correspondent at that time, Shibaev was implicated in a number of illegal activities, including the illegal building of a private *dacha* and participation in sex orgies. He was accused, though, of corrupt practices at the AUCCTU and the mismanagement of union funds.[29] The announcement in *Pravda* of Shibaev's ouster was typically vague; on March 6, 1982, it was announced that "In connection with his transfer to other work, the plenary session [of the AUCCTU] relieved A.I. Shibaev of his duties as Chairman of the All-Union Central Council of Trade Unions."

The key to understanding the motive of the Andropov faction in attacking Shibaev, who by all accounts was a non-factor in the power distribution of the day and, as such, was probably not worth the effort, may lie not so much in Shibaev himself, but in information he may have been able to provide on other members of the elite. According to Doder, during interrogation and later in his trial testimony, Shibaev implicated Sergei Medunov, the corrupt first secretary of the Krasnodar *kraikom,* a close political ally of Leonid Brezhnev, and the focus of a great deal of scorn by a political upstart from a neighboring region—Mikhail Gorbachev.

The Attack against the Party Boss of Krasnodar Krai

Sergei Fedorovich Medunov was born on October 4, 1915, of Russian parents, but little else is known about his early childhood years. He graduated in 1931 from the Kizlyar Agro-Pedagogical Technicum, located in the Dagestan Autonomous Republic within the Russian Federation, and commenced a career as a teacher. World War II saw Medunov enter the Red Army, where he served between 1939 and 1947. In 1942, while in the Red Army, Medunov was admitted into membership in the Communist Party. He was twenty-six years of age.

Immediately after his discharge from military service, Medunov embarked upon a career as a Communist Party *apparatchik,* working first in *raion* party organizations. Within four years, he was named a department head in the Crimean *oblast* Communist Party Committee, but was quickly promoted to become first secretary of the Communist Party Committee of the city of Yalta, where the famous wartime Big Three summit took place between Stalin, Churchill, and Roosevelt. He held this post until 1958. Like many rising party officials, Medunov's career often tacked back and forth between party and state jobs. This purposeful aspect of the Soviet cadres policy aimed at producing a corps of "generalist" officials who had a wide breadth of administrative experience. In 1958, then, Medunov was transferred over to the state apparatus, becoming the second-ranking state official in his previous region, the Crimea. He held the post of first deputy chairman of the Executive Committee of the Crimea *oblast* Soviet. His stint as a ranking *oblispolkom* official, though, was short-lived as in 1959 Medunov was transferred back to the party apparatus, this time in the Krasnodar Territory *(krai),* as the first secretary of the Sochi City Party Committee *(gorkom).* Sochi is famous in Russia as a splendid resort town on the Black Sea; under Medunov, it would become infamous for a very high level of corruption and crime.

Medunov was placed in his post in Sochi while Khrushchev was *primus inter pares* in Moscow. Later, some five years after Khrushchev's ignominious fall from power, Medunov was moved back to the state apparatus again. It is worth noting that in most instances in Soviet political history, a change in the national leadership as happened in 1964 usually carries with it a ripple effect throughout the locales; new general secretaries in Moscow have relied on the so-called "cadres weapon" to build personal followings among the lower-level party and state *apparatchiki*. However, the five-year lapse between the rise of the Brezhnev–Kosygin team in the Moscow Kremlin and Medunov's elevation should not be considered anomalous. As was described in the previous chapter, Brezhnev implemented a very conservative personnel policy, called "Trust in Cadres," that was at the cornerstone of his tacit agreement with the Soviet power structure. Also, any general secretary embarking on a conservative cadres replenishment would in any case take some time to focus attention on the first secretary of a city party organization of rather low importance in the overall scheme of things. Medunov had had at that time no real connection with the powerful men of the Kremlin, so "coattails" were not really in evidence.

Medunov's next position certainly was a promotion, however. In 1969 he was named chairman of the Executive Committee of the Krasnodar Krai Soviet, in Soviet parlance, chairman of the Krasnodar *kraiispolkom*, making him the highest ranking state official in this territory of 83,600 square kilometers and, in the late 1960s, slightly over 4 million inhabitants. In Krasnodar's neighboring region, Stavropol', another regional figure was at this same time forging his own impressive career: in 1970, Mikhail Gorbachev was named first secretary of the Stavropol' Krai Party Committee *(kraikom)*. Three years later, Medunov himself was promoted again, to the parallel party boss post in Krasnodar. Throughout the remainder of the 1970s, Gorbachev and Medunov, as neighboring "prefects," developed what can only be called an antagonistic and competitive relationship. The first steps in the chain of events that led to Medunov's eventual political demise in 1982, in fact, can be traced to the person of Mikhail Gorbachev.

During Medunov's reign as Krasnodar party boss, he willfully supported the policies of Brezhnev, especially the latter's agricultural line. Both Krasnodar and Gorbachev's Stavropol' are primarily agricultural regions, and Medunov's support for Brezhnev's rural policies was well rewarded by the general secretary. The basis of Medunov's poor relations with his neighbor Gorbachev was the latter's resentment at the overt corruption, extravagant life-style, and arrogance evidenced by Medunov. During Medunov's period in Krasnodar, the general level of illicit and criminal activity in the territory became quite elevated. As Solovyov and Klepikova put it,

In the Krasnodar Territory, and especially in the famous resort city of Sochi, graft and other kinds of corruption in Party and government organizations had attained an almost official status. One had to pay a bribe in order to buy a car, get an apartment, a promotion, or even a hotel room. There wasn't a single system that would function without bribery.[30]

Despite the reputation of the city and the territory as a whole, very little energy on the part of Medunov and the region's leadership was put into the process of addressing the problem. Medunov's neighbor Gorbachev, though, was intent on bringing these acts of official misconduct to the attention of the central leadership. Solovyov and Klepikova describe how Yuri Andropov would vacation in Stavropol, where he would be met by Gorbachev.

On the way from the airport to the resort, Gorbachev would complain to his influential friend about his neighbor and counterpart, Medunov, with whom he was competing in terms of all indexes, economic and cultural. . . . Gorbachev had gradually put together a thick dossier on Medunov; and after completing his regular course of treatment at Krasnye Kamni [the elite party sanatorium near Kislovodsk], Andropov tried to exploit it.[31]

The program to get rid of Sergei Medunov was initiated by Andropov for a number of reasons, not the least of which was the opportunity it provided to weaken Brezhnev, Medunov's patron. As many have pointed out, the anti-corruption campaign initiated by Andropov and the KGB in the late 1970s was inextricably tied to the KGB chief's simultaneous effort to challenge Brezhnev and thus to maneuver himself into prime position for the upcoming leadership succession. Based on the dossier on Medunov and the corruption in Krasnodar compiled by Gorbachev, Andropov initiated in 1978 an anti-corruption campaign in the territory aimed at crippling one of Brezhnev's clients and, at the same time, revealing Brezhnev's lack of ability to protect his friends. The logical starting place was Sochi.

In 1978, four individuals associated with the city housing authority were arrested and charged with embezzlement and bribery in their administration of housing in Sochi. As reported in the national labor publication *Trud*, the four arrested were involved in embezzling funds through submitting false repair bills and the hiring of non-existent ghost workers.[32] B.M. Dudnikov, director of the Polar Fisherman Resort Hotel, V.N. Magalentsev, an engineer at the hotel, L. Batalov, allegedly a carpenter attached to the local construction administration, and B.K. Cherkezia, the local construction administration's chairman, were convicted and sentenced to 15, 12, 15, and 10 years' deprivation of freedom, respectively, as well as the confiscation of their property. The prosecutor's office estimated the amount of the embezzlement to be 80,864 rubles.

The stakes were ratcheted upwards as the "mayor" of Sochi was soon thereafter implicated in a separate charge of official corruption. Viacheslav Aleksandrovich Voronkov, the chairman of the Sochi *gorispolkom*, was charged in 1980 by the local prosecutor (on secret orders from Andropov) with accepting bribes of 3,000 rubles on each apartment rented. In the short run, though, Andropov's strategy backfired; the city prosecutor, not the mayor, was removed from office, expelled from the Communist Party, and placed under house arrest. Andropov's response, to leak the news of Voronkov's deceit to both Soviet and Western news sources, thus violating one of the sacred tenets of the leadership—to avoid washing dirty laundry in public—succeeded in shining a sufficiently bright light on the situation to cause problems. Voronkov was arrested in November and put on trial for bribery and abuse of office. *Literaturnaya Gazeta* reported that the convicted mayor of Sochi had received a sentence of thirteen years deprivation of freedom and the confiscation of his property.[33]

The fact that Andropov had succeeded in getting rid of the Sochi mayor against the wishes of Medunov and Brezhnev did not mean that Brezhnev was without recourse. Brezhnev marshaled all his troops to fight the "get rid of Medunov" movement; the general secretary's wrath came down on Vitalii Vorotnikov, who as a first deputy premier of the Russian Republic had supported Andropov's campaign against Medunov. Vorotnikov was demoted and shipped to one of the worst possible ambassadorial posts: Havana. However, Mikhail Gorbachev had by this time been promoted to Moscow as party secretary for agriculture, and he held a seat on the Politburo. Given his past dealings and attitude regarding Medunov, he served as an ally of Andropov against Brezhnev. Finally, with Gorbachev's support, Andropov prevailed in July 1982.

Pravda reported the following development on July 24, 1982: "The plenary session [of the Krasnodar *kraikom*] released S.F. Medunov from his duties as first secretary of the Krasnodar Territory Party Committee in connection with his transfer to other work." The fact that Medunov was replaced as the party boss of Krasnodar Krai by the very same Vitalii Vorotnikov reveals just how powerful Andropov had become by the middle of 1982, still a few months short of Brezhnev's death in November of that year. The powerful Brezhnev patron Mikhail Suslov had died earlier in the year, and his death signified open season on attacks on Brezhnev and his family and followers. Within a year, in the immediate aftermath of Brezhnev's death and the elevation of Andropov to the general secretaryship, Vorotnikov was further rewarded for his support in the anti-corruption campaign against Medunov: he was elevated to position of chairman of the Russian Republic Council of Ministers, thus having completed the full circle back to Moscow between 1979 and 1983. As RSFSR premier, Vorotnikov was elevated, after a brief tenure as a candidate member, to full voting status in the Politburo of the Central Committee of the CPSU later in 1983.

The disgrace of Andropov's and Gorbachev's nemesis Sergei Medunov was completed during the same time. In June 1983, *Pravda* reported on its front page the results of a Central Committee plenary session and quoted from its statement: "The Central Committee's plenary session removed N.A. Shchelokov and S.F. Medunov from the CPSU Central Committee for mistakes in their work" (*"za dopushchennye oshibki v rabote"*).[34] At the same time, Vorotnikov was instituting his own anti-corruption effort back in Krasnodar. Both M. Shmatov, the chief of the Gelendzhik office of the OBKhSS (the MVD's anti-corruption department), as well as his senior inspector, R. Mitina, were arrested and charged with extortion of bribes. The two were convicted and sentenced to eleven and eight years, respectively, in an intensive-regime corrective labor camp. Each had his personal property confiscated.[35] In addition, in the same location and probably tied to the above prosecution, B. Borodkina, the manager of the Gelendzhik Restaurant and Cafeteria Trust of the local municipal administration, was arrested and convicted of receiving some 561,834 rubles worth of bribes. Miss Borodkina was executed for her crimes.

The decision of the Central Committee plenum to expel Medunov from the ranks of the political elite has been explained with respect to the politics of corruption and anti-corruption in the Soviet system. This interpretation is further supported by Peter Reddaway, who highlighted the links between localized instances of anti-corruption prosecutions and Andropov's efforts to undermine Brezhnev and his cronies:

> At least one of the roots of the anti-corruption campaign goes back to 1978 or beyond. For it was in September 1978 that Deputy Fishing Industry Minister Rytov was dismissed in disgrace for his key role in what came to be known as 'the fish case' or 'the caviar case.' This enormous scandal, involving several hundred suspects and witnesses, must have been handled from an early stage by Andropov's KGB, both because, as a long-term caviar racket, it involved economic crime on a grand scale, and also because it had international dimensions. It seems likely that Andropov persistently, over several years, pushed the case through to a number of convictions, because he knew that some of the threads led to an associate of Brezhnev's, [Sergei] Medunov, the first party secretary of the Krasnodar Territory.[36]

The fact that the Central Committee, in expelling Sergei Medunov, also expelled Nikolai Shchelokov, the erstwhile USSR minister of Internal Affairs, is no coincidence. His fate, too, was caught up in Andropov's drive to weaken Brezhnev and his "mafia" through the mechanism of anti-corruption.

The Campaign against Shchelokov and the MVD

General Nikolai Anisimovich Shchelokov was born the son of a mine worker on November 26, 1910, in Almaznaya, Ukraine. From the age of sixteen, he, like his father, worked in the local mines. In 1931, at the age of twenty, he was admitted into the Communist Party. It is very likely that Shchelokov first met his future political patron Leonid Brezhnev, the son of a Russian steel worker living in the Ukraine, at about this time. Shchelokov was matriculating at the Dnepropetrovsk Metallurgical Institute in the early 1930s while Brezhnev was the secretary of the party committee at the Dzerzhinsky Metallurgical Institute, and a fitter and chairman of the trade union committee at the Dzerzhinsky Metallurgical Plant in nearby Kamenskoe (after 1936: Dneprodzerzhinsk). Like Shchelokov, Brezhnev also entered the Communist Party in 1931, and both of these later national political figures worked as metallurgical engineers in the Ukraine. These kindred spirits certainly became well acquainted in the late 1930s, as their professional paths crossed in Dnepropetrovsk. In 1938 both men received their first major party assignments. Brezhnev was appointed to a position as department head within the Dnepropetrovsk *oblast* Communist Party apparatus, while Shchelokov was named first secretary of the "Red Guard" (*Krasnogvardeiski*) *raion* party committee located within Dnepropetrovsk *oblast*. From this point on, the careers of Leonid Brezhnev and Nikolai Shchelokov proceeded in tandem.

Between 1939 and 1941, while Brezhnev served as a secretary of the Dnepropetrovsk *Oblast* Party Committee *(obkom)*, Shchelokov chaired the Dnepropetrovsk City Soviet *(gorispolkom)*. During World War II, both engaged in political roles in the Red Army. At the end of the war, they worked closely again: Brezhnev served in 1945–1946 as chief of Political Administration of the Carpathian Military District, while his friend Shchelokov was secretary of the Party Commission of the Carpathian Military District. When Brezhnev was named first secretary of the Moldavian Communist Party in 1950, he called Shchelokov to a key role in the republic as well. In 1951, Shchelokov was named Moldavia's first deputy premier, a position he was to hold through the early to middle 1960s. At this time, Brezhnev and his protégé Shchelokov both sat as full voting members of the Moldavian Communist Party Politburo. The close working relationship between the two men, broken during the Khrushchev period when Brezhnev assumed more national prominence, was reestablished within months of Brezhnev's rise to ultimate power in the Soviet Union.

In 1966, Brezhnev named his friend Shchelokov, a man who had absolutely no experience in police work, to the post of chief policeman of the Soviet Union. Shchelokov's elevation to the position of USSR minister of Internal Affairs in 1966[37] guaranteed Brezhnev a close political ally and friend in this sensitive post. Nikolai Shchelokov packed up his family and belongings and moved from Kishinev to Moscow, where he moved into the same apartment building as his friend Brezhnev. By the time Shchelokov's troubles began in 1982, his career had been tied to the fortunes of Leonid Brezhnev for some fifty years. It may, in that sense, be fitting that the two exited the political scene in the Soviet Union within three weeks of each other.

While political expediency was certainly at the root of the timing of Shchelokov's travails, one should not get the impression that the MVD chief was an innocent pawn in the struggle for power. Shchelokov most certainly used his position as the top police official in the Soviet

Union to enrich his life-style and that of his family. He allegedly procured sixteen Mercedes and Volvo sedans for his extended family, who drove around the bleak Moscow streets as if they were members of the *dvorianstvo*. In addition, the MVD chief had the habit of viewing the fruits of criminal investigations as so much personal booty. He would frequently send his deputies to raid Moscow Custom Office's storeroom of confiscated items for things he or his family wanted. In many ways, Shchelokov's attitude was typical of the selfish arrogance of the Brezhnev-era political elite. As a result, within a month of Brezhnev's death and Andropov's ascension to supreme power, few neutral observers shed a tear when they read in the December 18, 1982, issue of *Pravda* that "the presidium of the USSR Supreme Soviet has relieved Comrade Nikolai Anisimovich Shchelokov of his duties as USSR Minister of Internal Affairs in connection with his transfer to other work." Vitalii Fedorchuk, Andropov's hand-picked successor as KGB chief earlier in the year (in May 1982 Andropov moved out of the KGB post and into the Party Secretariat, poising himself for the imminent succession to Brezhnev's post), was named in the article as the new USSR Minister of Internal Affairs.

The euphemism "in connection with his transfer to other work" meant political disgrace. After being ousted from the MVD, Shchelokov worked in a low-level post in the General Inspectorate of the USSR Ministry of Defense as chief of a police unit at a Siberian gas pipeline construction site.[38] As the investigators prepared a legal case and tightened their grip on Shchelokov and his family's misdeeds, his wife committed suicide in March 1983. Three months later, Shchelokov, along with Sergei Medunov, a second disgraced Brezhnevite, were expelled from the party Central Committee; the wording of the communiqué was, by Soviet standards, revealing. As cited above, the notice explained that the two were expelled for "mistakes in their work."[39] The process of disgrace continued in the following year. In November 1984, Shchelokov was stripped of his military rank by the USSR Supreme Soviet "for abuse of official position and for discrediting the military rank of Soviet general."[40] Rather than face a trial and further public disgrace himself, the seventy-four-year old former head of the Soviet internal police apparatus likewise committed suicide five weeks later, on December 13, 1984.[41] No mention of it was made in the Soviet press.

It is interesting that Brezhnev had kept Andropov (KGB) and

Shchelokov (MVD) as co-equals and close at hand. All three resided in the same apartment building, Andropov living directly above Brezhnev and Shchelokov directly below him. The first thing Andropov accomplished upon achieving the general secretaryship of the Communist Party was to destroy any semblance of their previous co-equal status and to place a political protégé at the head of the Soviet police. As shall be discussed below, the attack on the MVD continued, with the second episode coming after Brezhnev had left the scene.

Attacks on Brezhnev's Family

Even while Brezhnev was still alive and serving as the general secretary of the Communist Party, the anti-corruption campaign used to weaken his power and that of his followers began what must be considered bold approaches close to his immediate family. As one after another of those family members was implicated in the anti-corruption campaign, the impression was created that Brezhnev himself was unable to slow the politically motivated activities centered in the KGB and MVD. Brezhnev's practice of placing family members in critical "watchdog" posts in each of these organizations eventually came back to harm the general secretary when they themselves were targeted for political destruction. The morale of the so-called Brezhnev mafia must have plummeted as those leading figures of Brezhnev's political cohort, despite their powerful posts and kinship to Brezhnev, were chewed up in the anti-corruption campaign that coincided with the end of an era. One can infer that Andropov's purpose in revealing the weakness of the general secretary was to facilitate among the foot soldiers of the Brezhnev network a greater willingness to shift political loyalties away from any Brezhnevite heir presumptive, such as Konstantin Chernenko, and toward the newly emerging network of Yuri Andropov. The history of the 1978–1982 period shows that Andropov was indeed successful in this effort.

It may be tempting when reviewing the events of the 1978–1982 period to conclude that Brezhnev was throughout his career rather naive with respect to the more unsavory aspects of high politics in the Soviet Union. For history of the period reveals a general secretary who, despite his obvious institutional and personal advantages, was unable to protect even members of his immediate family from the anti-corruption campaign of one of his own appointees. The impression of naivete, of course, would be wholly incorrect. Brezhnev's inability at the final stage of his career to fend off Andropov was more closely tied to his own physical problems than to any political naivete.

Such an evaluation of Brezhnev is validated not merely by the fact that he was one of the few individuals of any political stature to emerge from the Stalin period with his life, although this feat should certainly not be underestimated. Specific to the present discussion, Brezhnev was quite aware of the potentialities of Kremlin politics and did indeed take measures to ensure that both the KGB and Internal Affairs machines were kept under control. Brezhnev kept up with the internal developments of each of these organizations by placing close relatives in the number-two spots of each. When Yuri Andropov was named chairman of the KGB in 1967, Brezhnev named his own brother-in-law Semen Kuz'mich Tsvigun, as first deputy chairman to serve as his "eyes and ears" in the KGB. In like fashion, in 1980 Brezhnev appointed his son-in-law Yuri Churbanov first deputy USSR Minister of Internal Affairs. These two Brezhnevite "number twos" became obvious targets for Andropov in his drive to discredit Brezhnev and his network.

Semen Tsvigun at the KGB

A significant amount of debate still surrounds the events that led to the first deputy chairman of the KGB being found dead in his office with a bullet wound in his temple, an apparent suicide. Certain other facts are, however, relatively clear. Born in September 1917 to a Ukrainian peasant household, Semen Kuz'mich Tsvigun began his early career as a school teacher, having been trained at the history faculty of the Odessa Pedagogical Institute. This brief chapter in his career ended two years after it began; in 1939 Tsvigun entered the security organs, where he toiled away the next forty-three years of his life.

In 1950 Leonid Brezhnev was placed in the post of party first secretary of the Moldavian Republic, and found Tsvigun a capable young Chekist. Brezhnev elevated Tsvigun, then thirty-four years of age, to the post of Moldavian deputy minister of State Security in 1951. In 1955, Tsvigun was moved to a parallel post in the KGB organization of Tadzhikistan, and became chairman of the Tadzhik KGB apparatus between 1957 and 1963. As detailed above in the discussion of Geidar Aliev's role in the "Caucasian strategy," Tsvigun served as chairman of the Azerbaidzhan KGB during 1963–1967; Geidar Aliev was his first lieutenant and succeeded Tsvigun in that post upon the latter's 1967 promotion to become Brezhnev's spy in Andropov's all-union KGB organization. The close ties between Brezhnev and Tsvigun were, of course, strengthened by the fact that Tsvigun was married to Vera Petrovna, the younger sister of Brezhnev's wife Viktoria Petrovna.

The details surrounding Tsvigun's demise are still somewhat murky, and the nature and official explanation of his death have even led some observers to speculate that he was murdered.[42] What is clear, though, is that the series of events that led to his death were closely connected to Andropov's drive to tighten the anti-corruption grip on others close to Brezhnev.

The official line on the Tsvigun affair, proffered by the KGB but evidently rejected by Brezhnev himself, was that Tsvigun committed suicide as a response to his being ordered by Mikhail Suslov to stop the investigation of a local Moscow diamond caper that threatened to entangle Leonid Brezhnev's daughter Galina. Tsvigun allegedly wished to arrest a famous Moscow circus clown named Boris Buriatia, or "Boris the Gypsy," after tsarist diamonds stolen from fellow circus performer Irina Bugrimova were found in Buriatia's apartment.[43] A portent of things to come, Galina Brezhneva, who herself was previously married to a Soviet circus administrator, had been since 1971 Galina Churbanova, the wife of Yuri Churbanov, the first deputy USSR minister of Internal Affairs. As the story goes, Mikhail Suslov refused to allow the arrest of Buriatia, and castigated Tsvigun for over-stepping his authority. According to this account, Suslov indicated that Tsvigun's career was now in serious difficulty and that he should consider himself on notice. Tsvigun allegedly committed suicide as a result.

The *Pravda* obituary ran on January 21, 1982 and explained that at the age of sixty-four Tsvigun had died "after a serious and lengthy illness" ("*posle tiazheloi prodolzhitel'noi bolezni*"); the rumors of suicide were only complicated by the fact that Leonid Brezhnev did not sign the obituary, despite the fact that Tsvigun was both the first deputy chief of the KGB and a member of the Central Committee of the CPSU, and his brother-in-law. The absence of Brezhnev's name among the twenty-six people who signed the obituary, and the fact that a large number of KGB and police figures dominated the list, lend credence to the theory that Brezhnev himself had refused to support the official version of Tsvigun's suicide.[44]

Solovyov and Klepikova are of the opinion that this rendition of the Tsvigun affair was a lie, that Tsvigun's death was not a suicide. In their view, Brezhnev refused to sign the obituary because it would sanctify the KGB's version of events, which he knew to be false. In their opinion, Brezhnev's refusal to sign the obituary was "perhaps the most courageous act of his lifetime."[45]

The official version of Tsvigun's death and the details that led up to it made Brezhnev look even worse, of course, in that it entailed his squelching of a legitimate investigation for purely selfish reasons. Solovyov and Klepikova have chosen to view the affair as a murder to eliminate Brezhnev's spy in the KGB. From their point of view, Andropov at the time needed desperately to leave the KGB apparatus for the Party Secretariat in order to be considered a prime contender for the upcoming succession to Brezhnev's post. But this necessary strategy would have meant that Tsvigun, the number-two man at KGB, would get the KGB top job once Andropov left. Thus, Andropov's promotion out of the KGB, so necessary for his quest to the top party job, would in actuality be the beginning of the end for him. As a result, Andropov would have to get rid of Tsvigun before he could move to the Secretariat; hence the motive to have Tsvigun killed.

This view of events, while difficult to validate one way or the other, deserves serious consideration. It is interesting in this respect that (a) Andropov's prospects looked much better after Suslov suddenly died of a heart attack six days after Tsvigun's suicide; (b) the anti-corruption campaign to weaken Brezhnev picked up markedly after Suslov's death; and (c) the arrest of Boris the Gypsy, over which Tsvigun and Suslov had allegedly had sharp words leading to Tsvigun's suicide, took place on the very day of Suslov's funeral. By all accounts, Brezhnev was extremely emotional in delivering his eulogy to Mikhail Suslov; perhaps it was due to a combination of both his sense of loss of the close friend he had known for many decades, as well as for his realization that without Suslov on the scene, the beginning of the end of the Brezhnev era was that much closer at hand.

The Soviet Circus and the Diamond Affair

While the high-level anti-corruption campaign gathered increased momentum with the death of Mikhail Suslov in late January 1982, the groundwork had been established two months earlier. In November 1981 the Party Central Committee approved a new phase in the law and order drive. A secret Central Committee letter was sent to each republic and local party committee, informing them of the new anti-corruption campaign and advising them of the Central Committee's areas of emphasis. One such area was to involve a crackdown on the extravagant life-styles of the privileged "new class." This focus presented a significant problem for Brezhnev in that a number of politically embarrassing skeletons were still actively rattling around in the Brezhnev family closet. Andropov's intent, it seems, was to bring them into the full light of day.

The highest-profile target of the 1982 anti-corruption campaign was Brezhnev's family, specifically the activities of his daughter Galina Churbanova. However, such a high-profile target required that Andropov proceed with some caution. During January 1982, the campaign focused its attention on the illegalities prevalent in the administration of the world famous Soviet circus. By all accounts, leading figures in the circus administration have been blatantly flaunting both Soviet law and any informal code of behavior that governed the privileged class in Moscow.

On January 29, 1982, while Leonid Brezhnev was eulogizing his long-time comrade and protector Mikhail Suslov, the famous circus clown Boris Buriatia was finally being arrested in connection with his possession of stolen tsarist diamonds. As the story goes, a certain circus lion tamer, Irina Bugrimova, had somehow come to own a substantial collection of diamonds once part of the Romanov family jewels. She had discovered them missing from her apartment in December 1981 upon returning from the funeral of the former Soviet National Circus chief Nikolai Asanov. As described above in connection with the suicide of Semen Tsvigun, the KGB had wanted to arrest "Boris the Gypsy" immediately, but Suslov allegedly intervened and refused to allow it. How a lion tamer with the Soviet circus could afford to own a cache of tsarist diamonds in the first place seems to be somewhat curious, and its improbability has led some to seek other motives in the entire scenario. Upon a search of Buriatia's apartment, the stolen diamonds were discovered and he was arrested.

The plot in the diamond affair thickens with Buriatia's interrogation, during which he allegedly implicated two rather highly placed figures in the Moscow social scene: first, Anatolii Kolevatov, the director of *Gostsirk* (State Circuses), the Soviet Ministry of Culture department in charge of administering the eighty-plus Soviet state circuses, and second, Galina Churbanova, Leonid Brezhnev's socialite daughter and the wife of Yuri Churbanov, the number two man at the MVD. According to one source, Galina and Boris Buriatia were lovers.[46] The arrest of the circus clown led investigators to uncover an intricate system of corruption at the head of the national circus administration.

That Buriatia's information implicated Galina Churbanova is supported by a curious February 22, 1982, *Pravda* letter to the editor which sent a not-so-subtle signal to those keeping up with the growing rumors of a high-level purge: it complained in generic terms about the morality of contemporary youth and how they reflect the declining morality of their parents. Churbanova's close ties to the circus and her alleged relationship with the arrested Buriatia made the seemingly innocuous letter published in the party newspaper much more ominous.

Acting on information supplied by Buriatia, the OBKhSS—the special department of the MVD that focused on corruption—arrested Soviet circus boss Kolevatov on February 26, 1982; upon a search of his apartment, the police discovered approximately $1 million worth of diamonds and approximately $280,000 in foreign currencies. As the story came to be detailed, Kolevatov was allegedly extorting bribes from circus performers who wished to travel abroad. His role as director of the Soviet circuses placed him in a position of arranging all foreign travel for the members of the various circuses, as well as deciding which individuals would be assigned to specific tours. Kolevatov allegedly used his power to extract bribes from those circus performers who wished to travel abroad. Kolevatov's deputy, Viktor Gorskii, was also arrested on corruption charges. Under questioning, Gorskii too allegedly implicated Galina Churbanova.

John F. Burns, the Moscow correspondent for the *New York Times*, chronicled the scandal that "had all Moscow abuzz."[47] His article argued that the diamonds and foreign currency found with Kolevatov were worth 1.2 million rubles, or 1.7 million dollars. It seems as though Kolevatov was known by many as "the millionaire" due to his overtly extravagant life-style, which included a gold Mercedes sedan and his sporting of ten-gallon hats and cowboy boots. According to his version of events, Kolevatov was exporting diamonds for sale in the West, and using Buriatia as some sort of courier or "keeper" of the diamonds. Burns also reported that the general secretary's daughter was indeed hauled in for questioning: "Miss Brezhnev had been questioned by the police after she was implicated in the affair by Boris the Gypsy. . . . Miss Brezhnev was said to have denied the allegation and there was no indication that she was still under investigation." Regardless of either the validity of the entire investigation (Solovyov and Klepikova suggest the possibility that the entire diamond affair was an Andropov setup) or Galina Churbanova's involvement—if any—in it, the very fact that Galina Churbanova née Brezhneva could be interrogated in the capital of the USSR while her father was general secretary of the Communist Party reveals both the seriousness of Andropov's effort to discredit Brezhnev as well as the uses to which anti-corruption campaigns can be put in a society riddled with illegalities. In such a system, the timing and targets of anti-corruption crackdowns reveal a great deal more than the sundry charges brought.

Simultaneous with the investigation of corruption in the Soviet circus, additional inquiry was taking place into the activities of important MVD officials. Linked to the circus scandal were illegalities in the visa division of the MVD. General Konstantin Zotov, since 1977 the director of the ministry of Interior's Visa Office (OVIR), had in January 1982 resigned for unspecified reasons; later word specified that Zotov had resigned because, while not personally tied to any specific misdeeds, corruption was out of control in the MVD's OVIR offices. The OVIR officials, it seems, were routinely selling exit visas for three or four thousand dollars apiece. The fact that Kolevatov's troubles revolved around bribes connected to foreign travel and that they coincided with the general purging of the MVD's office in charge of issuing exit visas for Soviet citizens, raises the probability that the two were quite closely connected.

The news of the legal difficulties of Zotov and Kolevatov was *not* reported in Soviet papers, but the gossip storm in the Soviet Union was severe. Such gossip was only exacerbated by the coincidence of a March 1, 1982, interview in *Pravda* with the famous Moscow circus clown Yuri Nikulin, whose comments are revealing. In the article, Nikulin indirectly implicated Circus Director Anatolii Kolevatov; when asked, given all his extensive experience in the circus, if he would change anything, he lamented the selfishness and lack of dedication of some individuals in the Soviet circuses. To make matters worse, this article, titled "A Conversation with Yuri Nikulin," was by-lined, a rarity in *Pravda*, to a writer named Galina Kozhukhova.[48] Few readers failed to catch the innuendo and raise an eyebrow upon seeing the author's first name. Later in 1982, Boris the Gypsy joined the growing list of suicide victims associated with the 1978–1992 anti-corruption campaign.

Brezhnev's Response: Promoting Chernenko

In the face of these challenges to his authority and to his office, Brezhnev responded by attempting to arrange the developments of the coming succession in such a way that favored the candidacy of one of his most loyal followers, Konstantin Chernenko.[49] Chernenko's ties to Brezhnev can be traced all the way back to the latter's stint in Moldavia during the early 1950s. Chernenko worked in the Moldavian party Central Committee during the time Brezhnev was the Moldavian party first secretary. Ever since this time, Chernenko's career was tied inexorably to that of Brezhnev. It is worth noting, however, that for many years Chernenko was not taken seriously at all as a major power broker among the elite. He was elected to the CPSU Central Committee at the advanced age of sixty, and by and large entered most of the stepping-stone posts later than other major political figures.[50] In fact, up until the final few years of Brezhnev's life, Chernenko was considered little more than the general secretary's valet, propping up Brezhnev in public (both literally and figuratively). In the face of Andropov's ambitious program to succeed Brezhnev, Chernenko was selected by Brezhnev as the man to promote as his own heir apparent.

In October 1977, the already sixty-six-year-old Chernenko was finally elected to a non-voting slot in the Politburo; within thirteen months, though, and no doubt due to the developments that occurred during 1978, Chernenko was elevated to full voting status in the Politburo. It seemed at the time that Brezhnev was in a hurry to provide Chernenko with all the necessary institutional *bona fides* required of all serious candidates for the top party slot. As most students of Soviet politics know, those individuals who are both party secretaries and full voting members of the Politburo are usually considered the most serious candidates for the general secretaryship. This fact explains why Andropov, already a full voting member of the Politburo, left his post of KGB chairman in January 1982 in favor of filling Suslov's vacant slot in the party secretariat. The timing of events with respect to

Chernenko seems to indicate that Brezhnev was maneuvering him into a position to contend for leadership. Given that Chernenko had been a party secretary (responsible for party administration) since 1976, with his elevation within the Politburo in November 1978, Chernenko now possessed the institutional prerequisites to compete with Andropov.

Brezhnev aided and abetted Chernenko's chances for success in this competition by doing all that he could to demonstrate that Chernenko was his personal choice to replace him after his death. As Sidney Ploss put it, Chernenko was "depicted as a kind of acting General Secretary, closely involved in military, police, agricultural, and foreign affairs."[51] On Chernenko's seventieth birthday in late September 1981, Brezhnev referred to him as a "restless man," seemingly attempting to indicate that Chernenko was physically rigorous for his advanced age and thus able to be taken seriously as a possible successor.[52] By the last year of Brezhnev's life, many analysts considered Chernenko the current "heir presumptive" to Leonid Brezhnev.

During the last decade or so of his life, Brezhnev's attitude toward other talented people in the leadership, however, may well have placed him in the predicament he faced by the end of the 1970s. Basically a man of mediocre talents but bent on creating a mini-cult around his own accomplishments, Brezhnev kept all men of independent ability or talent out of the top leadership. By the late 1970s, in his battle with Andropov, Brezhnev was forced by this cadres policy of promoting loyal mediocrity to promote the quintessence of such a cadre: Konstantin Chernenko. In a sense, then, Brezhnev's elevation of his own interests and those of his subordinate "clerks" over those of the state backfired on him. As one of the keenest observers of Kremlin politics and succession put it at the time,

> By keeping vigorous and able men out of the top leadership in the late 1970's and by grooming Chernenko as his new heir presumptive, Brezhnev made it possible for Andropov, despite the latter's numerous handicaps, to contest Chernenko in the succession process, and indeed to challenge Brezhnev himself. . . . Brezhnev's advocacy of Chernenko weakened Brezhnev not only politically but physically as well. His efforts to fight off Andropov's challenge taxed his strength, leading to a medical setback in Tashkent in March [1982] and contributing to his death in November. . . . [Andropov] capitalized on Brezhnev's physical frailty and on his political vulnerabilities: his longstanding strategy of favoring cronies (leaders like Chernenko, Nikolay Tikhonov, and

Kunayev) over more able leaders who might threaten his position; his increasing promotion of Chernenko as his heir; and the progressive failure of his major domestic policies in agriculture, in public health, and in industrial investment.[53]

Brezhnev's policy of promoting incompetent toadyism among his lieutenants certainly had ramifications for the post-Brezhnev period in Soviet politics. Six years before Brezhnev's death, Jerry F. Hough detected such a program and understood its implications: "If Brezhnev has been following an 'after me, the deluge' line instead of trying to guarantee his policies after he has gone (a distinct possibility in this observer's opinion), some type of deluge cannot be ruled out."[54] Of course, the deluge did come, in at least two phases. The first entailed the challenge to his leadership while Brezhnev was still alive and the destruction of his network immediately after his death; the second "deluge," of course, was much more devastating to Soviet power in Russia.

It is a testament to the scale of the crisis in Soviet politics that Chernenko was even a serious candidate to succeed Brezhnev in 1982, which at first he failed to do. What is more damning is the fact that even after Andropov had made his run through the political establishment during the 1978–1982 period and continued to do so after becoming general secretary between November 1982 and February 1984, the seventy-two-year-old Chernenko was still seen by a sufficient number of power brokers as a reasonable choice to lead the country upon Andropov's death.

The Politics of Anti-Corruption After Brezhnev

The death of Leonid Brezhnev on November 10, 1982, resulted in Andropov's elevation to supreme power in the USSR. However, it did not end his program to use the anti-corruption campaign as a political tool to deal with remaining members of the generally corrupt Brezhnev royal court. Without Brezhnev to provide even a minimal level of protection, Andropov's drive to combat the cynical and opulent lifestyles of the Brezhnev elite led to the unearthing of several additional major scandals.

Yuri Sokolov and Gastronom No. 1

One of the perquisites of public office in the Soviet Union entailed exclusive access to special stores stocked with Western goods, as well as a number of institutionalized yet informal arrangements concerning the procurement of the best food Moscow had to offer. First among the "restaurateurs to the Kremlin stars" was Yuri Sokolov, the director of what was known officially as "Store Number One of the Gastronom Trade Association of the Moscow City Soviet Executive Committee's Chief Administration for Trade." It was better known among its customers by its pre-1917 name, "Eliseev's." Arkady Vaksberg described Director Sokolov as "the man who had so zealously taken care of the cosmonauts, generals and actors and had looked after the nomenklatura and gone to endless trouble for the staff at the Moscow city soviet."[55] His work for the *nomenklatura,* of course, entailed massive riches for himself and his colleagues engaged in the black market food marketing scheme. According to *Washington Post* Moscow Bureau Chief Dusko Doder, when police entered and searched Sokolov's premises, the equivalent of $4 million was found in a safe box hidden under his apartment floor.[56]

The store director—a close friend of Moscow city party boss and Politburo member Viktor Grishin, Galina Brezhneva, and her husband, First Deputy USSR Minister of Internal Affairs Yuri Churbanov—was arrested in the fall of 1983 along with his immediate boss, Nikolai Tregubov; both were charged with accepting bribes in exchange for providing an illicit supply of foodstuffs. Within weeks, *Izvestiia* reported the verdict:

> The defendants were found guilty of regular bribe-taking over a prolonged period of time, as members of a criminal group organized by Sokolov, while abusing their official positions and perpetuating various illegal machinations involving food products.[57]

While Tregubov's sentence was not mentioned at the time (he later received fifteen years in a Soviet prison camp), Sokolov was given the death penalty and, failing in his appeal for clemency from the USSR Supreme Soviet, was executed in 1984.

Yuri Churbanov

The final family member of the Brezhnev "mafia" to fall in the anticorruption campaign was Yuri Churbanov. As mentioned above, Churbanov, like Brezhnev's brother-in-law Nikolai Tsvigun of the KGB, was a close family member of Leonid Brezhnev named to a sensitive "number-two" post for the purpose of serving as Brezhnev's source of information in the Ministry of Internal Affairs. In Churbanov's case, his 1971 marriage to Galina Brezhneva had provided yet another opportunity for Brezhnev-inspired nepotism.[58] Churbanov, a career Chekist, was named first deputy USSR Minister of Internal Affairs in 1980, but would be proven unable to survive politically after the death of his father-in-law patron. In Churbanov's case, however, it would take many years to bring the negative campaign to a conclusion.

In the aftermath of Andropov's success in replacing Brezhnev, Churbanov was, as might be expected, removed from his post in the MVD and transferred by Andropov to a lowly post far from Moscow: Yuri and Galina were forced to move to Murmansk, a frigid port city above the arctic circle, where Churbanov was named the new police chief. Such internal exile, though, would not be the end of the story for Churbanov, for his activities as an MVD official would come under severe scrutiny when what was perhaps the biggest political scandal of the 1980s, centered in the Soviet republic of Uzbekistan, came to light.

As Americans were in the final days of the 1988 election campaign that would make George Bush president, Yuri Churbanov was arrested by the police he used to command. A November 2 *Pravda* article titled "In the Procuracy of the USSR: Inexorable Logic of the Law," reported the arrest of several extremely visible members of the old Brezhnev regional network: Yuri Churbanov, Inamzhon Buzrukovich Usmankhodzhaev (the former Uzbek party boss), A. Salimov (former chairman of Presidium of Uzbek Supreme Soviet), Ismail Dzhabbarovich Dzhabbarov (former first secretary of Uzbekistan's Bukhara *obkom)* and Nazir Radzhabovich Radzhabov (former first secretary of Samarkand obkom).[59] In addition, many members of the Uzbek Ministry of Internal Affairs were implicated in the charges. Churbanov and the leading figures of what came to be called the "Uzbek mafia" were charged with bribe taking on an extremely high scale.

A tremendous amount of public interest surrounded the case; with Gorbachev's *glasnost'* in full swing at that time, the Soviet press covered this high-level trial that included virtually the entire political leadership of Uzbekistan. The trial venue was the USSR Supreme Court, presided over by Justice M.A. Marov, and proceedings began on December 12, 1988. Churbanov and his associates were charged with (1) bribe taking on a particularly large scale (RSFSR Criminal Code Article 173), and (2) use of official position for personal gain (Article 170). The Soviet press articles at the time stated that Churbanov was personally charged with taking 680,000 rubles in bribes. In the course of the trial, though, the prosecutors dropped the total by 275,000 rubles on grounds that only 405,000 rubles worth of bribes could actually be verified. In presenting these charges against Churbanov, the Soviet Prosecutor asked the court to sentence Churbanov to fifteen years deprivation of freedom in a strict-regime corrective labor colony (with the first five years to be served in prison).[60]

The outcome of the trial with respect to Churbanov was predictable. On December 30, 1988, after a two-and-a-half-week trial that brought over 200 witnesses to the stand, Churbanov was convicted of accepting bribes in the amount of 90,960 rubles and of abusing his official position for mercenary purposes. He was sentenced immediately to twelve years deprivation of freedom in a strict-regime corrective labor colony, the confiscation by the state of his personal property, and a fine equal to the amount of bribes received.[61] The conviction and sentencing of Yuri Churbanov can be considered the final chapter of that aspect of Andropov's anti-corruption campaign, initiated in 1978, which sought to weaken Brezhnev personally through an attack on his close friends and family. However, details of the case that involved Churbanov with the power brokers of Uzbekistan and the so-called cotton mafia, described below, merit attention as a quintessential example of official corruption in the Brezhnev-era Soviet Union.

The Uzbek Mafia

Between 1976 and 1983 the political and economic leadership of Uzbekistan defrauded the Soviet central bank out of some 3 billion rubles by falsely inflating the yields of the Uzbek cotton harvests. This so-called "cotton scandal" was but the most notorious of a series of scandals that permeated Uzbekistan during the tenure of Uzbek party boss Sharaf Rashidovich Rashidov. During his extended tenure as Uzbek political chieftain between 1959 and 1983, by intelligence and guile Rashidov successfully survived each of the Moscow leaders who served ostensibly as his boss. Outlasting Khrushchev, Brezhnev, and (almost) Andropov, Rashidov had developed an intricate political machine centered in the Uzbek capital of Tashkent, some 3,330 kilometers removed from Moscow. Rather than being a powerful prefect of

Moscow, Rashidov had indeed become a Central Asian "paladin."[62] Only after his death did the structure of his "mafia" come under direct attack by Moscow. Despite these developments, and his temporary posthumous eclipse, Rashidov's power in Uzbekistan exists into 1993, some ten years after his death.

Because of Moscow's desire to integrate the national economies of each of the constituent Soviet republics to match the overall needs of the society, the economies of many republics became, in a sense, single-product systems. This was the case with Uzbekistan, which produced the majority of Soviet cotton. Given this state of affairs, the enormous cotton fraud that developed in the latter Brezhnev years would come to ensnarl virtually the entire Uzbek power structure. For many years, as Uzbekistan's cotton production increased dramatically (at least on paper), Rashidov would be the focus of adulation from the central leadership. In addition, Rashidov would pay the expected homage to Brezhnev. Under Brezhnev, "adulation" usually meant at least two things: personal enrichment and state awards. By the end of his life, Rashidov had received plenty of each. He had been awarded by the Soviet state 10 Orders of Lenin, 2 Gold Stars, a Lenin Prize, 2 Hero of Socialist Labor medals, a Red Banner of Labor, an Order of the Red Star, 2 Sickle and Hammer Gold Medals, and the Badge of Honor, among a great many others. For his part, Rashidov presented valuable tokens of homage to Brezhnev and massaged the latter's insatiable ego in public. His reference to Brezhnev at the 1976 Twenty-fifth Party Congress as "the most outstanding and most influential political figure of contemporary times," is but one of a large number of outlandish examples of Rashidov's toadyism toward the general secretary.[63]

Rashidov was a candidate member of the central Politburo, and exercised considerable power at the national level. In Uzbekistan, he was a god. In addition, he enriched himself and his republic from Moscow coffers at mind-boggling levels. The problem, of course, was that each of these wonders was based on a chimera, a conscious lie: make-believe cotton.

Upon gaining power, Andropov was determined to get to the bottom of the Uzbek cotton scandal, but gaining reliable information from the far-away republic when all its own security and police officials were part of the conspiracy was almost impossible. Thus, a bizarre scenario came into existence: Andropov rerouted Soviet spy satellites usually focusing on the country's external enemies and aimed them at the

Uzbek cotton fields. (This represented the degree to which the Uzbek mafia controlled events in the republic; the Soviet head of state was forced to use spy satellites to garner accurate estimates of the real Uzbek cotton harvest!) With Andropov intent on destroying the political corruption of Brezhnev-era high officials, the prospects of Rashidov and the Uzbek mafia began to dim. Only after years of in-depth investigation did sufficient evidence present itself to allow for the prosecution of the republic's leading political figures.

The entire list of individuals caught up in the anti-corruption campaign in Uzbekistan numbers in the hundreds, to be sure. An accurate indication of the level and scope of the corruption, though, is evident from naming just a few of the prominent officials indicted on the scandal: USSR First Deputy Minister of Internal Affairs Yuri Churbanov, Uzbek Party first secretary Inamzhom B. Usmankhodzhayev, Chairman of the Uzbek Council of Ministers Narmakhonmad D. Khudaiberdyev, Uzbek Party Secretary Ye. Aitmuratov, the Chairman of the Uzbek Supreme Soviet A. Salimov, Uzbek Minister of Internal Affairs Khaidar Yakhyayev, Uzbek Deputy Ministers of Internal Affairs Kakhramanov and Petr Begelman, the top MVD officials in the Uzbek regions of Khorezm (Sabirov), Tashkent (Dzhamalov), Kashka-Darya (Norbutayev), Namangan (Makhamadzhanov), and Bukhara (Norov), as well as the former party first secretaries of Bukhara *obkom* (Ismail D. Dzhabbarov), Samarkand *obkom* (Nazir R. Radzhabov), and Khorezm *obkom* (Madair Khudaibergenov). In addition, the sitting party boss of Kashka-Darya *obkom* (Abduvakhid K. Karimov) was arrested, as was Kudrat Ergashev, Yakhyayev's successor as Uzbek minister of Internal Affairs. Karimov was executed; Ergashev committed suicide, as did his first deputy Gennadi Davidov. The head of the Bukhara *oblast* MVD's anti-corruption squad (OBKhSS), Akhat Muzaffarov, was arrested for taking bribes. The director of the Papskii Cotton Combine, Akhmadzhan Adylov, known as "the godfather" in Uzbekistan, had an underground headquarters in which he imprisoned and tortured his political opponents, passed judgment on political appointments throughout the republic, and accepted riches of all types as homage. One commentator referred to Adylov, a hero of Socialist Labor, as "the quintessence of a 'Central Asian variant' of the corruption of Brezhnevism at its apogee."[64] The Uzbek KGB chief Melkumov was fired and shipped off to a diplomatic post outside the USSR; his deputy, General Lagunov was likewise transferred out of

Uzbekistan. Literally every major institution in Uzbekistan—party, state, and government—was rocked by prominent corruption charges.

One of the accused in the Uzbek case summed up the situation well from the defendant's dock:

> Crimes like bribery and inflated production reports, and theft have become the norm. There is no serious attempt to combat these things. . . . Thus not a single question gets resolved without paying a bribe. The question is put thus: Either you resign from your post, or you live according to the laws of criminals. . . . The mafia stopped short of nothing, even giving tacit assent to the active growth of Islam, which, as is well known, preaches submission and humility before those who are senior in rank and age.[65]

As for Rashidov himself, he was the source of some official scorn during the remainder of the Soviet period. But, as shown below, even the post-Rashidov Uzbek leaders criticized their predecessors from the perspective of Moscow's role in creating local problems. At the June 1988 Nineteenth Party Congress, the sitting Uzbek party boss R.N. Nishanov argued:

> The people of Uzbekistan have directly experienced the results of cruel diktat, unbridled lawlessness during the reign of Stalin's repressions. A deep moral wound was inflicted on them during the years of the triumphant march backward, when servility, perfidy, and deception allowed a leader and medal grabber like Rashidov to acquire 10 Orders of Lenin and 2 Gold Stars and, on top of that, to pick up a Lenin Prize. Who gave these orders to Rashidov? Brezhnev, of course, and his closest associates. Why did they award them? Simply because they themselves were money grabbers.[66]

With the demise of Soviet power and the disintegration of the formerly centralized Soviet state, the period of self-criticism in Uzbekistan is seemingly over. Reports from Uzbekistan in the summer of 1992 revealed that Rashidov was undergoing a thorough rehabilitation. A front-page story in the June 8, 1992 issue of *Izvestiia* reported some enlightening developments:

1. the ten-story high Lenin monument, erected at the initiative of Sharaf Rashidov years earlier in the central square of Tashkent, was removed under cover of darkness on the night of June 7, 1992;

2. Lenin Street in Tashkent was renamed Rashidov Street;
3. the large bust of Rashidov, removed after his death and legal denunciations a few years earlier, was put back in place.

Two days later, again on *Izvestiia*'s front page, additional news appeared. It reported that the Uzbek government was planning a November 1992 national celebration on the seventy-fifth jubilee anniversary of the birth of Sharaf Rashidov; the celebration was to be organized by a recently established Jubilee Commission. In addition, at the beginning of 1992, filmmakers had started work on a film about Rashidov's life, titled "The Triumph and Drama of Sharaf Rashidov." Finally, in May 1992 the Presidium of the Supreme Soviet of Uzbekistan announced that the Ilyichevksy *raion* within Syr-Darya *oblast* would henceforth be called the Sharaf Rashidov *raion*. With the demise of Soviet power, the attack on the Uzbek mafia may have come to an end.

The Strange Case of Gdlyan and Ivanov

The two individuals most closely associated with the prosecution of the individuals connected to the Uzbek cotton scandal in particular, and with a principled stance against high-level corruption in general, are investigators Telman Kh. Gdlyan and Nikolai V. Ivanov. Throughout the decade, these two men became lightning rods for social reactions to the massive corruption unearthed at the time.

In the early 1980s Gdlyan was the chief of the USSR Prosecutor's Office's Investigative Group for Particularly Important Cases; Ivanov was his closest associate in the investigation of the Uzbek mafia. Together, these men are credited with bringing down the major members of that organizations, including Yuri Churbanov, the second-in-command at the USSR Ministry of Internal Affairs. Their acclaim at successfully battling organized crime and corruption in high places won them the respect of the nation and propelled them to election to the USSR Congress of People's Deputies in 1989. On these points, there is little debate. However, serious disagreements still exist with respect to the investigatory tactics employed by Gdlyan and Ivanov, the veracity of their later claims, and their political motivations. The case of Gdlyan and Ivanov provides another useful microcosm of the politicization of anti-corruption in the Soviet Union.

In September 1983, on the heels of the criminal proceedings in

Uzbekistan against Bukhara *oblast*'s anti-corruption (OBKhSS) chief, Akhat Muzaffarov, the USSR Prosecutor's Office created a special investigative group headed by Telman Gdlyan. Over the next several years, this special group employed some 200 people in the investigation of the Uzbek mafia, and their efforts certainly resulted in some rather significant legal actions: (a) criminal charges were brought against seventy people, (b) nineteen separate cases were brought to trial, and (c) forty people were convicted.[67] However, during the time this investigatory group was engaged in its probe of the Uzbek criminal element, a number of complaints and statements from citizens alleging questionable tactics by Gdlyan and his team began to appear at various party and soviet organs. These complaints continued to increase in number throughout the five or six years of the team's investigation.

Summarizing such a large list of allegations against Gdlyan and Ivanov is difficult, but the complaints fall into a number of categories. The two allegedly:

1. sought to expand artificially the true number of Uzbek officials involved in the corruption,
2. flagrantly violated the norms of socialist legality in attempting to get information from those under investigation,
3. illegally detained and arrested innocent citizens,
4. knowingly fabricated evidence against those they suspected of being involved in corruption,
5. manipulated and reworded official testimony,
6. illegally attempted to intervene in the court proceedings of the cases they investigated,
7. used the investigation as a tool of personal power and a means of settling political scores,
8. sought, through wanton and groundless accusations, to compromise the Central Committee as the leading body of the party, and
9. willfully aimed at undermining the authority of the Communist Party itself.[68]

In several instances, individuals arrested and convicted on the basis of their investigations were set free on the grounds that Gdlyan and Ivanov had violated proper legal procedures in the investigation.

Many, including Gdlyan and Ivanov, saw these attacks as the expected reaction of those in power most threatened by their anti-corruption activities. What is more, given the fact that Gdlyan and Ivanov had developed quite a significant amount of public support and had created within Soviet society the demand for further investigations into official corruption, even those not yet under direct scrutiny may have felt that this movement needed to be cut short as soon as possible. In any event, the Congress of People's Deputies created an extraordinary commission to investigate the charges against Gdlyan and Ivanov. The so-called "Commission to Examine Materials Relating to the Activity of the Investigative Group of the USSR Prosecutor's Office Headed by T. Gdlyan," was thus created, and, in an effort to present an objective hearing, Roy Medvedev was selected to be its chairman. Its other members included the USSR prosecutor general, representatives of the law-enforcement agencies, prominent legal scholars, and USSR People's Deputies.

Gdlyan and Ivanov responded to the creation of this commission by detailing at length how their investigations were hampered by higher-ups at virtually every step. In addition, they upped the ante on May 12, 1989, by publicly accusing on Leningrad television a number of national political figures of being involved in the Uzbek bribery and corruption case. Of particular importance, of course, was their accusation that the former chairman of the USSR Supreme Court, Vladimir Terebilov, and present or former Politburo members Yegor Ligachev and Grigorii Romanov were accomplices of the Uzbek mafia. Within days, the name of Mikhail Solomentsev, another Politburo member, was publicly added to the list. Ligachev and Solomentsev charged Gdlyan and Ivanov with issuing libelous statements and demanded that action be taken against them.

In September 1989 a Central Committee plenum heard a report by USSR Prosecutor General A. Ye. Sukharev on the investigation of the charges made by the investigators.[69] The two major conclusions appeared very early on in the report:

> First, the numerous statements by the investigators Gdlyan and Ivanov containing hints and allegations of Comrade Ligachev's involvement in bribe-taking are totally unfounded. Second, Comrades Gdlyan and Ivanov knew very well that they were not only violating elementary norms of investigative ethics and the presumption of innocence but also spreading a dangerous lie that they themselves had fabricated.[70]

In an interview that took place five days after the Central Committee statement by Prosecutor General Sukharev, the chairman of the commission looking into the allegations of impropriety against Gdlyan and Ivanov, Roy Medvedev, while assuming a generally "wait-and-see" attitude on the veracity of the charges, did admit that Gdlyan and Ivanov's troubles stemmed in some part from their violation of a cardinal tenet of Soviet political life; his statement that "We still have a kind of unwritten rule that people above a certain position must not be drawn into an investigation," revealed quite a bit about the *modus operandi* of anti-corruption in the Soviet Union.[71] Within a week, Medvedev was effectively replaced as chairman of the commission as a new controlling triumvirate (including Medvedev himself) was installed. One of the new co-chairmen of the commission, People's Deputy Nikolai Strukov, a senior investigator in the Kursk *oblast* prosecutor's office, explained in *Moskovskiye novosti* that the changes in the commission's leadership were made because "Medvedev sometimes indulges in wishful thinking when speaking on the commission's behalf, [and] has not always been able to organize the purely technical process of our work."[72]

This high-level confrontation between fearless investigators and their prominent political targets certainly captured the attention of the Soviet public. Many supporters of Gdlyan and Ivanov in the community feared that the new triumvirate at the commission would not be impartial in their investigations of Gdlyan and Ivanov. A photo appeared in the same issue of *Moskovskiye novosti* showing a human chain of supporters, locked hand to hand, in the middle of a Moscow street. The caption described the protesters as "a chain in defense of Gdlyan." Public support remained quite high for the two. During this same time, *Argumenty i fakty* published the results of a public opinion survey that asked respondents to identify those members of the Congress of People's Deputies they considered "the very best" and those they considered "the worst."[73] Both Gdlyan and Ivanov fared quite well in this survey: Gdlyan was considered among "the very best" deputies by 187 respondents, and among "the worst" by a mere 15. For Ivanov, the corresponding numbers were 156 and 11. Such popularity did not, however, prevent further trouble for the two.

After being fired from their posts in the all-union Ministry of Internal Affairs, the USSR Prosecutor's Office was involved in an investigation of the criminal charges against the two. At a public rally on

February 4, 1990, the two men called for the resignation of the entire ruling Politburo on the grounds of their protection of the mafia and corruption. Four days later, on February 8, 1990, the Collegium of the USSR Prosecutor General's Office presented to the USSR Supreme Soviet a request that Gdlyan and Ivanov, both people's deputies, be stripped of their parliamentary immunity in order to be charged with criminal offenses.[74] Shortly thereafter, on February 21, Gdlyan and Ivanov were expelled from the Communist Party "for committing flagrant violations of the law and the requirements of the CPSU Statutes."[75] On April 18, 1990, the USSR Supreme Soviet refused the aforementioned request by the USSR Prosecutor's Office, but did issue a warning to the former investigators to tone down their inflammatory public statements about corruption in high places. As a result, no criminal proceedings were instituted against Gdlyan and Ivanov at this time. Undeterred, Gdlyan and Ivanov persisted in making headlines with their accusations; by early May 1990 Gorbachev himself had been accused by the two of protecting the Soviet mafia.[76]

Finally, on July 12, 1991, USSR Prosecutor General Nikolai Trubin signed a letter on behalf of Mikhail Gorbachev asserting that sufficient evidence against Gdlyan and Ivanov had now been accumulated to charge the two with the crime of exceeding their official powers. Inexplicably, however, six weeks later all charges were dropped. In the immediate aftermath of the failed August coup against Gorbachev, Prosecutor General Trubin issued a decision on August 31, 1991, withdrawing the criminal case against Gdlyan and Ivanov. The charges were dropped, the decision read, on the basis of "rehabilitating circumstances—the absence of elements of a crime in their actions."[77] Suddenly, the evidence that supported a criminal indictment in July was deemed in August, after the coup attempt, to be vacuous. In the Soviet press, more than a few people wondered about political motives in the decision to drop all charges against the two firebrands.

In one of their final major controversies a few week later, Gdlyan and Ivanov issued a statement, printed in *Pravda*, requesting satirically that the Communist Party at its next Central Committee plenum consider seriously issuing a full pardon to all the convicted members of the Uzbek mafia. Since the equally corrupt and equally guilty high officials in Moscow who attempted to protect their Uzbek colleagues had managed to stay unindicted and out of jail, it was only fair, they suggested bitterly, that the poor Uzbeks be released also.[78] Gdlyan and

Ivanov's parting shot was clear: admit that the mafia and official corruption are officially sanctioned and protected, and drop all the pretense of a serious campaign to uproot corruption from Soviet society. With the demise of the Communist Party and Soviet Union in December 1991, the strange case of Gdlyan and Ivanov receded from the front pages.

While the exact truth with respect to the activities of Telman Gdlyan and Nikolai Ivanov is certainly worth pursuing for any number of reasons, the point worth emphasizing at present is the high degree of politicization visible in the Gdlyan and Ivanov affair. It is almost certain that in some fashion, these ambitious and energetic investigators did violate certain legal procedures in attempting to combat corruption among the political elite of Uzbekistan. As Arkady Vaksberg aptly puts it, "both of them were themselves products of that system of 'socialist legality' (to be more exact, illegality), under which people were none too fussy about exact observation of the procedures they disparagingly referred to as 'legal formalism.' "[79] It is even possible that these transgressions occurred at the urging of their superiors within the USSR Ministry of Internal Affairs.

Conclusion

Returning to our central concern in this chapter, once again a great deal of evidence points to the conclusion that arbitrariness and political expediency are fundamental factors that need to be taken into consideration in any analysis of corruption and anti-corruption as they existed under Soviet rule. Regarding one of the central characters of this story, Yuri Andropov, one is left to concur with Richard Sakwa, who argued that "it must be presumed that as head of the KGB he [Andropov] knew of the pervasive corruption in Central Asia and elsewhere, but kept quiet until it suited his purposes to lift the cover on the corruption in Brezhnev's immediate entourage."[80]

That the Andropov campaign against high-level corruption in the Soviet Union sent shudders through the elite is certainly demonstrated by the rash of suicides during this time. Vaksburg's exposé of Soviet corruption dedicated an entire chapter to the "epidemic" of suicides in the early 1980s that claimed both Nikolai Shchelokov (the USSR minister of Internal Affairs) and his wife, Viktor Paputin (the first deputy USSR minister of Internal Affairs), Semen Tsvigun (the first deputy chairman of the USSR KGB), General Sergei Krylov (head of the Academy of the USSR Ministry of Internal Affairs), and Boris Buriatia (the famous Soviet clown also known as "Boris the Gypsy"). In Vaksberg's words, this rash of suicides "speaks not only of the enormous psychological pressure on their top people, but also of the endless web of intrigue in which even the most experienced can become confused, and of those permanently double and triple lives in which the slightest loss of concentration can lead to catastrophe."[81]

That such corruption was so pervasive at all levels of Soviet society—both among the common man and among the *nomenklatura*—made anti-corruption an extremely attractive vehicle for calculated intrigue against one's enemies. In such an environment, it is not surprising that certain individuals situated in certain control organs might have been better suited to master such a methodology of political practice. With political expediency and arbitrariness driving a significant portion of anti-corruption in Soviet society, it is not at all surprising that the more routinized and legitimate functions of maintaining law and order became corrupted as well. The somewhat sanguine conclusion that remains as a residue of the analysis of this period of Soviet political history is best captured in Richard Sakwa's statement that by the final years of the Brezhnev period, "the Soviet . . . ruling classes had become one of the most venal, incompetent and useless ruling classes in history."[82]

Notes

1. F.J.M. Fedlbrugge (1979), "Does Soviet Law Make Sense?: Rationality and Functionality in Soviet Law," pp. 399–407 in Donald D. Barry, et al., eds., *Soviet Law after Stalin: Soviet Institutions and the Administration of Law* (Alphen aan den Rijn: Sijthoff & Noordhoff): p. 404.

2. Gordon B. Smith (1979), "Procuratorial Campaigns against Crime," in Donald D. Barry, et al., eds., *Soviet Law after Stalin: Part 3: Soviet Institutions and the Administration of Law* (Alphen aan den Rijn: Sijthoff & Noordhoff), pp. 143, 154, 162.

3. Ibid., p. 153.

4. For example, see Michael E. Urban (1989), *An Algebra of Soviet Power: Elite Circulation in the Belorussian Republic 1966–1986* (Cambridge: Cambridge University Press), especially chapters 5, 6, 7.

5. Michel Tatu (1975), "Decision Making in the USSR," in Richard Pipes, ed., *Soviet Strategy in Europe* (New York: Crane, Russak): p. 55.

6. Vladimir Solovyov and Elena Klepikova (1983), *Yuri Andropov: A Secret Passage into the Kremlin* (London: Robert Hale), p. 83–121.

7. See for example, the work of John P. Willerton, Jr. (1979), "Clientelism in the Soviet Union: An Initial Examination," *Studies in Comparative Communism,* Vol. 12 (Nos. 2–3): 159–183; and (1987), "Patronage Networks and Coalition Building in the Brezhnev Era," *Soviet Studies,* Vol. 39 (No. 2): 175–204.

8. Gyula Jozsa (1983), "Political 'Sielschaften' in the USSR," in T.H. Rigby and Bohdan Harasymiw, eds., *Leadership Selection and Patron–Client Relations in the USSR and Yugoslavia* (London: George Allen & Unwin), p. 139.

9. Grey Hodnett (1975), "Succession Contingencies in the Soviet Union," *Problems of Communism,* Vol. 24 (No. 2): 11.

10. Solovyov and Klepikova (1983), *Yuri Andropov,* p. 105.

11. Arkady Vaksberg (1991), *The Soviet Mafia* (New York: St. Martin's Press), p. 179.

12. Ibid., p. 177.

13. Ibid., p. 187.

14. Gabriel A. Almond and G. Bingham Powell (1978), *Comparative Politics: System; Process and Policy* (Boston: Little, Brown).

15. Representative of this school of thought are the following: Stephen D. Krasner (1984), "Approaches to the State: Alternative Conceptions and Historical Dynamics," *Comparative Politics,* Vol. 16 (No. 2): 223–246; Eric A. Nordlinger (1981), *On the Autonomy of the Democratic State* (Cambridge, MA.: Harvard University Press); Theda Skocpol (1979), *States and Social Revolutions* (Cambridge: Cambridge University Press); and Charles Tilly, ed. (1975), *The Formation of National States in Western Europe* (Princeton, NJ: Princeton University Press).

16. Graham T. Allison (1971), *Essence of Decision: Explaining the Cuban Missile Crisis* (Boston: Little, Brown).

17. *Pravda,* July 6, 1978, pp. 1–3.

18. Peter Reddaway (1984), "Soviet Policies on Dissent and Emigration: The Radical Change of Course since 1979," Occasional Paper No. 192, Kennan Institute for Advanced Russian Studies (Washington, D.C.: Woodrow Wilson International Center for Scholars).

19. *V Tsentral'nom Komitete KPCC: Ob uluchshenii Raboty po Okhrane Pravoporiadka i Usilenii Bor'by s pravonarusheniiami," Pravda,* August 11, 1979, pp. 1, 3.

20. *Pravda,* August 31, 1979.

21. *Izvestiia,* October 24, 1979, p. 3; emphasis added.

22. Peter Reddaway (1984), "Soviet Policies on Dissent and Emigration," pp. 11, 12–13.

23. See Brezhnev's speech in *Pravda,* February 23, 1981, pp. 2–9.

24. It is worth remembering, though, that KGB representation in the CPSU Central Committee has traditionally been quite modest. Even with the 1981 increase, this pattern of low representation remained: even with these elevations at the Twenty-sixth Party Congress, the KGB still has but four of the 319 full members, less than 2 percent of the Central Committee.

25. *"Nash Kriterii Nravstvennosti," Pravda,* November 9, 1981, p. 3.

26. Cited in *Newsweek,* November 22, 1982, p. 39.

27. Michel Tatu (1968), *Power in the Kremlin* (New York: Viking Press).

28. Solovyov and Klepikova (1983), *Yuri Andropov,* p. 224.

29. Dusko Doder (1988). *Shadows and Whispers: Power Politics inside the Kremlin from Brezhnev to Gorbachev* (New York: Penguin Books), p. 62.

30. Solovyov and Klepikova (1983), *Yuri Andropov,* p. 191.

31. Ibid., p. 191.

32. *Trud,* March 10, 1978, p. 4.

33. *Literaturnaya gazeta,* November 12, 1980, p. 12.

34. *Pravda,* June 16, 1983, p. 1.

35. *Sovetskaya Rossia,* April 1, 1983, p. 2.

36. Peter Reddaway (1984), "Soviet Policies on Dissent and Emigration," p. 14.

37. In 1966 the internal police organization was called the USSR Ministry for the Maintenance of Public Order. Its name was changed to the USSR Ministry of Internal Affairs in 1968.

38. Solovyov and Klepikova (1983), *Yuri Andropov,* p. 276.

39. *Pravda,* June 16, 1983, p. 1.

40. *Izvestiia,* November 9, 1984, p. 6.

41. For confirmation of the suicide, see Richard Sakwa (1990), *Gorbachev and His Reforms, 1985–1990* (Englewood Cliffs, NJ: Prentice Hall), p. 84; and John L. Scherer, ed. (1985), *USSR Facts and Figures Annual* (Gulf Breeze, FL: Academic International Press), p. 402.

42. Solovyov and Klepikova (1983), *Yuri Andropov,* p. 228.

43. *Newsweek,* November 22, 1981, p. 39.

44. The following people signed the obituary (in order): Andropov, Gorbachev, Ustinov, Chernenko, Aliev, Bugaev, Shchelokov, Pavlov, Savinkin, Ageev, Alidin, Antonov, Bobkov, Grigorenko, Dushin, Emokhonov, Ermakov, Kriuchkov, Lezhepekov, Matrosov, Nosyrev, Pirozhkov, Suplatov, Fedorchuk, Tsinev, and Chebrikov.

45. Solovyov and Klepikova (1983), *Yuri Andropov,* p. 228.

46. Ibid., p. 225.

47. See John F. Burns, "2 Scandals Have All Moscow Abuzz," *New York Times,* February 27, 1982; and Dusko Doder, "Soviets Said to Arrest, Fire Officials in Scandal," *Washington Post,* February 27, 1982.

48. *"Proshchanie s Klounom: Rasskazyvaet Yurii Nikulin," Pravda,* March 1, 1982, p. 3.

49. Solovyov and Klepikova describe rumors circulating through Moscow in the fall of 1982 of Brezhnev's attempts to arrest Andropov on September 10, leading to gunfire between MVD forces acting under the command of Yurii Churbanov and Andropov loyalists among the KGB. It is difficult to assess the validity of such rumors. See Solovyov and Klepikova (1983), *Yuri Andropov,* pp. 255–258.

50. For example, when comparing Chernenko (born 1911) and Andropov (born 1914) before the prelude to the Brezhnev succession accelerated Chernenko's career, it is clear that Andropov had a much more impressive history: Andropov entered the Central Committee in 1961 at age 47, Chernenko in 1971 at age 60; Andropov became a candidate member of the Politburo in 1967 at age 53, Chernenko in 1977 at the age of 66. It seems as though Chernenko, despite being three years older than Andropov, was ten years behind in a political sense.

51. Sidney Ploss (1982), "Soviet Succession: Signs of Struggle," *Problems of Communism,* Vol. 31 (No. 5): 45.

52. *Pravda*, September 25, 1981.

53. Myron Rush (1983), "Succeeding Brezhnev," *Problems of Communism*, Vol. 32 (No. 1): 3.

54. Jerry F. Hough (1976), "The Brezhnev Era: The Man and the System," *Problems of Communism*, Vol. 25 (No. 2): 17.

55. Arkady Vaksberg (1991), *The Soviet Mafia*, p. 213.

56. Dusko Doder (1988). *Shadows and Whispers*, p. 200.

57. *Izvestiia*, November 25, 1983, p. 6.

58. Besides the cases of Tsvigun (KGB) and Churbanov (MVD), Brezhnev had named his son Yuri Leonidovich Brezhnev to a post as USSR deputy minister, later USSR first deputy minister, of Foreign Trade. After his father's death, Yuri was transferred to other work in Kazakhstan. Brezhnev's daughter, the infamous Galina, was employed in the Novosti Press Agency.

59. "*V Prokurature SSSR: Neumolima Logika Zakona*," *Pravda*, November 2, 1988, p. 6.

60. "*V Verkhovnom Sude SSSR: Nachalis' Preniia Storon*," *Pravda*, December 14, 1988, p. 6.

61. "*V Verkhovnom Sude SSSR: Prigovor*," *Pravda*, December 31, 1988, p. 3.

62. This distinction between "prefect" and "paladin" is borrowed from Gregory Gleason (1987), "Prefect or Paladin?: Centrist and Nationalist Leaders in Soviet Central Asia," paper presented at the nineteenth annual convention of the American Association for the Advancement of Slavic Studies, Boston, Massachusetts.

63. Cited in Jerry Hough (1976), "The Brezhnev Era," pp. 2–3.

64. Boris Rumer (1988), "Trouble in Samarkand," *World Monitor* (November): 46.

65. Ibid., p. 49.

66. Baruch A. Hazan (1990), *Gorbachev's Gamble: The 19th All-Union Party Conference* (Boulder, CO: Westview Press), p. 279.

67. *Pravda*, May 20, 1989, p. 3.

68. See, for example, the charges contained in *Pravda*, May 13, 1989, p. 2; *Pravda*, May 20, 1989, p. 3; *Pravda*, May 21, 1989, p. 3; *Izvestiia*, May 21, 1989, p. 4; *Pravda*, September 22, 1989, pp. 6–7; *Izvestiia*, September 28, 1989, p. 6; *Izvestiia*, October 5, 1989, p. 6; *Izvestiia*, October 15, 1989, p. 15; and *Izvestiia*, October 29, 1989, p. 2.

69. *Pravda*, September 22, 1989, pp. 6–7.

70. Ibid., p. 6.

71. *Izvestiia*, September 28, 1989, p. 6.

72. *Moskovskiye novosti*, October 15, 1989, p. 15.

73. *Argumenty i fakty*, October 7–13, 1989, p. 1.

74. *Pravda*, February 9, 1990, p. 7; *Izvestiia*, February 9, 1990, p. 3.

75. *Argumenty i fakty*, February 24–March 2, 1990, p. 8. The article reported that 351 persons had attended a general meeting of Communists in the Prosecutor's Office apparatus and there considered the question "On Violations of the Law and the Requirements of the CPSU Statutes Committed by Communists T.Kh. Gdlyan and N.V. Ivanov."

76. *Pravda*, May 8, 1990, p. 3.

77. *Izvestiia*, September 3, 1991, p. 8.

78. *Pravda,* September 25, 1991, p. 2.
79. Arkady Vaksberg (1991), *The Soviet Mafia,* p. 116.
80. Richard Sakwa (1990), *Gorbachev and His Reforms,* p. 86.
81. Arkady Vaksberg (1991), *The Soviet Mafia,* p. 104.
82. Richard Sakwa (1990), *Gorbachev and His Reforms,* p. 85.

6

OFFICIAL CORRUPTION, THE SOFT STATE, AND THE FUTURE OF REFORM

In terms of economic growth, the only thing worse than a society with a rigid, overcentralized, dishonest bureaucracy is one with a rigid, overcentralized, honest bureaucracy.

—Samuel P. Huntington[1]

The January 1991 Soviet currency reform, which initiated a policy of extracting large-denomination ruble bills from the economy, was aimed, at least according to official pronouncements, at undercutting the thriving profiteers and speculators engaged in corrupt activities. While the real reasons behind the withdrawal of fifty- and one hundred–ruble notes from the economy in all likelihood have more to do with the goals of deflating the economy and its pent-up demands on consumption, the couching of the policy rationale in terms of a campaign against illegal economic activity highlights the traditional concern of the Soviet leadership with the systemic corruption that has marked Soviet society for decades. The corrupt nature of Soviet politics and economy became especially prominent and, one might argue, intrinsic to the system in the post-Khrushchev period.

From a number of important perspectives, the eighteen-year rule of Leonid Brezhnev witnessed a crucial watershed in the history of the Soviet Union and the world socialist movement. On the positive side, it was during this time that the USSR became recognized as a great global power on a military par with the United States. In addition, the détente policy, closely associated with Brezhnev, dramatically changed the nature of East–West relations. However, the Brezhnev administration will best be remarked upon as the period during which the economic and ideological bankruptcy of the Soviet Union became manifest. It can truly be said that the actions of Leonid Brezhnev are much more responsible for the present crisis and change in the USSR than are those of Mikhail Gorbachev.

The fundamental characteristic of this period in Soviet history was the failure of the Brezhnev leadership to maintain what Aleksandr Solzhenitsyn has called "the great conscious lie"—the ability to perpetuate the myth of Soviet economic, ideological, and moral superiority in the face of the harsh realities of social life in the USSR. The same system that produced extreme economic dislocation, maldistribution, and blatant inefficiency also ensured the development of a level of official corruption at the top of the political leadership pyramid that was (and remains) almost unimaginable. From an economic standpoint, the level of corruption that obtained in the Soviet system was no less a logical product of that system than were the queues of citizens seeking scarce food items. Given the nature of the Soviet system, the structure of its economic activity, and the administration of Soviet power, the creation of "the corrupt society" was absolutely inevitable. This inescapable characteristic of Soviet governance has led one émigré scholar to refer to the system as a "kleptocracy."[2]

Despite the fact that official corruption (to say nothing of the illegal economic activities of everyday citizens who were forced to barter, steal, and hoard goods to maintain their meager standard of living) was as much a characteristic of Soviet politics as the elaborate system of economic planning, the Communist Party apparatus, or the force structure of the Soviet Army, scant attention has been paid to official corruption *as a logical requisite and administrative inevitability in the Soviet mode of politics.* I have attempted to address this issue here. This is not to say that the social phenomenon of corruption in the Soviet Union has been ignored in the extant literature. A modest body of research has focused on the "second economy" or the "black market" in the USSR; émigré literature has highlighted the social conditions created by an economy that provides meager investments in consumer goods and services; and a long-standing theme from observers has been to expose the privilege associated with public office in the system.[3] However, little scholarly attention has been paid to the structural nature of official corruption, to the forces in the USSR that encouraged and rewarded corrupt and illegal activities by Soviet officials, to the political motives behind "anti-corruption" campaigns, and to the impact of this structure of official corruption on any efforts to reform the system.

This final chapter seeks to shed some analytical light on the nature of crime and official corruption in the post-1985 Soviet Union, with special emphasis on evaluating its impact on the workings of the socio-economic system during perestroika and beyond. Of specific interest in this respect will be the potential role of official policies toward corruption in the continued restructuring of the economy of the former Soviet Union. Toward these ends, the decades-old legacy of Soviet official corruption will be subjected to a cost–benefit analysis in an attempt to establish the socio-economic effect of the phenomenon on Soviet and post-Soviet society in general. Additionally, we shall speculate on the possible ways in which aspects of the established corrupt patterns within Soviet officialdom, and by extension the Soviet *homo economicus*, may influence the further development of the system in a more liberal economic and political direction.

The Soviet Soft State: Past and Future

The notion of the "soft state" was first put forward by Gunnar Myrdal in his work on world poverty.[4] Essentially, the concept describes a social environment marked by indiscipline, both on the part of private citizens and public officials. This indiscipline manifests itself in deficiencies in legislation and, in particular, in law observance and enforcement. Private citizens ignore the proscriptions of the law; public officials ignore the rules and directives passed down to them from their superiors. Very often, public officials in the soft state are co-opted or "captured" by those they are supposed to regulate. The soft state is marked by corruption, racketeering, bribery, black markets, arbitrariness and political expediency in the enforcement of laws, and the abuse of power. It is interesting that Myrdal identifies the soft state as typical of underdeveloped nations struggling to build authority and legitimate institutions.

According to Myrdal, certain forces tend to facilitate the development of soft state characteristics in Third World settings: mistrust of government, exaggerated bureaucratization, and the unequal distribution of political power; each of these ingredients was very much in evidence in the Soviet setting. In describing the soft state in the developing world, Robert P. Clark uses language very familiar to students of the Soviet Union:

> It appears as if the hidden cause of political softness and public immorality in the Third World lies in the comparatively underdeveloped state of countervailing powers in these societies. Perhaps the chief characteristic of Third World power systems is the relative lack of power anywhere in the system. Coercion, force and authoritarian rule are all present in abundance, but power is a genuinely scarce commodity. . . . There are few freely operating opposition political parties or independent judiciary systems. Most legislatures are of the rubber stamp variety. Interest groups are primitive and are mostly under the control of the government itself. Press freedom is rare. . . . Laws are made or unmade and enforced or unenforced not according to some master guide, such as a constitution, but according to the whim of the administrator and the special access enjoyed by traditional elites. . . . This lack of a system of countervailing powers paradoxically encourages Third World leaders to try to accumulate more and more force and authority. It is paradoxical because even as they violate their own laws and abuse their own supporters to gain more power, in the long run they condemn themselves to further weakness and softness.[5]

At least with respect to confronting this "softness" and establishing solid authoritative institutions, the post-Soviet states share much in common with the Third World.

Many of the problems connected with the corruption, black markets, and organized crime detailed in the previous chapters of this book can be traced, then, to the weaknesses of the Soviet state. Solovyov and Klepikova assert this very fact in their discussion of corruption in Georgia under Eduard Shevardnadze:

> The fact is that illegal businesses in Georgia, from private distilleries to under-the-counter sales in shops—that black-market capitalism he had combated with all his vigor and tireless inventiveness—filled in gaps left by the state. *The state's weakness favored private initiative.*[6]

It is rather ironic, given sovietology's general orientation throughout the past decades to emphasize the coercive power of the state, that in eulogizing Soviet power a year or so after its demise commentators should point to weaknesses of the state as being both a cause and, in some ways, a product of corruption. But the fact of the matter is that official and societal corruption in the Soviet Union, totaling some 400 billion rubles per year[7] in the late 1980s, were both a system and a symptom of Soviet power.

This volume has attempted to demonstrate the structural forces in the Soviet mode of government that made societal and official corrupt behavior the rational behavior of the day. This is certainly not to argue that somehow Soviet power created official corruption in Russia; our review of tsarist administrative practices disproves such a notion. On the other hand, one can argue that the specific types of administrative practices adopted by the Soviet regimes over the roughly seven-decade history of the USSR certainly exacerbated the situation regarding corruption. In this sense, a certain proportion of private and public forms of illicit behavior can be traced to the characteristics of Soviet power. The level of corruption, both among the citizenry and public officials, rose as the state became "softer." A vicious circle of increased cynicism and corruption developed as the increasing "softness" of the state compelled rational actors in such a system to engage in increasingly illicit behavior. Note that this description does not speak to the issue of motive; a testament to the decline of authority, or state softness, in the final decades of the Soviet period is the fact that even unselfish and patriotic individuals could not themselves escape from the necessity of participating in the informal mechanisms society had created to solve everyday problems. At a certain point, but one that is difficult to ascertain with any accuracy, the informal, illicit system became more important than the soft, formal system. At such a point, it is accurate to describe the USSR as a corrupt system; the formal institutions of the state, as well as the behavior of individuals in both public and private concerns, became corrupted by the fact that the informal institutions of society were more authoritative (less "soft") that the formal ones. Such a situation, whether in the Soviet Union or a developing "new state," cannot persist over the long run.

In the post-Soviet period of rapid change, confronting the problems associated with these phenomena in an environment of radically reduced state power[8] will present the respective leaders of the resultant states with a set of issues not dissimilar to those instances of state building in newly emerging states. In many ways, it may be fruitful to consider the states of the former Soviet colonial empire to be, as in Africa and elsewhere, concerned primarily with authority building and institutionalization. In the case of the so-called "new states" associated with the decolonialization drive of the late 1960s and early 1970s, the role of corruption in society and in public office was a major and significant variable in state-building efforts; such will also be the case in the "new states" of the former Soviet Union.

An interesting and potentially provocative question, then, revolves around an evaluation of the possible role of official corruption in the continuing societal reform movement in the former Soviet Union. There is little doubt as to the pervasive nature of official corruption as it existed in the Soviet system. Moreover, the major manifest causes of corruption in that system were readily obvious: a centrally planned economy marked by artificially low prices, the scarcity of goods, and the overabundance of uncommitted currency, all governed by a pervasive bureaucratic apparatus.[9] Less clear, however, is the impact that such corruption has had for Soviet society in the past and what role it might play in any future, reformed society emerging from the ashes of the USSR.

A Balance Sheet

One scholar with a significant amount of first-hand exposure to the pattern of Soviet practices has stated that "the corruption of higher-ranking officials takes place on a mass scale and is more or less harmless."[10] The body of literature focusing on the societal impact of corruption in the developing world, however, suggests that official corruption is not merely "harmless" in these settings, and can in many cases exert quite a powerful influence on the development of society. In fact, a debate has taken place over the nature of this impact on society, with different scholars seeing positive and negative consequences.[11] That literature suggests a number of alleged benefits as well as a number of supposed costs that obtain as a result of official corruption. While much of this debate has centered on the prevalence of corruption in what were referred to in the 1960s and 1970s as the emerging "new states," it is perhaps instructive to note that quite a few of the political and economic problems that confronted these developing nations are certainly germane to the contemporary former Soviet Union: a legacy of colonial, patriarchical rule; only nascent entrepreneurialism; underdeveloped economic infrastructures; rudimentary market mechanisms; weakly organized labor; and a general population unaccustomed to democratic political institutions. In many senses, if liberalizing developments in the Soviet Union are permitted to proceed apace, the post-Soviet states may well be considered "emerging" states.[12]

Alleged Positive Aspects of Soviet Official Corruption

1. Corruption encourages capital formation. If governments are unwilling or unable to generate investment capital through normal means, such as taxation, the operation of a corrupted governmental bureaucracy may allow for the accumulation from the populace of a sizable amount of private capital through the extraction of bribes. In the Soviet case, inflation assumed the form not of market price increases, but of the accumulation among the general population of exaggerated amounts of currency, which can be considered as unmet claims on consumption. Since the leadership has had an interest in deflating the economy by withdrawing the excess currency, the paying of unofficial fees or bribes may succeed in doing so. As others have pointed out, however, in order to ensure useful capital formation for the state, it is important that much of the accumulated capital be used to promote economic development and not be siphoned off to individual Swiss bank accounts.[13] Nevertheless, a properly controlled system of bribe-taking may be seen as an attractive substitute for higher levels of taxation for the accumulation of investment capital in the former Soviet Union.

2. Corruption cuts red tape and reduces bureaucratic rigidity. The frequency with which bribes were offered to, and accepted by, state officials was quite high in the Soviet Union. The extreme level of bureaucratization meant for the average citizen that virtually all aspects of daily life required the official intervention of one or another Soviet bureaucracy. This applied to the procurement of such basic commodities as housing, transportation, health care, and education. According to James Scott, herein lies a major cause of the high level of corruption that existed in the USSR.[14] Soviet citizens (and subjects of the Russian empire before them) have come to accept the proposition that bribes will be necessary to facilitate the procurement process—to grease the machine's wheels, as it were. Through *baksheesh* one can overcome the barriers raised by the bureaucratic apparat.[15] Indeed, for the Soviet citizenry, the ability to influence the bureaucracy through the use of bribes afforded some level of psychological comfort to the process in that through the use of bribes one could indeed control one's fate in the face of what would otherwise be an overly centralized and unwieldy governmental bureaucracy. The government's de facto acceptance of official corruption in this sense humanized the interaction between the population and the public organs that went so far in controlling most aspects of social life in the country.

3. Corruption promotes entrepreneurial behavior. In an ideological atmosphere that discourages and indeed tends to punish private economic incentive, corruption may be the major source of entrepreneurialism in the system. In that a certain "market" existed with respect to the system of bribery in the USSR, and that this market, like most others, tended to reward the most efficient actor, the successful entrepreneur was required to maintain a certain level of efficiency in his activities. Higher bribes win out over lower ones; enterprises that are consistently able to offer higher bribes (i.e., consistently more efficient in their activities) win out over enterprises unable to do so (i.e., enterprises consistently less efficient in their activities). In the Soviet case, the persistence of an entrenched system of *baksheesh* compelled economic actors to acquire a set of economic skills more consistent with the liberalized open market systems of the West. While the official system of the command economy discouraged entrepreneurialism, the unofficial system encouraged it.

4. Corruption militates against elite cleavages. That the Soviet elite enjoyed special privileges not at all consistent with their adopted political ideology and Soviet law itself is well established.[16] Members of the elite were allowed special access to better health care, educational opportunities, consumer goods, housing, foreign travel, and the like. The maintenance of such a life-style and the distribution of the "spoils" of officialdom tended to mitigate intra-elite conflict. A sense of solidarity within the elite based on its special status within society served as a tie that bound the elite together. In this manner, the emergence of destructive conflict within the elite was made less probable.

5. Corruption helps overcome ethnic discrimination and promotes national integration. Like many multi-ethnic states based on a form of colonial rule, the governance of the Soviet Union, the distribution of its high offices, and other structural privileges tended to accrue to the dominant national groups. In the USSR, the Russians especially, but also the Ukrainians and Belorussians, who combined to form the Slavic core of the country, were politically, economically, linguistically, culturally, and religiously predominant. The existence of a system of corruption, which in this case was perhaps less discriminatory than the official governing system, allowed the less powerful national groups to "buy in" to the system. To the degree that the Soviet black market, the openness of Soviet officialdom to economic compromise, and other aspects of corruption in the USSR constituted an alternative system for the distribution of goods and services, this unofficial system was better suited to the integration of non-dominant areas of the Soviet colonial empire. In this manner, groups that would be less sympathetic to Soviet power were co-opted into the unofficial, but very real, system of economic and political activity.

   6. Corruption substitutes economic activity for political violence. In the absence of the aforementioned economic co-optation of minority social groups in the Soviet Union, the probability of inter-ethnic violence would have increased precipitously. Indeed, as the events of recent years in Armenia and Azerbaidzhan have shown, such violence, no matter how powerful the *pax sovietica* became, resided just below the surface. The economic activity associated with official corruption, however, militated against such violent extra-political activities. It does so by providing a means for the diminution of the colonial flavor of center–periphery relations through the development of an alternative set of "rules of the game" that discriminate among claimants less on ethnic or religious grounds, and more on strict economic criteria. In the eyes of many ethnic leaders in the Soviet Union, the latter state of affairs was much preferable to the built-in biases of the official alternative, and constituted a system within which they could channel their "legitimate" national aspirations.

   7. Corruption attracts quality personnel to government service. Many states have experienced difficulty in recruiting quality individuals to responsible positions in government. Relatively low salaries, especially in states subscribing to socialism's more egalitarian precepts, have hampered the best efforts to elevate the professional qualifications of many members of the state bureaucracy. The Soviet Union suffered further in this regard by virtue of its avowed philosophy of leveling incomes to a significant degree. Moreover, Soviet ideology tended to exaggerate the incomes of blue collar workers relative to white collar employees and members of the intelligentsia. Corruption rendered this problem almost inconsequential in that it provided ample opportunities for individuals in the government bureaucracy to supplement their official salaries with the fruits of official corruption. In this sense, the informal system of official corruption allowed for the augmentation of legal material incentives by corrupt ones. Because of the abundant opportunities provided by corruption, sufficient material incentives may exist to attract a higher quality of individual into government service, while maintaining for ideological reasons the facade of austerity.

8. *Corruption in electoral politics indicates the advance of popular democracy.* Even the presence of electoral corruption has been seen as beneficial in a number of political settings. In systems experiencing the early stages of democratic political mechanisms, the existence of electoral corruption—the buying and selling of votes, for example—reveals that the regime is no longer in a position merely to dictate results or to engineer them by force or intimidation. Of course, until recently Soviet elections functioned less for the articulation of public choice than for that of public unanimity and obligation. With elections in the former Soviet Union becoming actual mechanisms for filling the responsible posts of the state and government, the potential for electoral corruption will rise, even while the more coercive elements associated with past elections decline. Even under these conditions, popular democracy will be seen as advancing due to the fact that the very existence of electoral corruption would entail both the bona fide electioneering and reciprocal give-and-take sorely lacking in the Soviet past.

Alleged Negative Aspects of Soviet Official Corruption

1. *Corruption entails the outflow of capital.* Against the favorable argument that corruption helps to build investment capital for the future economic development of the national economy, there is considerable evidence that in Third World settings much of the capital extracted from the population through official corruption has been dedicated overwhelmingly to the personal enrichment of high government officials. Money has been deposited in Swiss bank accounts, invested in real estate abroad, or simply converted to support lavish life-styles at home. The well-publicized cases of the Somoza family in Nicaragua and the Marcoses in the Philippines highlight the tendency of domestic wealth to flow outside the national borders to safe havens abroad. In the case of the Soviet Union, however, there was little evidence that

whatever wealth accumulated through official corruption was exported abroad for personal or selfish reasons. Most official corruption in the USSR took the form of monetary transfers, which, given the non-convertibility of the Soviet ruble, were difficult to translate into wealth abroad. As a result, the bulk of corrupt receipts in such a system parlayed into individual advantage within the Soviet Union proper.

2. *Corruption distorts investment.* In order to disguise the fruits of official corruption, much of the capital that is garnered through official corruption and is eventually invested in the domestic economy is often invested in sectors of the economy that provide the best chances of its not being detected, not necessarily in those sectors that are in need of investment. In addition, investment capital is often allocated to grandiose projects that reap political rather than development gains. Soviet elites tended to direct corrupted funds into the procurement of dachas, liquor, consumer goods, and other creature comforts. In this way, then, a portion of the money extracted from the population through bribes and favors went toward the maintenance of elite privileges.

3. *Corruption diverts administrative activity.* Given the pervasiveness of corruption in the Soviet Union, and that much of the attractiveness associated with the holding of a responsible government position resided with its incumbent opportunities for corrupt gains, a disproportionate amount of the everyday activity of the Soviet apparat was dedicated to the search for further personal aggrandizement. To the degree that such activity was allowed to take place, the proper and legitimate functions involved in the running of the Soviet state went unsatisfied. In examining the incentive system that governed the personal activities of Soviet bureaucrats, it is clear that a minimalist ethos obtained—one that sought to guarantee only the maintenance of the system to the degree that was necessary to ensure their future opportunities for personal gain. Aggregating such individual motivations, the collective professional ethos becomes one of simply muddling through.

4. *Corruption decreases administrative capacity.* Contradicting the argument that the inherent opportunities for corruption associated with official positions in the Soviet system would have helped to attract quality individuals to "public" service, an equally plausible argument can be made that the persistence of self-regarding activity by members of the administrative apparatus would serve actively to discourage not only the development of professional standards within the administrative organs but also the recruitment of honest, civic-oriented profes-

sionals into public service. Over time, of course, the quality of those individuals within public organs decreased, thus entailing a decline in the organizations' effectiveness in dealing with national problems.

5. *Corruption reduces external aid.* The states of the former Soviet Union, not unlike a number of developing countries, will be reliant for the foreseeable future on sizable grants of external aid. Germany, for example, has committed itself to aid the post-Soviet reform agenda with the infusion of massive amounts of direct aid. History is replete, however, with examples of the withdrawal of economic and/or military aid by a state's benefactor because of the latter's disgust with the rampant corruption of those governments receiving the aid. In addition, it is difficult to estimate the opportunity costs involved with the non-awarding of aid in the first place due to the stigma of corruption on the part of needy regimes.

6. *Corruption weakens the legitimacy of the system.* A system that requires a vigorous underground or illegal economy to distribute goods and services efficiently, that manifests a corrupted officialdom, that elevates bribery to a national art form, soon fosters a level of cynicism in the population that calls into serious question the regime's legitimacy. It was difficult for President Gorbachev to call for austerity measures[17] from the population when people could read in the press criticisms of the lavishness of his new dacha on the Georgian coast, complete with imported sand from Bulgaria for its beachfront.[18] No matter how powerful the coercive organs of a state, no regime can persist in the long run without the majority of the population seeing it as a legitimate entity. The Soviet population was perhaps willing to do so when the economy succeeded in providing at least the basic staples of life, but such support could not be counted upon in times of trouble. On the other hand, some have argued that a tradition of official corruption, if it has been a hallmark of the state's political history, can serve to absolve the corrupt activities of the present regime. That is, a fatalistic attitude toward corruption tends to short-circuit the development of public umbrage over the current perpetrator of official high crimes.[19]

7. *Corruption invites military coups.* The evident corruption of civilian regimes has certainly provided at least a pretext and a rationale for military leaders to institute military coups in a number of states. While it might be difficult to ascertain the true motivations for these coups, it is clear that in many cases the population welcomed such military action due to their own distaste for the corruption of civilian

rule. At a minimum, civilian governments in states with a politicized military apparatus engage in overt official corruption only at some risk to their rule (and their lives). While the notion of Bonapartism in the Soviet Union was for many years considered only a negligible possibility, events in 1990 and 1991 raised it to the level of public discussion. Indeed, during his final days Gorbachev himself publicly discussed (and discounted) the rumors of a military coup in the Soviet Union. If corruption has provided even a pretext for military coups in other locales, the extent and persistence of official corruption in the USSR in the late 1980s gave civilian politicians and military figures alike some pause.

Official Corruption, Perestroika, and Beyond

Official corruption in the Soviet Union was, for at least the last quarter-century, a structural prerequisite of the political and economic system of the country. While, to be sure, bribery has been a traditional social phenomenon in both tsarist and Soviet Russia, since the mid-1960s official corruption assumed an almost unprecedented scope in the USSR. It is not exaggerating to argue, moreover, that the nature of the Soviet system itself almost guaranteed the pervasiveness of official misconduct, the development of a thriving black market, and the corrupting of society in general. As Gregory Grossman argued,

> there can be little doubt with regard to the magnitude of illegal economic activity and corruption, the USSR is far from "underdeveloped" by world standards. It would be surprising, indeed a miracle, if it were otherwise, for the Soviet Union possesses every favorable condition for the appearance of a large illegal economy and of corruption of officialdom.[20]

Corruption thus became an integral and functional characteristic of the operation of the Soviet system. In the post-Khrushchev period, official corruption became an officially accepted and, in some respects, encouraged manifestation of the Soviet system of governance. Acts of official corruption became *necessary* attempts to rationalize the irrationalities of the socialist economic and administrative system in that country. Indeed, the phenomenon of corruption in the USSR is most productively analyzed as an active and, given the nature of the formal mechanism, attractive alternative to the official system for the production and distribution of goods and services. It was an alternative system that was utilized by virtually every citizen in the Soviet Union, that enhanced the efficiency (such as it was) of the formal system, and was recognized by the political elite as a benefit not only to the living standards of the general population but also, by extension, to the stability of its own rule.

From this perspective, it is instructive to distinguish between official corruption for *private* gain and official corruption for *bureaucratic* gain.[21] The Soviet planning system, its method of allocating the necessary production materials to factory managers, the problems that inhere in enterprise procurement measures, and other factors, combined to force Soviet officials at virtually all levels to engage in illegal economic activities that were aimed less at personal aggrandizement and more at the simple satisfaction of their production quotas. As Joseph Berliner described over three decades ago, such conditions led managers to engage in blatant over-reporting or falsification *(pripiski)* of production reports to their superiors, the hiring of "pushers" *(tolkachi)* who act as independent procurement officers and bribe-givers for Soviet enterprises, and the predominance of influence peddling *(blat)*, theft, and barter.[22] These illegal activities took place not because Soviet managers were any less honest as human beings than are enterprise managers in the West, but because that system forced them into such behavior if they were to satisfy their superiors, provide the necessary salary supplements to their workers, and, ultimately, keep the Soviet economy muddling through.

The higher authorities in the Soviet Union were consistently more interested in economic plan fulfillment than in the enforcement of many laws that allegedly governed the behavior of economic and administrative personnel. In a word, administrators were very often compelled by circumstances, as well as the instructions of party officials, to break the law; the enforcement organs were encouraged, likewise, to look the other way, reflecting the elite perception that these forms of corruption often performed vital system functions.[23]

To the degree that the Soviet leaders were wedded to the old system, they could not afford to do away with many of the illegal activities that flourished both in officialdom and among the general populace.[24] Indeed, on a more systemic level, it has been suggested that the Brezhnev leadership accepted this necessary "ideological retrenchment" with respect to a wide range of economic activities. In describing what he labeled Brezhnev's "Little Deal," James R. Millar has argued,

> The Brezhnev leadership struck a new but tacit bargain with the urban population: to tolerate the expansion of a wide range of petty private economic activities, some legal, some in the penumbra of the legal, and some clearly and obviously illegal, the primary aim of which was the reallocation by private means of a significant fraction of Soviet national income according to private preferences. . . . In any event, the Little Deal included tolerance of an expansion of private enterprise, especially in the service activities, . . . of illegal middleman activity, of nepotism, and of the conversion of public property for personal use or for private pecuniary gain.[25]

This compact allowed the Brezhnev regime to avoid, as it consistently sought to do, any significant structural reform of the official Soviet economic system—reform that was without a doubt necessary at that time.

It is clear that official corruption and illicit economic activity by the masses helped rationalize the old system. While it may be difficult, given the secretive nature of these activities, to gauge the exact impact on the Soviet economy, in one scholar's words, "undeniably, corruption has made important contributions to its efficient functioning."[26] What contribution can these activities make, if any, to the present efforts by the new post-Soviet states to reform the institutions inherited from the USSR?

Primarily, the pseudo-market elements of the second economy succeeded in the past, and theoretically, can continue to succeed even in the midst of ongoing structural economic reform, in avoiding precisely the types of economic dislocation now being experienced in the post-Soviet economy. Writing prior to the initiation of Gorbachev's reforms, Richard Ericson showed a degree of optimism about the prospects for the relatively smooth transition from a centrally planned economy (CPE) to an economy that relies more directly on market mechanisms. He argued that what is legally considered "corrupt" behavior on the part of Soviet enterprise managers and the second economy in general "could consistently and (second-best) efficiently allocate productive material inputs among competing uses in spite of the institutional constraints (e.g., fixed prices) peculiar to a CPE."[27] In addition, even in the presence of lagging institutional reforms such as are taking place in the early part of 1993, the second economy is capable of developing further as a supplement to the present official economy. It is "sufficiently developed and 'monetized' so that it is meaningful to speak of the operation of organized markets with generally available information as to prices and trade opportunities."[28]

Indeed, the major restriction to the further development of many aspects of this mechanism is, of course, their proscribed status under law. According to Gregory Grossman, the dynamic of this alternate economic mechanism is constrained in its ability to supply goods and services at market-clearing prices primarily by two forces: the personal risks involved in participating in these illegal activities, and the imperfect mobility of "underground" resources.[29] As legal changes herald new "rules of the game" in the post-Soviet states, more and more formerly illegal "corrupt" practices will be legalized. The newly emerging formal system will adopt an increasing number of characteristics of the previously illegal, informal system.

What these evaluations point to is the potential benefit to the post-Soviet economy of the large-scale legalization of much of the activity that is now considered official corruption and illegal black market activity. A significant percentage of the official corruption for *personal* gain and virtually all of the official corruption for *administrative* gain were a result of Soviet economic practices that have been shown to be ill-suited to the task of meeting the needs of the population. As has been argued, these illegal activities, many of which would be considered absolutely proper economic behavior in market economies, were countenanced by the Soviet leaders for years. The practices of virtually all second economy actors, as well as the illicit policies of the enterprise managers who operated under the old system, have already been institutionalized to a degree that would allow for their relatively rapid incorporation into a new reformed economy.

The economic skills that have been developed *na levo* in the Soviet Union by the "corrupt" activities of recent decades, if liberated from legal prejudice, could provide for the much needed restructuring of prices, distribution, and supply in the post-Soviet economy. A legalization of certain already prevalent economic activities does not require the wholesale restructuring of the economic and administrative system in one step, but rather allows for the incremental introduction of various measures as deemed necessary by the respective post-Soviet political leaderships. Given the fact that (a) such activity has, within bounds, been tolerated and even encouraged in the past, (b) the political leaders in the Soviet Union did not possess the power or, evidently, the inclination to combat useful corruption, (c) evidence from other developing market economies suggests that, at a minimum, significant and necessary entrepreneurial and resource allocation skills are already in place within the alternative system, and (d) the states of the former Soviet Union are rapidly approaching a point when the worsening economic crisis in the country may threaten the stability of the civilian regimes themselves, the costs associated with the piecemeal and selective legalization of presently illicit economic activity seem trivial in comparison. As Aleksandr Yakovlev accurately put it, "if a majority constantly repeats specific acts, it will be in vain to describe it as a crime."

Conclusion

Returning to the definition of corruption defended in the early portions of this book, which viewed the concept as the legal manifestation of the system's *institutionalized* values, the case can be made that post-Soviet society is perfectly ready to embrace the legal redefinition of many economic behaviors. The persistence of corruption, among both the political and ideological vanguard as well as the masses, points to the fact that "socialist morality" never really took root in the Soviet Union.[30] To be sure, popular and elite cynicism with respect to the old system and its values has reached epidemic levels. In addition, the drastic social and political changes that are under way in Eastern Europe will certainly continue to attract the attention of reformers in the leadership posts of the post-Soviet states. Economic necessity at home has already proven powerful enough in this environment to allow for the rewriting of many elements of the criminal codes that govern economic activity in the former Soviet Union.

The local economies in the former USSR have experienced tremendous dislocation, marked by supply shortages, rationing, local economic warfare, and whispers of famine. In such an environment, corruption can only increase. Corruption at the level that was evident in the Soviet Union for over a quarter of a century has been portrayed here as primarily the *product,* not the cause, of Soviet economic malfeasance. For the Soviet elite as well as the masses, it has for some length of time been a "major regular method of solving one's problems in the social environment."[31] The social and economic reforms that have been initiated over the past two or three years have altered this social environment significantly and, if they are permitted to proceed, may allow for the legal institutionalization of the now prevailing social values regarding private economic activity and "corruption" in the former Soviet Union.

Official corruption in the Soviet Union, to be sure, entailed many negative consequences for the system. It perpetuated the creation and maintenance of a privileged class of political and economic elites in the country. It diverted the energies of relatively competent bureaucrats from the administration of state policies to the orchestration of self-aggrandizement. It elevated bribery, secrecy, and selfishness to the status of an official ethos. Finally, it forced a generally honest population into massive illicit activity for the sole purpose, in most cases, of maintaining a minimal standard of living. However, in the final analysis, official corruption in the USSR may be seen as having been a net benefit to the system. It helped ensure the maintenance of minimal living standards for the state's population. It allowed for the marginal improvement of the economy as a system for the distribution of goods and services. Moreover, it humanized (albeit at a base level) the relationship between the public organs and the mass of the population by providing the latter with some predictable means of influencing their own social environment. Perhaps most important of all, it allowed for the development of economic skills that may well serve—if they are allowed to be practiced without fear of reprisals—to militate against the massive economic dislocation that will accompany any transition from a centrally planned to a more mixed market economy.

Notes

1. *Political Order in Changing Societies* (New Haven, CT: Yale University Press, 1968), p. 69.

2. Konstantin Simis (1977–78), "The Machinery of Corruption in the Soviet Union," *Survey*, Vol. 23, (No.4): 35.

3. See, for example, Gregory Grossman (1977), "The 'Second Economy' of the USSR," *Problems of Communism*, Vol. 26, No. 5 (September–October): 25–40; Aron Katsenelinboigen (1977), "Coloured Markets in the Soviet Union," *Soviet Studies*, Vol. 29, No. 1 (January): 62–85; John M. Kramer (1977), "Political Corruption in the USSR," *Western Political Quarterly*, Vol. 30, No. 2 (June): 213–224; J.M. Montias and Susan Rose-Ackerman (1980), "Corruption in a Soviet-type Economy: Theoretical Considerations," Kennan Institute Paper No. 110;

Charles A. Schwartz (1979), "Corruption and Political Development in the USSR," *Comparative Politics*, Vol. 11 (No. 4): 425–442; Dmitrii K. Simes (1975), "The Soviet Parallel Market," *Survey*, Vol. 21 (No. 3): 42–52; Konstantin Simis (1982), *USSR: The Corrupt Society* (New York: Simon and Schuster); and Steven J. Staats (1972), "Corruption in the Soviet System, *Problems of Communism*, Vol. 21, No. 1 (January–February): 40–47.

4. Gunnar Myrdal (1970), *The Challenge of World Poverty* (New York: Random House), especially chapter 7.

5. Gary K. Bertsch, Robert P. Clark, and David M. Wod (1991), *Power and Policy in Three Worlds* (New York: Macmillan), p. 629–630.

6. Vladimir Solovyov and Elena Klepikova (1983), *Yuri Andropov: A Secret Passage into the Kremlin* (London: Robert Hale), p. 112; emphasis added.

7. Arkady Vaksberg (1991), *The Soviet Mafia* (New York: St. Martin's Press), p. 133.

8. Overall crime rates have jumped drastically since 1985. In each year since, double-digit increases in overall crime have been the norm. Compared to the respective previous years, crime rose in 1988 by 9.5 percent, in 1989 by an additional 31.8 percent, and in 1990 by an additional 13.2 percent.

9. For a thorough review of the forces at work in the Soviet Union that make such a high level of corruption almost inevitable, refer to Gregory Grossman (1979), "Notes on the Illegal Private Economy and Corruption," pp. 834–854 in *Soviet Economy in a Time of Change* (Washington, D.C.: Joint Economic Committee of the U.S. Congress).

10. Aron Katsenelinboigen, *Tsvetniya rynki i sovetskaya ekonomika. SSSR. Vnutrennie protivorechiya*, 1981, (2): 97; cited in Mikhail Heller (1988), *Cogs in the Wheel: The Formation of Soviet Man* (New York: Alfred A. Knopf), p. 139.

11. For more on this argument, see Gabriel Ben-Dor (1974), "Corruption, Institutionalization, and Political Development: The Revisionist Theses Revisited," *Comparative Political Studies*, Vol. 7, No. 1 (April): 63–83; Edward C. Banfield (1975), "Corruption as a Feature of Governmental Organization," *Journal of Law and Economics*, Vol. 18 (December): 587–605; David H. Bayley (1966), "The Effects of Corruption in a Developing Nation," *Western Political Quarterly*, Vol. 19 (December): 719–732; Nathaniel H. Leff (1964), "Economic Development through Bureaucratic Corruption," *American Behavioral Scientist*, Vol. 8, No. 3 (November): 8–15; Colin Leys (1965), "What Is the Problem about Corruption?" *Journal of Modern African Studies*, Vol. 3 (No. 2): 215–230; Joseph S. Nye (1967), "Corruption and Political Development: A Cost–Benefit Analysis," *American Political Science Review*, Vol. 51 (June): 417–429; and John Waterbury (1973), "Endemic and Planned Corruption in a Monarchical Regime," *World Politics*, Vol. 25, No. 4 (July): 533–555.

12. Consider for example, the following. In the late 1980s, USSR ranked 103 in the world in telephones per capita, and 88 in the world in automobiles per capita; hardly the numbers associated with an advanced economy.

13. Joseph Nye (1967), "Corruption and Political Development," p. 420.

14. While not referring directly to the Soviet case, Scott (1972) argues that "foremost among the structural factors that encourage corruption in new states is the tremendous relative importance of government in these nations as a source of goods, services, and employment," *Comparative Political Corruption* (Engle-

wood Cliffs, NJ: Prentice-Hall), p. 12. Scott's comments are certainly applicable to the state of affairs in the former USSR.

15. For more on this theme, please refer to chapter 10, "Corruption," in Mikhail Heller (1988), *Cogs in the Wheel: The Formation of Soviet Man* (New York: Alfred A. Knopf); and chapter 3, "Corruption: Living *Na Levo,*" in Hedrick Smith (1976), *The Russians* (New York: Quadrangle).

16. Refer to Mervyn Matthews (1978), *Privilege in the Soviet Union: A Study of Elite Lifestyles under Communism* (London: George Allen & Unwin); Milovan Djilas (1957), *The New Class: An Analysis of the Communist System* (New York: Frederick A. Praeger); and David K. Willis (1985), *KLASS: How Russians Really Live* (New York: St. Martin's Press).

17. At the time of this writing, such basics as milk, bread, and eggs are being rationed in the former Soviet Union.

18. "'Chaika' nad 'zolotymi peskami'," *Zerkalo,* No. 13 (September 1990).

19. In his examination of corruption in Morocco, John Waterbury has argued that "There is a general level of cynicism running throughout—the cynicism of the non-participant masses who fall back on the traditional reflex, 'government has ever been thus'; the cynicism of the participants who partake of the system individually while refusing any responsibility for it; and the cynicism of the King who plays on the weakness and greed of his subjects. In this system, corruption serves only one 'positive' function—that of the survival of the regime." From "Endemic and Planned Corruption in a Monarchical Regime," p. 555.

20. Gregory Grossman (1979), "Notes on the Illegal Private Economy and Corruption," p. 843.

21. For more on this important distinction, see John M. Kramer (1977), "Political Corruption in the U.S.S.R.," pp. 214–217.

22. Joseph Berliner (1957), *Factory and Manager in the USSR* (Cambridge, MA: Harvard University Press), especially chapters 10, 11, and 12. See also Steven Shenfield (1983), "Pripiski: False Statistical Reporting in Soviet-Type Economies," pp. 239–258 in Michael Clarke, ed., *Corruption: Causes, Consequences, and Control* (London: Francis Pinter).

23. John M. Kramer (1977), "Political Corruption in the U.S.S.R.," p. 221.

24. On a more practical level, anti-corruption procedures should be created and maintained only if the costs involved in doing so are more than made up for by the benefits received. It makes no sense economically, for example, to spend a billion rubles a year on an anti-corruption campaign if the results of such a campaign save the state only a percentage of that total. Anti-corruption measures should be considered an investment, and should be evaluated on these grounds.

25. James R. Millar (1985), "The Little Deal: Brezhnev's Contribution to Acquisitive Socialism," *Slavic Review,* Vol. 44, No. 4 (Winter): 697.

26. John M. Kramer (1977), "Political Corruption in the U.S.S.R.," p. 223.

27. Richard E. Ericson (1984), "The 'Second Economy' and Resource Allocation under Central Planning," *Journal of Comparative Economics,* Vol. 8 (No. 1): 2–3.

28. Ibid., p. 4.

29. Gregory Grossman (1979), "Notes on the Illegal Private Economy and Corruption," p. 852.

30. This assertion is, of course, more valid in some areas of the Soviet Union (e.g., the Caucasus and Central Asia) than in others, for a variety of reasons, not the least of which is the persistence in these comparatively less developed areas of strong "patrimonial" tendencies. For more on this aspect of corruption, see Ken Jowitt (1983), "Soviet Neotraditionalism: The Political Corruption of a Leninist Regime," *Soviet Studies,* Vol. 35, No. 3 (July): 275–297; Gerald Mars and Yochanan Altman (1983), "How a Soviet Economy Really Works: Cases and Implications," pp. 259–267 in Michael Clarke, ed., *Corruption: Causes, Consequences, and Control* (London: Francis Pinter); C.A. Schwartz (1979), "Corruption and Political Development in the USSR," *Comparative Politics,* Vol. 11, (No. 4): 425–442; and Robin Theobold (1990), *Corruption, Development and Underdevelopment* (Durham, NC: Duke University Press).

31. Gregory Grossman (1979), "Notes on the Illegal Private Economy and Corruption," p. 840.

References

Adams, Jan S. (1977). *Citizen Inspectors in the Soviet Union: The People's Control Committee.* New York: Praeger Publishers.

Allison, Graham T. (1971). *Essence of Decision: Explaining the Cuban Missile Crisis.* Boston: Little, Brown).

Almond, Gabriel A., and G. Bingham Powell (1978). *Comparative Politics: System, Process and Policy.* Boston: Little, Brown.

Babaev, V. (1979). " 'Povyshat' kachestvo otchetnykh dannykh." *Vestnik statistiki,* Vol. 8: 40.

Banfield, Edward C. (1975). "Corruption as a Feature of Governmental Organization." *Journal of Law and Economics,* Vol. 18 (December): 587–605.

Bauman, Zygmunt (1974). "Officialdom and Class: Bases of Inequality in Socialist Society," In *The Social Analysis of Class Structure,* ed. Frank Parkin, pp. 129–48. London: Tavistock.

Bayley, David H. (1966). "The Effects of Corruption in a Developing Nation." *Western Political Quarterly,* Vol. 19 (December): 719–732.

Beissinger, Mark R. (1990). "The Party and the Rule of Law." *Columbia Journal of Transnational Law,* Vol. 28 (No. 1): 41–58.

Belikova, Galina, and Aleksandr Shokhin (1989). "The Black Market: People, Things, Facts." *Soviet Sociology,* Vol. 28 (Nos. 3–4).

Ben-Dor, Gabriel (1974). "Corruption, Institutionalization, and Political Development: The Revisionist Theses Revisited." *Comparative Political Studies,* Vol. 7, No. 1 (April): 63–83.

Benson, Bruce L., and John Baden (1985). "The Political Economy of Governmental Corruption: The Logic of Underground Government." *Journal of Legal Studies,* Vol. 14 (June): 391–410.

Berger, Peter L., and Thomas Luckmann (1967). *The Social Construction of Reality.* New York: Penguin.

Berliner, Joseph (1983). "Entrepreneurship in the Soviet Period: An Overview." In *Entrepreneurship in Imperial Russia and the Soviet Union,* ed. Gregory Guroff and Fred V. Carstensen, pp. 191–299. Princeton, NJ: Princeton University Press.

Berliner, Joseph (1957). *Factory and Manager in the USSR*. Cambridge, MA: Harvard University Press.

———— (1952). "The Informal Organization of the Soviet Firm," *Quarterly Journal of Economics*. Vol. 66: 342–365.

Berman, Harold J., and James W. Spindler (1972). *Soviet Criminal Law and Procedure: The RSFSR Codes*. 2nd ed. Cambridge, MA: Harvard University Press.

Bertsch, Gary K., Robert P. Clark, and David M. Wood (1991). *Power and Policy in Three Worlds*. New York: Macmillan.

Black, Cyril E. (1964). "The Nature of Imperial Russian Society." In *The Development of the USSR: An Exchange of Views*, ed. Donald W. Treadgold, pp. 173–190. Seattle: University of Washington Press.

Blackwell, Robert E., Jr. (1979). "Cadres Policy in the Brezhnev Era." *Problems of Communism*, Vol. 28 (No. 2): 29–42.

Boim, Leon, and Glenn G. Morgan (1978). *The Soviet Procuracy Protests, 1937–1973: A Collection of Translations*. Alphen aan den Rijn: Sijthoff & Nordhoff.

Bonin, John (1976). "On the Design of Managerial Incentive Structures in a Decentralized Planning Environment." Middletown, CT: Wesleyan University (Mimeograph).

Bregman, Randy, and Dorothy C. Lawrence (1990). "New Developments in Soviet Property Law." *Columbia Journal of Transnational Law*, Vol. 28 (No. 1): 189–206.

Breslauer, George W. (1986). "The Nature of Soviet Politics and the Gorbachev Leadership." In *The Gorbachev Era*, eds. Alexander Dallin and Candoleeza Rice, pp. 11–30. Stanford, CA: Stanford Alumni Association.

———— (1982). *Khrushchev and Brezhnev as Leaders: Building Authority in Soviet Politics*. London: Allen & Unwin.

British Broadcasting Corporation Monitoring Service (1979). *Composition of the USSR Supreme Soviet, March 1979*. Reading, England: Newspaper Archive Developments.

Brown, Archie (1983). "Andropov: Discipline *and* Reform?," *Problems of Communism*, Vol. 32 (No. 1): 18–31.

Butler, William E., ed. (1983). *Basic Documents on the Soviet Legal System*. New York: Oceana Publications.

Caiden, Gerald, and Naomi Caiden (1977). "Administrative Corruption," *Public Administration Review*, Vol. 37, No. 3 (May–June): 301–308.

Carstensen, Fred V., and Gregory Guroff (1983). "Economic Innovation in Imperial Russia and the Soviet Union: Observations." In *Entrepreneurship in Imperial Russia and the Soviet Union*, eds. Fred V. Carstensen and Gregory Guroff, pp. 347–360. Princeton, NJ: Princeton University Press.

Chalidze, Valerii (1977). *Criminal Russia: Essays on Crime in the Soviet Union*. New York: Random House.

Chibnall, Steven, and Peter Saunders (1977). "Worlds Apart: Notes on the Social Reality of Corruption." *British Journal of Sociology*, Vol. 28 (No. 2): 138–155.

Clark, William A. (1991). "Token Representation in the CPSU Central Committee." *Soviet Studies*, Vol. 43, (No. 5): 913–929.

Clarke, Michael, ed. (1983). *Corruption: Causes, Consequences, and Control*. London: Francis Pinter.

Conn, David (1979). "A Comparison of Alternative Incentive Structures for Centrally Planned Economies." *Journal of Comparative Economics*, Vol. 3 (September): 261–276.

Daniels, Robert V. (1980). "Evolution of Leadership Selection in the Central Committee, 1917–1927." In *Russian Officialdom: The Bureaucratization of Russian Society from the Seventeenth to the Twentieth Century*, eds. Walter McKenzie Pintner and Don Karl Rowney, pp. 355–368. Chapel Hill: The University of North Carolina Press.

Desai, Padma (1989). *Perestroika in Perspective: The Design and Dilemmas of Soviet Reform*. Princeton, NJ: Princeton University Press.

Deutscher, Isaac (1969). "Roots of Bureaucracy." *Canadian Slavic Studies*, Vol. 3, No. 3 (Fall): 453–472.

Djilas, Milovan (1957). *The New Class: An Analysis of the Communist System*. New York: Praeger Publishers.

Doder, Dusko (1988). *Shadows and Whispers: Power Politics inside the Kremlin from Brezhnev to Gorbachev*. New York: Penguin Books.

Downs, Anthony (1967). *Inside Bureaucracy*. Boston: Little, Brown.

Eckstein, Harry. (1982). "The Idea of Political Development: From Dignity to Efficiency." *World Politics*, Vol. 34 (No. 4): 451–486.

Eisenstadt, S.N. and Lemarchand, R., eds. (1981). *Political Clientelism, Patronage and Development*. London: Sage.

Eisenstadt, S.N. and Roniger, L. (1984). *Patrons, Clients and Friends*. Cambridge: Cambridge University Press.

Ericson, Richard (1984). "The 'Second' Economy and Resource Allocation under Central Planning." *Journal of Comparative Economics*, Vol. 8, (No. 1): 1–24.

———— (1983). "On an Allocative Role of the Soviet Second Economy." In *Marxism, Central Planning, and the Soviet Economy*, ed. Padma Desai, pp. 110–132. Cambridge: The MIT Press.

Etzioni, Amitai (1961). *A Comparative Analysis of Complex Organizations*. New York: The Free Press.

Feldbrugge, F.J.M. (1984). "Government and the Shadow Economy in the Soviet Union. " *Soviet Studies*, Vol. 36 (No. 4): 528–543.

————. (1979). "Does Soviet Law Make Sense?: Rationality and Functionality in Soviet Law." In *Soviet Law after Stalin: Soviet Institutions and the Administration of Law*, ed. Donald D. Barry, et al., pp. 399–497. Alphen aan den Rijn: Sijthoff & Noordhoff.

————, ed. (1973). *Encyclopedia of Soviet Law*. Dobbs Ferry, NY: Oceana Publications.

Feldbrugge, F.J.M., G.P. Van Den Berg, and William B. Simmons, eds. (1985). *Encyclopedia of Soviet Law*. 2d rev. ed. Dordrecht: Martinus Nijhoff.

Ford, Robert A. D. (1984). "The Soviet Union: The Next Decade." *Foreign Affairs*, Vol. 62 (No. 5): 1132–1144.

Friedgut, Theodore H. (1979). *Political Participation in the USSR*. Princeton, NJ: Princeton University Press.

Friedrich, Carl J. (1972). *The Pathology of Politics: Violence, Betrayal, Corruption, Secrecy, and Propaganda*. New York: Harper and Row.

————. (1966). "Political Pathology." *Political Quarterly*, Vol. 37 (January–March): 70–85.

Fuller, E. (1980). "Georgian Official Sentenced to Death for Bribery." *Radio Liberty Research* (290/80).

Gellner, Ernest, and Waterbury, John eds. (1977). *Patrons and Clients in Mediterranian Societies*. London: Duckworth.

Giddens, Anthony (1981). *The Class Structure of the Advanced Societies*. London: Hutchinson.

Givens, Robert D. (1980). "Eighteenth Century Nobiliary Career Patterns and Provincial Government." In *Russian Officialdom: The Bureaucratization of Russian Society from the Seventeenth to the Twentieth Century,* ed. Walter McKenzie Pintner and Don Karl Rowney, pp. 106–129. Chapel Hill: The University of North Carolina Press.

Glazer, Myron (1983). "Ten Whistleblowers and How They Fared." *The Hastings Center Report,* Vol. 13 (December): 33–41.

Gleason, Gregory (1987). "Prefect or Paladin?: Centrist and Nationalist Leaders in Soviet Central Asia." Paper presented at the 19th annual meeting of the American Association for the Advancement of Slavic Studies, Boston, MA.

Graham, Jill W. (1986). "Principled Organizational Dissent: A Theoretical Essay." *Research in Organizational Behavior,* Vol. 8: 1–53.

Granick, David (1961). *The Red Executive*. Garden City, NY: Doubleday.

Grechin, A.S. (1983). "Experiment in the Sociological Study of People's Feelings on Law and Order." *Sotsiologicheskiye issledovania,* No. 2 (April–June): 121–126.

Gregory, Paul R. (1990). *Restructuring the Soviet Economic Bureaucracy*. Cambridge: Cambridge University Press.

Grossman, Gregory (1987). "The Second Economy: Boon or Bane for the Reform of the First Economy?" *Berkeley–Duke Occasional Papers on the Second Economy in the USSR* 11, No. 2 (December).

———. (1985). "The Second Economy in the USSR and Eastern Europe: A Bibliography." *Berkeley-Duke Occasional Papers on the Second Economy in the USSR* 1 (September).

———. (1984) *Studies in the Second Economy of Communist Countries*. Berkeley: University of California Press.

———. (1979). "Notes on the Illegal Private Economy and Corruption." In *Soviet Economy in a Time of Change*, pp. 834–854. Washington, D.C.: Joint Economic Committee of the U.S. Congress.

——— (1977). "The 'Second Economy' of the USSR." *Problems of Communism,* Vol. 26, No. 5 (September–October): 25–40.

Guroff, Gregory, and Fred V. Carstensen, eds. (1983). *Entrepreneurship in Imperial Russia and the Soviet Union*. Princeton, NJ: Princeton University Press.

Harasymiw, Bohdan (1984). *Political Elite Recruitment in the Soviet Union*. London: Macmillan.

Hazan, Baruch A. (1990). *Gorbachev's Gamble: The 19th All-Union Party Conference*. Boulder, CO: Westview Press.

Hazard, John (1990). "Gorbachev's Attack on Stalin's Etatism of Ownership." *Columbia Journal of Transnational Law,* Vol. 28 (No. 1): 207–223.

Heidenheimer, Arnold J., ed. (1970). *Political Corruption: Readings in Comparative Analysis*. New York: Holt, Rinehart and Winston.

Heller, Mikhail (1988). *Cogs in the Wheel: The Formation of Soviet Man*. New York: Alfred A. Knopf.

Hewett, Ed A. (1988). *Reforming the Soviet Economy: Equality Versus Efficiency.* Washington, D.C.: The Brookings Institution.

Hill, Ronald J., and Peter Frank (1986). *The Soviet Communist Party.* 3d ed. Boston: Allen & Unwin.

Hodnett, Grey (1975). "Succession Contingencies in the Soviet Union." *Problems of Communism,* Vol. 24 (No. 2): 1–21.

Hough, Jerry F. (1982). "Changes in Soviet Elite Composition." In *Russia at the Crossroads: The 26th Congress of the CPSU,* ed. Seweryn Bialer and Thane Gustafson, pp. 39–64. London: George Allen & Unwin.

——— (1980). *Soviet Leadership in Transition.* Washington, DC: The Brookings Institute.

———. (1979). "The Generation Gap and the Soviet Succession." *Problems of Communism,* Vol. 28 (No. 4): 1–16.

———. (1977). *The Soviet Union and Social Science Theory.* Cambridge, MA: Harvard University Press.

———. (1976). "The Brezhnev Era: The Man and the System." *Problems of Communism,* Vol. 25 (No. 2): 1–17.

———. (1969). *The Soviet Prefects: The Local Party Organs in Industrial Decision Making.* Cambridge: Harvard University Press.

Hough, Jerry F., and Merle Fainsod (1979). *How the Soviet Union Is Governed.* Cambridge, MA: Harvard University Press.

Huntington, Samuel P. (1968). *Political Order in Changing Societies.* New Haven: Yale University Press.

Ionescu, Ghita (1977). "Patronage under Communism." In *Patrons and Clients in Mediterranian Societies,* ed. Ernest Gellner and John Waterbury. London: Duckworth.

Johnston, Michael (1986). "The Political Consequences of Corruption: A Reassessment." *Comparative Politics,* Vol. 18 (No. 2): 459–477.

Jos, Philip H. (1992). "Empirical Corruption Research: Beside the (Moral) Point?" Paper presented to the 1992 Annual Meeting of the South Carolina Political Science Association.

Jos, Philip H., Mark E. Tompkins, and Stephen W. Hays (1989). "In Praise of Difficult People: A Portrait of the Committed Whistleblower." *Public Administration Review,* Vol. 49 (No. 6): 552–561.

Jowitt, Ken (1983). "Soviet Neotraditionalism: The Political Corruption of a Leninist Regime." *Soviet Studies,* Vol. 35, No. 3 (July): 275–297.

Jozsa, Gyula (1983). "Political 'Sielschaften' in the USSR." In *Leadership Selection and Patron-Client Relations in the USSR and Yugoslavia,* ed. T.H. Rigby and Bohdan Harasymiw, pp. 139–173. London: George Allen & Unwin.

Juviler, Peter H. (1976). *Revolutionary Law and Order: Politics and Social Change in the USSR.* New York: The Free Press.

Katsenelinboigen, Aron (1983). "Corruption in the USSR: Some Methodological Notes." In *Corruption: Causes, Consequences, and Control,* ed. Michael Clarke, pp. 220–228. London: Francis Pinter.

———. (1981). *Tsvetniya rynki i sovetskaya ekonomika. SSSR. Vnutrennie protivorechiya* (Vol. 2).

———. (1978). *Studies in Soviet Economic Planning.* White Plains, NY: M.E. Sharpe.

————. (1977). "Coloured Markets in the Soviet Union." *Soviet Studies*, Vol. 29, No. 1 (January): 62–85.

Kline, George L. (1987). *Capital Punishment for Crimes against Property in the USSR*. Washington, D.C.: Kennan Institute Occasional Paper.

————. (1965). "Economic Crime and Punishment." *Survey*, Vol. 57 (October): 67–72.

Klitgaard, Robert E. (1987). *Controlling Corruption*. Berkeley: University of California Press.

Kramer, John M. (1977). "Political Corruption in the USSR." *Western Political Quarterly*, Vol. 30, No. 2 (June): 213–224.

Krasner, Stephen D. (1984). "Approaches to the State: Alternative Conceptions and Historical Dynamics." *Comparative Politics*, Vol. 16 (No. 2): 223–246.

Lampert, Nicholas (1985). *Whistleblowing in the Soviet Union: A Study of Complaints and Abuses under State Socialism*. New York: Schocken.

————. (1984). "Law and Order in the USSR: The Case of Economic and Official Crime." *Soviet Studies*, Vol. 36 (No. 3): 366–385.

————. (1983). "The Whistleblowers: Corruption and Citizens' Complaints in the USSR." In *Corruption: Causes, Consequences, and Control*, ed. Michael Clarke, pp. 268–287. London: Francis Pinter.

LaPalombara, Joseph, ed. (1971). *Bureaucracy and Political Development*. Princeton, NJ: Princeton University Press.

Lapidus, Gail Warshovsky (1977). "The Brezhnev Regime and Directed Social Change: Depoliticization as Political Strategy." In *The Twenty-Fifth Congress of the CPSU: Assessment and Context*, ed. Alexander Dallin, pp. 26–38. Stanford, CA: Hoover Institution Press.

Leff, Nathaniel H. (1964). "Economic Development through Bureaucratic Corruption." *American Behavioral Scientist*, Vol. 8, No. 3 (November): 8–15.

Leggett, George (1981). *The Cheka: Lenin's Political Police*. Oxford: Clarendon Press.

Lemarchand, R., and Legg, K. (1972). "Political Clientelism and Development." *Comparative Politics*, Vol. 4 (No. 2): 149–178.

Leys, Colin (1965). "What Is the Problem about Corruption?" *Journal of Modern African Studies*, Vol. 3 (No. 2): 215–230.

Loeb, Martin, and W.A. Magat (1978). "Success Indicators in the Soviet Union: The Problem of Incentives and Efficient Allocation." *American Economic Review*, Vol. 68 (March): 173–181.

Los, Maria, ed. (1990). *The Second Economy in Marxist States*. New York: St. Martin's Press.

————. (1983). "Economic Crimes in Communist Countries." In *Comparative Criminology*, ed. I.L. Barak-Glantz and E.H. Johnson, pp. 39–57. Beverly Hills, CA: Sage Publications.

————. (1982). "Crime and Economy in the Communist Countries." In *White Collar and Economic Crime*, ed. P. Wickman and T. Dailey, pp. 121–137. Lexington, MA: Lexington Books.

Luryi, Yuri I. (1986). "The Use of Criminal Law by the CPSU in the Struggle for the Reinforcement of Its Power and in the Inner-Party Struggle." In *Ruling Communist Parties and Their Status under Law*, ed. Dietrich Andre Loeber, pp. 91–114. The Hague: Martinus Nijhoff.

Mars, Gerald, and Yochanan Altman (1983). "How a Soviet Economy Really Works: Cases and Implications." In *Corruption: Causes, Consequences, and Control,* ed. Michael Clarke, pp. 259–267. London: Francis Pinter.

————. (1983). "The Cultural Bases of Soviet Georgia's Second Economy." *Soviet Studies,* Vol. 35 (No. 4): 546–560.

Matthews, Mervyn (1989). *Patterns of Deprivation in the Soviet Union under Brezhnev and Gorbachev.* Stanford, CA: Hoover Institution Press.

————. (1978). *Privilege in the Soviet Union: A Study of Elite Lifestyles under Communism.* London: George Allen and Unwin.

Mazour, Anatole G. (1962). *Russia: Tsarist and Communist.* Toronto: D. Van Nostrand.

McMullen, M. (1961). "A Theory of Corruption." *Sociological Review,* Vol. 9: 181–201.

Meehan-Waters, Brenda (1980). "Social and Career Characteristics of the Administrative Elite, 1689–1761." In *Russian Officialdom: The Bureaucratization of Russian Society from the Seventeenth to the Twentieth Century,* eds. Walter McKenzie Pintner and Don Karl Rowney, pp. 76–105. Chapel Hill: The University of North Carolina Press.

Meier, Kenneth J., and Thomas M. Holbrook (1992). " 'I Seen My Opportunities and I Took 'Em': Political Corruption in the American States." *Journal of Politics,* Vol. 54 (No. 1): 135–155.

Merton, Robert K. (1957). *Social Theory and Social Structure.* Glencoe, IL: The Free Press.

Merton, Robert K., Ailsa P. Gray, Barbara Hockey, and Hanan C. Selvin, eds. (1952). *Reader in Bureaucracy.* Glencoe, IL: The Free Press.

Miceli, Marcia P., and Janet P. Near (1985). "Characteristics of Organizational Climate and Perceived Wrongdoing Associated with Whistleblowing Decisions," *Personnel Psychology,* Vol. 38: 525–544.

Millar, James R. (1985). "The Little Deal: Brezhnev's Contribution to Acquisitive Socialism." *Slavic Review,* Vol. 44 (Winter): 694–706.

Miller, John H. (1977). "Cadres Policy in Nationality Areas: Recruitment of CPSU First and Second Secretaries in Non-Russian Republics of the USSR." *Soviet Studies,* Vol. 29 (No. 1): 3–36.

Mitchell, R. Judson (1982). "Immobilism, Depoliticization, and the Emerging Soviet Elite." *Orbis,* Vol. 26 (No. 3): 591–610.

Monas, Sidney (1970). "Bureaucracy in Russia under Nicholas I." In *The Structure of Russian History: Interpretive Essays,* ed. Michael Cherniavsky, pp. 269–281. New York: Random House.

Monteiro, John B. (1966). *Corruption: Control of Maladministration.* Bombay: Manaktalas.

Montias, J.M., and Susan Rose-Ackerman (1980). *Corruption in a Soviet-type Economy: Theoretical Considerations.* Washington, D.C.: Kennan Institute Occasional Paper, No. 110.

Mousnier, Roland (1973). *Social Hierarchies, 1450 to the Present.* London: Croom Helm.

Murphy, Patrick (1985). "Soviet *Shabashniki:* Material Incentives at Work." *Problems of Communism,* Vol. 34, No. 6 (November-December): 48–57.

Myrdal, Gunnar (1970). *The Challenge of World Poverty.* New York: Random House.

Newcity, Michael (1990). "Perestroika, Private Enterprise and Soviet Tax Policy." *Columbia Journal of Transnational Law*, Vol. 28 (No. 1): 225–252.

Neznansky, Freidrich (1985). *The Prosecution of Economic Crimes in the USSR, 1954–1984*. Falls Church, VA: Delphic Associates.

Nordlinger, Eric A. (1981). *On the Autonomy of the Democratic State*. Cambridge, MA: Harvard University Press.

Nove, Alec (1975). "Is There a Ruling Class in the USSR?," *Soviet Studies*, Vol. 27, No. 4 (October): 615–638.

Nye, Joseph S. (1967). "Corruption and Political Development: A Cost–Benefit Analysis," *American Political Science Review*, Vol. 51 (June): 417–429.

Ofer, Gur, and A. Vinokur (1980). *Private Sources of Income of the Soviet Urban Household*. Santa Monica, CA: Rand Publications.

Orlovsky, Daniel (1976). "Recent Studies on the Russian Bureaucracy." *Russian Review*, Vol. 34 (October): 448–467.

Palmier, Leslie (1983). "Bureaucratic Corruption and its Remedies." In *Corruption: Causes, Consequences, Control*, ed. Michael Clarke, pp. 202–219. London: Francis Pinter.

Parkin, Frank (1971). *Class Inequality and Political Order: Social Stratification in Capitalist and Communist Societies*. New York: Praeger Publishers.

Pintner, Walter M. (1980a). "Civil Officialdom and the Nobility in the 1850s." In *Russian Officialdom: The Bureaucratization of Russian Society from the Seventeenth to the Twentieth Centuries*, ed. Walter McKenzie Pintner and Don Karl Rowney, pp. 227–249. Chapel Hill: The University of North Carolina Press.

———. (1980). "The Evolution of Russian Officialdom, 1755–1855." In *Russian Officialdom: The Bureaucratization of Russian Society from the Seventeenth to the Twentieth Centuries*, ed. Walter McKenzie Pintner and Don Karl Rowney, pp. 190–226. Chapel Hill: The University of North Carolina Press.

———. (1970). "The Social Characteristics of the Early Nineteenth-Century Russian Bureaucracy." *Slavic Review*, Vol. 29 (September): 429–443.

Pintner, Walter McKenzie, and Rowney, Don Karl (1980). *Russian Officialdom: The Bureaucratization of Russian Society from the Seventeenth to the Twentieth Century*. Chapel Hill, NC: University of North Carolina Press.

Pintner, Walter McKenzie, and Rowney, Don Karl (1980). "Officialdom and Bureaucratization: Conclusion." In *Russian Officialdom: The Bureaucratization of Russian Society from the Seventeenth to the Twentieth Centuries*, eds. Walter McKenzie Pintner and Don Karl Rowney, pp. 369–380. Chapel Hill: The University of North Carolina Press.

Ploss, Sidney I. (1982). "Soviet Succession: Signs of Struggle." *Problems of Communism*, Vol. 31 (No. 5): 41–52.

Pomorski, Stanislav (1978). "Crimes against the Central Planner: 'Ochkovtiratel'stvo'." In *Soviet Law after Stalin*, ed. Donald D. Barry, et al., Vol. 2, pp. 291–311. Alphen aan den Rijn: Sijthoff & Noordhoff, 1978.

——— (1977). "Criminal Law Protection of Socialist Property in the USSR." In *Soviet Law after Stalin*, ed. Donald D. Barry, Vol. 1. Alphen aan den Rijn: Sijthoff & Noordhoff, 1977.

Pomorski, Stanislav, and George Ginsburgs (1986). *Enforcement of Law and the Second Economy*. Washington, D.C.: National Council for Soviet and East European Research.

Powell, Raymond (1977). "Plan Execution and the Workability of Soviet Planning." *Journal of Comparative Economics*, Vol. 1: 51–76.

Radio Liberty Research (1977). "The 'Black' Millions." *RL* 179/77 (July 27).

Radio Liberty Research (1977). "Criticism of the Administration of Georgia." *RL* 60/77 (March 14).

Raeff, Marc (1985). *Understanding Imperial Russia: State and Society in the Old Regime.* New York: Columbia University Press.

———. (1979). "The Bureaucratic Phenomenon of Imperial Russia, 1700–1905." *American Historical Review*, Vol. 84 (No. 2): 399–411.

———. (1975). "The Well-Ordered Police State and the Development of Modernity in Seventeenth and Eighteenth Century Europe: An Attempt at a Comparative Approach." *American Historical Review*, Vol. 80 (No. 5): 1221–1243.

———. (1957). "The Russian Autocracy and Its Officials." In *Russian Thought and Politics*, ed. Hugh McLean, et al., pp. 77–91. Cambridge, MA: Harvard University Press.

Reddaway, Peter (1984). "Soviet Policies on Dissent and Emigration: The Radical Change of Course Since 1979." Washington, D.C.: Occasional Paper No. 192, Kennan Institute for Advanced Russian Studies, Woodrow Wilson International Center for Scholars.

———. (1975). "The Georgian Orthodox Church: Corruption and Renewal." *Religion in Communist Lands*, Vol. 3 (July-October): 14–23.

Redkina, N. (1981). " 'Pripiska' i otpiska." *Komsomolskaya pravda* (8 September): 2.

Remington, Thomas F. (1988). *The Truth of Authority: Ideology and Communications in the Soviet Union.* Pittsburgh, PA: University of Pittsburgh Press.

Riasanovsky, Nicholas (1977). *A History of Russia.* 3d ed. New York: Oxford University Press.

Rigby, Thomas H. (1978). "The Soviet Regional Leadership: The Brezhnev Generation." *Slavic Review*, Vol. 37 (No. 1): 1–24.

———. (1970). "The Soviet Leadership: Towards a Self-Stabilizing Oligarchy?" *Soviet Studies*, Vol. 22 (No. 2): 167–191.

———. (1968). *Communist Party Membership in the USSR, 1917–1967.* Princeton, NJ: Princeton University Press.

Rose-Ackerman, Susan (1978). *Corruption: A Study in Political Economy.* New York: Academic Press.

Rosner, Lydia S. (1986). *The Soviet Way of Crime: Beating the System in the Soviet Union and the U.S.A.* Boston: Bergin & Garvey Publishers.

Rowney, Don Karl, and Pintner, Walter M. (1980). "Officialdom and Bureaucratization: An Introduction." In *Russian Officialdom: The Bureaucratization of Russian Society from the Seventeenth to the Twentieth Century*, ed. Walter McKenzie Pintner and Don Karl Rowney, pp. 3–18. Chapel Hill: The University of North Carolina Press.

Rudolph, L.I., and Rudolph, S.H. (1979). "Authority and Power in Bureaucratic and Patrimonial Administration." *World Politics*, Vol. 31 (No. 1): 195–227.

Rumer, Boris (1988). "Trouble in Samarkand," *World Monitor* (November): 44–55.

Rush, Myron (1983). "Succeeding Brezhnev." *Problems of Communism*, Vol. 32 (No. 1): 2–7.

Sakwa, Richard (1990). *Gorbachev and His Reforms, 1985–1990.* Englewood Cliffs, NJ: Prentice Hall.

Schapiro, Leonard (1971). *The Communist Party of the Soviet Union.* New York: Vintage Books.

Schwartz, Charles A. (1981). "Economic Crime in the U.S.S.R.: A Comparison of the Khrushchev and Brezhnev Eras." *International and Comparative Law Quarterly,* Vol. 30: 281–296.

———. (1979). "Corruption and Political Development in the USSR." *Comparative Politics,* Vol. 11 (July): 425–442.

Scott, James C. (1972). *Comparative Political Corruption.* Englewood Cliffs, NJ: Prentice-Hall.

———. (1969). "Corruption, Machine Politics, and Political Change." *American Political Science Review,* Vol. 63, No. 4 (December): 1142–1158.

Seliunin, Vasilii, and Grigorii Khanin (1987). "Lukavaya tsifra," *Novy Mir,* No. 2 (February): 181–201.

Sharlet, Robert (1979). "The Communist Party and the Administration of Justice in the USSR." In *Soviet Law after Stalin: Soviet Institutions and the Administration of Law,* ed. Donald D. Barry, et al., pp. 321–392. Alphen aan den Rijn: Sijthoff & Noordhoff.

———. (1977). "Stalinism and Soviet Legal Culture." In *Stalinism: Essays in Historical Interpretation,* ed. Robert C. Tucker, pp. 155–179. New York: W.W. Norton.

Shelley, Louise I. (1990). "The Second Economy in the Soviet Union." In *The Second Economy in Marxist States,* ed. Maria Los, pp. 11–26. New York: St. Martin's Press.

———. (1980). "The Geography of Soviet Criminality." *American Sociological Review,* Vol. 45 (No. 1): 111–122.

Shenfield, Steven (1983). "Pripiski: False Statistical Reporting in Soviet-type Economies." In *Corruption: Causes, Consequences, and Control,* ed. Michael Clarke, pp. 239–258. London: Frances Pinter.

Siegelbaum, Lewis H. (1984). "Soviet Norm Determination in Theory and Practice, 1917–1941." *Soviet Studies,* Vol. 36 (No.1): 45–68.

Simes, Dmitrii K. (1975). "The Soviet Parallel Market." *Survey,* Vol. 21, No. 3 (Summer): 42–52.

Simis, Konstantin (1982). *USSR: The Corrupt Society: The Secret World of Soviet Capitalism.* New York: Simon and Schuster.

———. (1977–78). "The Machinery of Corruption in the Soviet Union." *Survey,* Vol. 23 (No. 4): 35–55.

Skocpol, Theda (1979). *States and Social Revolutions.* Cambridge, MA: Cambridge University Press.

Smelser, Neil J., ed. (1973). *Karl Marx on Society and Social Change.* Chicago: University of Chicago Press.

Smith, Gordon B. (1988). *Soviet Politics: Continuity and Contradiction.* New York: St. Martin's Press.

———. (1979). "Procuratorial Campaigns Against Crime." In *Soviet Law After Stalin: Soviet Institutions and the Administration of Law,* ed. Donald D. Barry, et al., pp. 143–167. Alphen aan den Rijn: Sijthoff & Noordhoff.

———. (1978). *The Soviet Procuracy and the Supervision of Administration.* Alphen aan den Rijn: Sijthoff & Noordhoff.

————. (1987). "Gorbachev's Council of Ministers." *Soviet Union*, Vol. 14 (No. 3): 343–363.

Smith, Hedrick (1976). "Corruption: Living 'Na Levo'." Chapter 3 in *The Russians*. New York: Quadrangle/New York Times Book Company.

Snyder, Mark (1974). "The Self-Monitoring of Expressive Behavior." *Journal of Personality and Social Psychology*, Vol. 30 (October): 526–537.

Solomon, Peter H., Jr. (1987). "The Case of the Vanishing Acquittal: Informal Norms and the Practice of Soviet Criminal Justice." *Soviet Studies*, Vol. 39 (No. 5): 531–555.

Solovyev, Vladimir, and Elena Klepikova (1983). *Yuri Andropov: A Secret Passage into the Kremlin*. London: Robert Hale.

Staats, Steven J. (1972). "Corruption in the Soviet System." *Problems of Communism*, Vol. 21, No. 1 (January-February): 40–47.

Sternheimer, Stephen (1980). "Administration for Development: The Emerging Bureaucratic Elite, 1920–1930." In *Russian Officialdom: The Bureaucratization of Russian Society from the Seventeenth to the Twentieth Century*, ed. Walter McKenzie Pintner and Don Karl Rowney, pp. 316–354. Chapel Hill: The University of North Carolina Press.

————. (1975). "Administering Development and Developing Administration: Organizational Conflict in Tsarist Bureaucracy, 1906–1914." *Canadian-American Slavic Studies*, Vol. 9, No. 3 (October): 227–301.

Tatu, Michel (1975). "Decision Making in the USSR." In *Soviet Strategy in Europe*, ed. Richard Pipes, pp. 45–64. New York: Crane, Russak.

————. (1968). *Power in the Kremlin*. New York: Viking Press.

Theobold, Robin (1990). *Corruption, Development and Underdevelopment*. Durham, NC: Duke University Press.

Tilly, Charles, ed. (1975). *The Formation of National States in Western Europe*. Princeton, NJ: Princeton University Press.

Tilman, Robert O. (1968). "Emergence of Black-Market Bureaucracy: Administration, Development, and Corruption in the New States." *Public Administration Review*, Vol. 28 (No. 5): 437–444.

Torke, Hans-Joachim (1988). "Crime and Punishment in the Pre-Petrine Civil Service: The Problem of Control." In *Imperial Russia, 1700–1917: State, Society, Opposition*, ed. Ezra Mendelsohn and Marshall S. Shatz, pp. 5–21. DeKalb: Northern Illinois University Press.

————. (1971). "Continuity and Change in the Relations between Bureaucracy and Society in Russia, 1613–1861." *Canadian Slavic Studies*, Vol. 5, No. 4 (Winter): 457–476.

Treml, Vladimir (1985). "Alcohol in the Soviet Underground Economy." *Berkeley–Duke Occasional Papers on the Second Economy in the USSR*, No. 5 (December).

Trotsky, Leon (1937). *The Revolution Betrayed*. New York: Doubleday.

Tucker, Robert C. (1990). *Stalin in Power: The Revolution from above, 1928–1941*. New York: W.W. Norton.

————. (1977). *Stalinism: Essays in Historical Interpretation*. New York: W.W. Norton.

Urban, Michael E. (1989). "Does Faction Make a Difference?" In *An Algebra of Soviet Power: Elite Circulation in the Belorussian Republic 1966–86*, pp. 98–115. Cambridge, MA: Cambridge University Press.

————. (1982). *The Ideology of Administration: Soviet and American Cases.* Albany, NY: SUNY Press.

Vaksberg, Arkady (1991). *The Soviet Mafia.* New York: St. Martin's Press.

Van Den Berg, Ger P. (1985). *The Soviet System of Justice: Figures and Policy.* Dordrecht: Martinus Nijhoff.

Voslensky, Michael (1984). *Nomenklatura: The Soviet Ruling Class.* Garden City, NY: Doubleday.

Waterbury, John (1973). "Endemic and Planned Corruption in a Monarchical Regime." *World Politics,* Vol. 25, No. 4 (July): 533–555.

Werner, Simcha B. (1983). "New Directions in the Study of Administrative Corruption." *Public Administration Review,* Vol. 43, No. 2 (March–April): 146–154.

Willerton, John P., Jr. (1987). "Patronage Networks and Coalition Building in the Brezhnev Era." *Soviet Studies,* Vol. 39 (No. 2): 175–204.

————. (1979). "Clientelism in the Soviet Union: An Initial Examination." *Studies in Comparative Communism,* Vol. 12 (Nos. 2–3): 159–183.

Willis, David K. (1985). *Klass: How Russians Really Live.* New York: St. Martins Press.

Wilson, James Q. (1961). "The Economy of Patronage." *Journal of Political Economy,* Vol. 69, No. 4 (August): 369–380.

Yaney, George L. (1973). *The Systematization of Russian Government: Social Evolution in the Domestic Administration of Imperial Russia, 1711–1905.* Urbana: University of Illinois Press.

Zelenov, V.P. (1964). *Borba s ochkovtiralstvom i pripiskami.* Moscow.

Zemtsov, Il'ya (1985). *The Private Life of the Soviet Elite.* New York: Crane Russak.

————. (1976). *Partiya ili Mafiya: Razvorovannaya respublika.* Paris: Les Editeurs Reunis.

Author Index

Subject Index

William A. Clark is Assistant Professor of Political Science and Director of Graduate Studies at Louisiana State University. He has also written *Soviet Regional Elite Mobility after Khrushchev.*

www.ingramcontent.com/pod-product-compliance
Ingram Content Group UK Ltd.
Pitfield, Milton Keynes, MK11 3LW, UK
UKHW020432010325
455677UK00029B/1117